Henry Ford's
Lean Vision

Henry Ford's Lean Vision

Enduring Principles From The First Ford Motor Plant

William A. Levinson

PRODUCTIVITY
productivity press

PRODUCTIVITY PRESS · NEW YORK

Most Productivity Press books are available at quantity discounts when purchased in bulk. For more information contact our Customer Service Department (800-394-6868). Address all other inquiries to:

Productivity Press
444 Park Avenue South, Suite 604
New York, NY 10016
United States of America
Telephone: 212-686-5900
Fax: 212-686-5411
E-mail: info@productivityinc.com

Cover design by Design Plus
Page design and composition by William H. Brunson, Typography Services
Printed and bound by Malloy Lithographing in the United States of America

Library of Congress Cataloging-in-Publication Data

Levinson, William A., 1957–
    Henry Ford's lean vision / by William A. Levinson.
        p.   cm.
    Includes bibliographical references and index.
    ISBN 1-56327-260-1
    1. Industrial relations.   2. Automobile industry and trade—Management.
3. Industrial management.   4. Production management.   5. Ford, Henry,
1863–1947—Influence.   I. Title.
    HD6976.A8 L485   2002
    658—dc21

                                                                    2002011252

06 05 04 03 02   9 8 7 6 5 4 3 2 1

Contents

Preface   ix

   Why This Book Was Written   xi

Introduction   xiii

   What to Expect from this Book   xiii

   Background Resources   xiv

   Chapter by Chapter Overview   xv

One: Brave New World: Changing How the
     World Works   1

   The Bottom Line: Ford's Results Speak for Themselves   3

   Defining Lean Enterprise   6

   Ford's Basic Principles   17

Two: Ford's Principles: The Foundation   21

   Natural Law   22

   Ford and Eastern Philosophy: The Japanese Connection   27

   Continuous Improvement: Kaizen   30

   Bringing Win-Win to the Workplace   41

   Service   47

   Summary   52

Three: Ford on Labor Relations   55

   Management and Labor as Partners   56

   No Free Lunch: A Key Concept   64

   Human Resource Practices   66

   Employee Housing and Stores   70

   Summary   73

**Four: Principles for Organizational and
Personal Success** 75
   Persistence 81
   Initiative 83
   Breaking Down Organizational Barriers 85
   Corporate Culture at the Ford Motor Company 88
   How the Ford Motor Company Lost Its Culture 96

Five: Perceiving Genuine Value 103
   A Warning to the United States 104
   Everything Must Add Value 113
   Middlemen Do Not Add value 113
   Advertising as Waste 120
   No Free Lunch 124

Six: Ford on Economics, Government, and Health Care 133
   Business Cycles 133
   The Stock Market Should Be Irrelevant to
     National Prosperity 135
   The Role of Inexpensive Energy 138
   The Role of Government 145
   Health Care 153

Seven: Eliminate Waste 161
   "Everything But the Squeal" 163
   ISO 14000 Is Free 178
   Summary 188

Eight: Ford's Factory 191
   The Factory and the Worker 194
   Continuous Improvement: Kaizen 195
   Lean Manufacturing 200
   5S-CANDO 201
   Just-In-Time (JIT) Manufacturing and
     Inventory Reduction 228
   Design for Manufacture and Design for Assembly 247
   Process Simplification and Improvement 254

Packaging and Delivery   267
Point-of-Use Assembly   268
Occupational Safety   270
Quality Control   281

Nine: Customer and Supplier Relationships   285
Identifying Markets and Creating Demand   285
Pricing Strategy   289
Supply Chain Management   292

Ten: Frederick Winslow Taylor and
    Scientific Management   301
Did Taylor Influence Ford?   303
Scientific Management, Lean Manufacturing,
    and Kaizen Blitz   304
Taylor and Motion Efficiency   305
The Truth Behind Taylorism   309
Principles for Change Management   319
An Experimental Design Tragedy   322

Eleven: The Influence of Benjamin Franklin   327
Franklin on Waste   328
Franklin on Initiative, Self-Reliance, and Persistence   331
Franklin on Money   333

Bibliography   335

Index   343

Preface

Henry Ford himself provides the best description of this book's mission, and he is the one who achieved it:

Every thoughtful man has an idea of what ought to be; but what the world is waiting for is a social and economic blueprint.

. . . We want artists in industrial relationships. We want masters in industrial method, both from the standpoint of the producer and the product. We want those who can mold the political, social, industrial, and moral mass into a sound and shapely whole (Ford, 1922a, 196–197).

Henry Ford was directly responsible for making the United States the wealthiest and most powerful country on earth. The United States superseded the British Empire during the 1910s— shortly after the introduction of scientific management and mass production—as the world's dominant power. Japan knew exactly what it was getting when it adopted Ford's lean enterprise system during the mid-twentieth century: a proven set of synergistic methods and practices for mass-producing any product or delivering any service cheaply but well.

Researching this book was like assembling the pieces of a puzzle to get a complete picture. Henry Ford's *My Life and Work* (1922), *Today and Tomorrow* (1926), and *Moving Forward* (1930) provided the framework. The notorious Harry Bennett's *Ford: We Never Called Him Henry* (1951) relates how Ford saw waste in rust-flecked slag from a steel mill. This work showed in an instant the importance of recognizing waste (in Japanese, *muda*) wherever

it appears, and that this talent may well have been Ford's principal success secret. Norwood's *Ford: Men and Methods* (1931)
stresses the expression, "it worried the men," in referring to waste
at the River Rouge plant. This shows that the ability to recognize
waste and an urgent desire to suppress it permeated the entire
organization; it was part of the organizational culture. Many other
references, most of which are out of print, supplied other valuable
pieces of the puzzle.

Once all the pieces were assembled, the complete picture
emerged: a lean enterprise system of synergistic and mutually
supporting methods that surpassed almost anything that exists
today. This book presents that complete picture. It is a history of
the Ford Motor Company and a biography of Henry Ford—and
plenty of books have treated both subjects—only so far as history
and biography can serve as teachers. This book's paramount goal
is to illuminate Henry Ford's thinking through the rediscovery and
consolidation into a single reference of the eminently sensible
principles that Ford developed more than 80 years ago. It is a
hands-on tool that the reader can put to work in any modern
activity: industry, service, health care, or government. It also supplies two powerful change management motivators for driving the
cultural transformation to lean enterprise:

1. Ford's bottom line speaks for itself. His lean enterprise
   system delivered proven and unprecedented results not
   only for manufacturing but also for transportation (the
   Detroit, Toledo, & Ironton Railroad), health care (the
   Henry and Clara Ford Hospital), agriculture, and freight
   management systems.
2. This book proves beyond doubt that the United States
   invented lean manufacturing. American workers are more
   likely to buy into the principles of lean manufacturing
   when they recognize the concept as having been "Made
   in the USA." Worker buy-in will, in turn, help preserve
   American manufacturing jobs and capability. This will keep

the "Made in USA" label on other manufactured products where it belongs.

WHY THIS BOOK WAS WRITTEN

If there is a Holy Grail of principles for managing human and physical resources in any manufacturing or service enterprise—with services including government, health care, and education—Henry Ford discovered it. He used it with unquestionable results, and he offered it to the world. It has always been ours to rediscover, and this project began with an article about a 1982 visit to Japan by some Ford Motor Company executives. The executives wanted to learn about Japanese quality and improvement methods. "One Japanese executive referred repeatedly to 'the book.' When Ford executives asked about the book, he responded: 'It's Henry Ford's book of course—your company's book'" (Stuelpnagel 1993, 91).

I thought it might be interesting to read *My Life and Work*, and its introduction alone revealed its awesome potential for application to today's economic and social issues. It was immediately clear that Ford was using the elements of Dr. Stephen Covey's *Principle-Centered Leadership* almost a century ago. This single chapter also revealed Ford's ideas about eliminating all forms of waste from agriculture as well as industry. That is how this project began.

A hope for the future: our nation's and the world's

There has not been a single example throughout recorded history of a great nation or empire that has not fallen. Egypt, a third-world country, was once the richest and most powerful nation on earth. Henry Ford warned that, because expensive corporate office buildings consume capital while producing nothing, they are likely to end up as tombs. The ancient Egyptians bypassed the phase of using massive and ornate edifices to house living executives: they stocked the Pyramids directly with dead ones.

A visitor to modern Macedonia would have trouble believing that this poor Balkan nation once ruled most of the known world. Only ancient ruins, along with aqueducts and roads—some of them are still usable—remind modern visitors that Italy also once ruled most of the known world. Living people can remember when the sun never set on the British Empire. The modern United Kingdom consists of little more than its home island, and its living standards are very modest compared to those in the United States.

Lawrence Miller's *Barbarians to Bureaucrats* (1989) describes the inexorable rise and fall of organizations. Businesses and nations follow the same cycle of growth and decline. The fact that both spouses often *must* work to afford a home and a family is evidence that the United States has already fallen into decline. Ford's principles offer a realistic hope that the United States can be the first nation to answer "No!" to history's demand that we, like all other great empires and nations, must pass into obscurity. *We need not, to quote Rudyard Kipling's Recessional, become "one with Nineveh and Tyre."* Henry Ford bequeathed us the tools we need to stand against the tides of history and turn them back. We need only take them up and use them.

What to Expect from This Book

This book's principal mission is to illuminate Henry Ford's thinking. The reader will learn to look at any job or business system—even a complete industry—from a new perspective. He or she will gain the ability to identify improvement opportunities that most people would overlook, and to see waste and inefficiency hiding in the job the way a chameleon hides among leaves. *One of Ford's principal success secrets was his unwillingness to take any aspect of a job or activity for granted. If the reader develops the same mindset, this book has done its job.* The best single-sentence condensation of this book's content is, "Examine the job or activity and ask, 'What would Henry Ford do?'"

HOW TO USE THIS BOOK

> No methods or formulas can be devised to substitute for human judgment and leadership.
> —Henry Ford, *Moving Forward* (1930, 146)

Most of Ford's principles were amazingly progressive for their time, and they still hold outstanding value today. Ford himself warns, however, against taking his writings as gospel and dogma:[1]

> Sometimes we of the Ford Motor Company meet men who have taken our books as their business Bibles and are trying to run their businesses as we ran ours ten years ago. They thought they had found in our books a complete system of management that only needed to be applied and it would automatically produce results....

What we want him to do is to disregard all systems, get to the wheel of his own business, and give himself to it (Ford, 1930, 140).

No book can be a substitute for independent thought, and it is futile to try to run an organization from a cookbook. Principles and concepts, in contrast, equip the practitioner to work out the problem. The idea is not to imitate Ford and his associates exactly, but rather to see what they did and apply the underlying methods and principles appropriately to one's own situation.

(Don't worry about Ford's and other references' use of the gender-specific word "men" to describe businesspeople and workers. The workforce of their day was primarily male.)

BACKGROUND RESOURCES

Every reference that might provide information or insight on the Ford thought process was obtained. Some references then led to others. The principal ones were the following.

1. Ford's own *My Life and Work* (1922), *Ford Ideals* (1922a, from "Mr. Ford's Page" in the *Dearborn Independent*), *Today and Tomorrow* (1926), *Moving Forward* (1930), and "My Philosophy of Industry" (1929, an interview with Ford) were the foundations of this book.
2. Charles E. "Cast-iron Charlie" Sorensen's *My Forty Years with Ford* (1956) describes the organizational culture of the company's early years.
3. Harry Bennett's *Ford: We Never Called Him Henry* (1951) recounts how Ford saw the waste in a pile of rust-flecked slag from a steel mill.
4. Arnold and Faurote's *Ford Methods and the Ford Shops* (1915) provides some detailed examples of processes at the Highland Park plant.
5. Norwood's *Ford: Men and Methods* (1931) shows that the River Rouge plant not only had a lockout-tagout safety

program, it empowered its workers to stop the line when there was trouble: a practice whose introduction most people attribute to Japan.

6. Frederick Winslow Taylor's *The Principles of Scientific Management* (1911) and *Shop Management* (1911a), and Frank Gilbreth's *Motion Study* (1911), show the American origins of lean manufacturing, along with standardization and best practice deployment. Taylor and Gilbreth also show how hard it is to see waste and inefficiency until one learns how to look for them.

CHAPTER BY CHAPTER OVERVIEW

Lean Manufacturing Is an American Invention

The first chapter, "Brave New World: Changing How the World Works," provides two valuable change management tools for cultural transformation. It:

- Describes the Ford Motor Company's profound expansion of the United States' wealth and power, and its role in other parts of the world. This should overcome typical barriers to change like, "How do we know it will work?" (It did.) "What's it going to do for the bottom line?" (Ford wrote with a straight face in 1930 that his biggest problem was keeping profits down.)
- Shows that Henry Ford, or at least his books, taught the Japanese how to make those inexpensive, high-quality cars that captured a large share of the American market during the 1970s and 1980s. Earlier scientific management practitioners like Taylor and Gilbreth laid the foundations of what we now call lean manufacturing; Ford systematized it on an unprecedented scale. He also took the lean concept beyond the shop floor and into his supply chain, thus creating the lean enterprise. American workers and

managers may be more receptive to lean manufacturing as the reintroduction of U.S. developed methods than as the importation of Japanese methods.

Ford and the Human Element

The next three chapters relate primarily to individual success, organizational behavior and culture, and organizational psychology—i.e., the "soft sciences." Engineers and managers who want to transform their organizations must understand and apply these chapters' contents to gain the workforce's enthusiastic participation.

"Ford's Principles: The Foundation," shows the close alignment of Ford's personal philosophies and values with Japanese culture. Japan's receptivity to Ford's ideas may have involved more than industrial engineering and technology.

"Ford and Labor Relations" shows what employers must do to earn and keep the loyalty and commitment of their workers. The basic idea is that managers, professionals, hourly workers, and stockholders are all partners in the enterprise. The only way for each stakeholder to get a bigger piece of the pie is to make the pie bigger.

"Principles for Organizational and Personal Success" discusses key characteristics for individuals and enterprises that want to succeed at anything. These include an internal locus of control (self-reliance), vitality, and persistence. The chapter also describes the corporate culture of the early Ford Motor Company and shows how the company later lost that culture.

Ford and Operational Effectiveness

The next five chapters describe Ford's principles for operational effectiveness in any organization. Chapter 7, "Eliminate Waste," and Chapter 8, "Ford's Factory," are of particular interest to lean practitioners because they focus respectively on waste reduction and lean methods. "Ford's Factory," the book's longest chapter, is full of specific examples of lean manufacturing techniques. Chapter 9,

"Marketing and Supplier Relationships," includes supply chain management and supplier development.

"Perceiving Genuine Value" discusses what adds value and what doesn't. Manufacturing is the backbone of national prosperity and security, and the United States *must* stem the loss of its manufacturing capability. Value comes from Ford's three principal arts: agriculture (to which we may add mining, lumbering, and other extractive industries that get raw materials from nature), manufacturing, and transportation. The stock market, retailing, and the government do not create value or add value to anything. Do not allow the cost accounting system to run a business enterprise.

"Ford on Economics and Government" discusses the role of monetary systems, business cycles, government, and the stock market on businesses and the creation of wealth. Ford was confident in the ability of a well-managed business to defy cyclical market effects. Both the government and the stock market can encourage dysfunctional behavior that undermines a value-creating enterprise.

"Eliminate Waste" is about how to make money—a lot of money. The elimination of waste from every aspect of a business enterprise adds the savings directly to the bottom line. This is how Ford increased wages while reducing car prices and expanding his business. *People often look straight at waste without recognizing it.* The reader will learn from this chapter how to look at any manufacturing or economic activity in a new light and recognize waste when he or she sees it. Registration to the ISO 14000 standard for environmental management systems should be not only free but profitable.

"Ford's Factory" covers Ford's introduction of most so-called Japanese management techniques, along with a number of ideas that we associate with W. Edwards Deming and Tom Peters. The former's include just-in-time (JIT) manufacturing, error-proofing, design for manufacture, motion efficiency, and process simplification. The latter's include flat, lean, and porous organizations.

"Marketing and Supplier Relationships" focuses on identifying and creating markets and working with suppliers. Ford's success began with a clear vision statement about his prospective market. He also described supply chain management and supplier development.

Influences on Ford

Henry Ford said, "I am going to see that no man comes to know me" (Gourley, 1997, 38), but it useful to trace and study the people and literature that influenced him.

"Frederick Winslow Taylor and Scientific Management" discusses the relationship between Ford's industrial methods and Taylor's *Principles of Scientific Management*. It dispels the myths and stereotypes about Taylor's desire to turn workers into mindless robots or automata. Taylor actually introduced many ideas that modern management science considers very progressive. Scientific management and Frank Gilbreth's motion efficiency studies are, in fact, the direct forerunners of modern lean management.

"The Influence of Benjamin Franklin" discusses another inventor, and one of Ford's fellow Freemasons. Ford wrote in his discussion of the economic depression that followed the First World War, "Nothing has happened in our history to render out of date the business philosophy of Benjamin Franklin. *Poor Richard's Almanac* is still the best business compendium. The old American virtues of thrift and industry have no successors or substitutes. Business success is still a matter of making friends by service, and not a case of cornering necessitous people in such a way that they will have to come to you" (Ford, 1922a, 282–283).

Footnotes

1. Major General J. F. C. Fuller warned, "Adherence to dogmas has destroyed more armies and lost more battles and lives than any other cause in war. No man of fixed opinions can make a good general ..." (Tsouras, 1992, 149). The French "knew" in 1940, for example, that German armor could not bypass the Maginot Line by moving

through the Ardennes Forest. (It did.) The United States believed in 1941 that Pearl Harbor was too shallow for airplane-dropped torpedoes. (It wasn't. Royal Navy torpedo planes had, in fact, attacked the Italians successfully in shallow water at Taranto on 11 November, 1940.) The same lesson applies to business. Swiss watchmakers, for example, invented the quartz watch movement but they considered it of little value. The best watches were, "of course," mechanical. They did not even bother to patent the invention and they soon lost most of their market share to Timex.

ONE

Brave New World: Changing How the World Works

The Ace of Spades—the Ace of Swords in the ancient tarot deck—symbolizes "the triumph of a great force, either love or hatred; may signify a birth of special significance" (*Aquarian Tarot*, 1975). Tarot cards have no supernatural powers, but their merit as symbols of concepts, principles, archetypes, and role models is another matter (Levinson, 1994). The Ace of Swords symbolizes a world-transforming event or innovation.[1]

Two such events framed the twentieth century. The first was Henry Ford's introduction of an automobile that could be an everyday tool instead of a luxury for the rich, and the manufacturing technology for its production. The second was Bill Gates's development of software that brought computers into individual households and changed the Internet from an obscure mainframe technology to an everyday tool.

The automobile transformed American society and created a host of supporting industries and jobs. Ford (1930, 177) said that, during nineteen years of production, the Model T was directly responsible for the generation of seven billion dollars of wages and income. This was at that time *more than the estimated wealth of thirty-five of the country's forty-eight states.* This figure supports the contention that Ford made the United States the wealthiest and most powerful nation on earth, and it does not even include railway workers, rubber workers, oil workers, and others for whom the Model T created jobs

Anne Stevens, Ford Vice President for North American Assembly Operations, used the phrase "brave new world" in her keynote address at the 6th Annual Lean Management and Total Productive Maintenance (TPM) Conference (Stevens, 2001). I don't know if she intended this to have a dual meaning for insiders, but in Aldous Huxley's book of that title, Henry Ford was God, Ford's book *My Life and Work* was the Bible, and the Sign of the T—the Model T—was a religious icon. People reckoned time (A.F., After Ford) from the introduction of the Model T and the moving assembly line in 1908.

It was easy to envision such a future when Huxley wrote *Brave New World* in 1932. Henry Ford's transformation of the modern world was as complete and profound as the fictional change of Arthurian England by Mark Twain's Connecticut Yankee. Until Gates did for computers what Ford did for industry, no single person had done as much to shape the world's future. Although it is unlikely that Henry Ford will ever become the religious icon depicted by Huxley, his achievements changed the course of history irrevocably—and for the better.

Ford is known best for making automobiles available to middle-class buyers. This in turn created the suburban lifestyle. The suburban shopping mall followed, superseding many downtown shopping districts. The construction of interstate highway systems led to the decline of the passenger train. The private automobile, a luxury in the early twentieth century, is a commonplace necessity today. The automobile industry created millions of related jobs that range from highway construction to parts manufacturing.

Ford's influence, however, extends well beyond the automobile. He grew up on a farm and experienced firsthand the waste of human and animal energy in farm labor. This led him to develop tractors for farm work and to experiment with industrial methods on his own farm in Dearborn, Michigan. He played a major role in mechanizing agriculture, which helped reduce hunger in many parts of the world. Ford took over the ailing Detroit, Toledo, & Ironton Railway and made it profitable, and he introduced industrial methods into the health care industry. The next section covers a major selling point for Ford's lean enterprise system: its proven results.

THE BOTTOM LINE: FORD'S RESULTS SPEAK FOR THEMSELVES

> Our problem has always been to keep profits down and not up.
>
> —Henry Ford, *Moving Forward* (1930, 11)

Ford proved that it is within the power of value-adding industries like manufacturing and the extractive industries (i.e., enterprises that get foodstuffs and raw materials from nature) to abolish poverty, eliminate hunger, and create almost limitless wealth. This is not hyperbole or speculation: he achieved this wherever he put his hand. He wrote of his methods, specifically continuous improvement and lean manufacturing:

> These fundamentals are not peculiar to the automobile industry and they apply to any business, large or small. They are universal. If they were adopted, a flood of properly-made goods would flow through every nook and cranny of the country, drive out high prices, produce employment everywhere at good wages, and make poverty impossible. The getting of these goods into consumption is the problem of business leadership (Ford, 1930, 11).

Now for the bottom lines, beginning with your company's bottom line. Ford increased his workers' pay while reducing his prices and expanding his business. His principles can even help your company make money by satisfying the ISO 14000 standard for environmental management systems. Ford increased his profits by reducing what we now call environmental waste. This was decades before the EPA, and he could have legally dumped into the river whatever wouldn't go up the smokestack. Instead, "He perfected new processes—the very smoke which had once poured from his chimneys was now made into automobile parts" (Sinclair, 1937, 61).

Next, consider the national bottom line—our gross domestic product (GDP), national standard of living, and national security. A high school graduate could own a house and support a family with one income during the 1950s and 1960s. Now a double income often achieves only the standard of living that a single income once provided. The real purchasing power of American wages and salaries has deteriorated, and Ford can tell us why. It's because most dot-com companies and service jobs produce nothing of real value. Government, which also creates nothing, takes an increasing share of the nation's production.

Ford quadrupled his workers' real wages in twenty years. This corresponds to an inflation-adjusted annual growth rate of 7.2 percent. By relearning what Henry Ford taught during the early twentieth century, the United States might achieve unprecedented national prosperity while eliminating many of its social problems. This is not speculation; Ford did it, and nothing except self-limiting paradigms prevents us from doing it again.

Ford's Breakthroughs in 1908 Won the Second World War

Mass production, to which Ford introduced the United States during the first quarter of the twentieth century, was the "sleeping giant" that Admiral Isoruku Yamamoto warned the Japanese government about as the Second World War approached[2]. Mass production made the United States the arsenal of democracy that supplied weapons and equipment to England and the Soviet Union. The United States' enormous manufacturing capability simply overwhelmed the Axis powers.

Admiral Yamamoto was not the only one who foresaw this. Taiichi Ohno, the father of the Toyota production system, learned in 1937 that German workers were three times more productive than Japanese workers. Americans were, in turn, three times more productive than Germans, thus making one American worth nine Japanese (Ohno, 1988, 3). Manufacturing is the backbone of military power, so the Axis's situation became hopeless as soon as the United States entered the war.

Ford production chief Charles E. Sorensen put it more succinctly: "The seeds of [Allied] victory in 1945 were sown in 1908 in the Piquette Avenue plant of Ford Motor Company when we experimented with a moving assembly line" (Sorensen, 1956, 273). He added that the Willow Run factory, which began as a pencil sketch in his California hotel room, put out one B-24 bomber per hour during the war.

A cartoon in the *London Times* recognized the connection between manufacturing and military power even earlier, in 1918. "The Fighting Pacifist" shows Ford hurling an inexhaustible stream of tanks, trucks, ships, airplanes, shells, and money (in the form of support for the Allied war effort) at the Kaiser. The caption anticipated Admiral Yamamoto's remark about antagonizing sleeping giants: "Henry Ford is the most powerful individual enemy the Kaiser has" (Alvarado and Alvarado, 2001, 74). This discussion underscores the importance of manufacturing to the United States' military security, and the extreme danger associated with the country's declining manufacturing capability.

Ford's Transformation of American Society

In Huxley's anti-Utopia, humanity evolves to serve the machinery of industry and to consume its output. In Ford's own vision of the future, industrialization relegates poverty and hunger to the history books, and thereby eliminates the root causes of war. His tractors actually played a major role in helping Russia grow enough food to feed its people.

Ford's tractors also changed American demographics. Rural populations declined while urban and suburban populations increased because it took fewer farmers to grow a given quantity of food. Ford also wanted to create leisure time for ordinary workers in an era when some people worked six days a week for up to twelve hours a day. We owe our five-day, forty-hour workweek to Henry Ford.

The End of Hunger

The food that our country air-dropped on Afghanistan is the most recent example of the United States' generosity in hunger relief abroad. Food shipments are a necessary containment action—the third step of the modern Ford Motor Company's eight-discipline problem-solving system—to prevent starvation. Henry Ford got at hunger's root cause long ago, his tractors created abundance where famine once reigned. Here is but one of many examples:

> In Armenia, ten of our tractors introduced by a relief committee plowed 1000 acres in eleven days. This work would have required 1000 oxen and 500 men—and neither the oxen nor the men were available (Ford, 1926, 164-165).

Russia was unable to use its rich farmland efficiently until Ford introduced automobiles. This led to the development of roads over which food could move easily. Tractors came next. The Soviet Union, which had asked Ford for help, calculated that one tractor did the work of fifty men and a hundred oxen. England discovered that it cost half as much to plow with tractors as with horses, and mechanization revived agriculture in Greece. One threshing machine in Morocco did the work of 135 men.

The next section lays the groundwork for this chapter's proof that Ford systematized lean enterprise. It begins with an easily remembered definition of lean.

DEFINING LEAN ENTERPRISE

Prevalent definitions of lean manufacturing and lean enterprise are unfortunately similar to a favorite definition of obscenity: "I know it when I see it." Other definitions cover its aspects but not its essence. Just-in-time (JIT) production, single-minute exchange of die (SMED), and *poka-yoke* (error-proofing) are all lean manufacturing tools, but they are not lean manufacturing. Excessive focus on the individual tools of lean manufacturing is like the error of the blind scholars who, in John Godfrey Saxe's tale, touched an elephant and concluded that the part they felt was the entire elephant. Lean enterprise is a system of mutually supporting and synergistic techniques and practices.

Lean Enterprise in a Single Word: Friction

It is useful to go even further and find a single word that encompasses the essence of lean enterprise. Darkness is absence of light, and the most convenient way to define lean enterprise is similarly through its opposite: *friction.*

Friction was General Carl von Clausewitz's (1976) term for "...the force that makes the apparently easy so difficult.... countless minor incidents—the kind you can never really foresee—combine to lower the general level of performance, so that one always falls short of the intended goal." Friction covers all non-value-adding efforts and activities; anything that does not add value to the product or service is friction. A lean enterprise is one from which friction is absent. Japan calls friction *muda* (waste): overproduction, waiting, transportation, inventory, extraneous motion, and the costs of poor quality (e.g., scrap, rework, and inspection).

Friction often hides in plain sight—for years or even centuries. When friction is discovered, we often can't believe we didn't notice it sooner because it is suddenly so obvious—that is, in retrospect. The joke about how underachievers install a light bulb—one worker holds the bulb while three or four others turn the ladder—is not as funny once we realize the procedure we've just improved was equally inefficient.

The ability to see such friction, and to teach his workers to see it, was among Henry Ford's principal success secrets. Chapter 7 explains the concept of friction and all it implies. This single word encompasses the true essence of the lean enterprise, and an organization that understands this has the closest thing to a magic word for organizational transformation. Any member of the organization can point to a method, procedure, piece of equipment, material—anything at all—say to another, "That's friction," and gain immediate understanding and cooperation. The organizational culture should demand the friction's prompt elimination, and this is exactly what happened under Ford. This was the key to the success of the original Ford Motor Company and the foundation of every lean manufacturing technique it developed.

Lean Enterprise, ISO 9000, and ISO 14000

Lean enterprise and the ISO standards for quality (9000) and environmental (14000) management systems are not separate activities that the organization must juggle (thus losing focus on any), but synergistic and mutually supporting ones. Aggressive use of lean enterprise techniques should result in smooth and natural achievement of ISO 9000 and ISO 14000 registration, although one must still document the programs to meet the ISO requirements.

Later chapters will cite synergies with ISO 9000 by citing the appropriate section of ISO 9001:1994. (The older standard consolidates requirements in a more convenient form for analysis.) The ISO 9000:2000 cross-reference is per the American Society for Quality's *Proposed U.S. Adoptions of Draft Standard International,* from late 1999.

Lean Manufacturing Is an American Invention

Now that the book has introduced lean enterprise (of which lean manufacturing is a subset), it will show that Ford and his associates:

- Invented or at least deployed on a massive scale all the so-called Japanese quality and productivity improvement methods like *kaizen* (continuous improvement), just-in-time (JIT) manufacturing, poka-yoke (error-proofing), 5S-CANDO, design for manufacture (DFM), benchmarking, and others.
- Systematized what we now call lean manufacturing.
- Described in explicit detail what Dr. Stephen Covey would later call principle-centered leadership—and defined

exceptionally progressive ideas about the relationship between employers, workers, and customers.

- Were decades ahead of W. Edwards Deming and Tom Peters in breaking down organizational barriers, creating a porous organization, and flattening the organizational structure.

Table 1-1 summarizes well-known modern business and social concepts and their origin (or at least their first large-scale application).

Ford did not actually invent all the items listed next to his name himself. He could not, for example, read or create blueprints despite his mechanical expertise. Charles Sorensen, who began his career with Ford as a patternmaker for iron casting, claims (1956, 6), "I could sense Henry Ford's ideas and develop them." He also states that Ford was the sponsor but not the father of mass production. Walter Flanders was responsible for inventory reduction and efficient arrangement of production machinery. The company would not have survived its early years without James Couzens' management of its finance and sales operations. Sorensen concludes that Henry Ford would have been nothing without people like Couzens, Flanders, C. Harold Wills, and himself, while they, including himself, would have been nothing without Ford. Ford's leadership was nonetheless responsible for creating what we now call lean enterprise.

Two of Japan's foremost lean manufacturing pioneers, Taiichi Ohno and Shigeo Shingo, make no secret of where they learned about lean manufacturing. Productivity Inc.'s former president, Norman Bodek, describes his introduction to Taiichi Ohno in 1980:

> I was first introduced to the concepts of just-in-time (JIT) and the Toyota production system in 1980. Subsequently I had the opportunity to witness its actual application at Toyota on one of our numerous Japanese study missions. There I met Mr. Taiichi Ohno, the system's creator. When bombarded with questions from our group on what inspired his thinking, he just laughed and said he learned it all from Henry Ford's book (Ford, 1926, vii).

Table 1-1. Origin of Leading-Edge Management Techniques

General principles	Origin	Major exponents and modern examples
Principle-centered leadership in business organizations	Ford	Dr. Stephen Covey (*Principle-Centered Leadership*)
Continuous improvement (kaizen) at every level: personal and organizational	Ford	Continuous personal improvement was always important in Japan. Masaaki Imai is a well-known exponent of organizational kaizen.
Social issues, human relations		
Common interests of employer and employee	Taylor, Ford	Also Basset (1919)
Equal pay for women[3]	Ford	Modern equal opportunity laws. A goal of the Equal Rights Amendment (ERA), which was never ratified.
Equal opportunity for minorities[4]	Ford	Modern equal opportunity laws
Opportunities for disabled workers and older workers	Ford	Americans with Disabilities Act (ADA), modern age discrimination laws
Environmental cleanliness (at a profit!)	Ford	"Green manufacturing," Environmental Protection Agency (EPA), ISO 14000
Systematic workplace safety	Ford	OSHA. Ford's River Rouge plant had lockout-tagout by 1931.
Education	Henry Ford Trade School: Graduates could command wages that exceeded those of most college graduates, or proceed to college. It was superior to most modern secondary schools and its graduation rate exceeded that of contemporary high schools.	
Health care	Henry and Clara Ford Hospital: high-quality and cost-efficient care through application of industrial principles to health care	
Organization and management		
Flat organization	Ford	Tom Peters
Elimination of restrictive job descriptions, breaking down organizational barriers	Ford	W. Edwards Deming (re: barriers), Tom Peters (advocacy of the porous organization)
Management by wandering around (MBWA)	(military origins)	Practiced by Ford, later described by Tom Peters

Table 1-1. Origin of Leading-Edge Management Techniques, *continued*

General principles	Origin	Major exponents and modern examples
Lean Manufacturing	**Ford**	**Gilbreth and Taylor laid the foundation.**
5S-CANDO (cleaning, organizing)	Ford, others	Elements appeared in American workplaces by 1911.
Small lot and single-unit processing	Ford	A key characteristic of the Toyota production system
Single-minute exchange of die (SMED)	U.S. per Gilbreth (1911)	Ford (1930) describes process improvements that reduce work handling (setup). Taylor (1911a) identified setup time explicitly but he focused on improving the value-adding part of the job. Shigeo Shingo is the best-known exponent of SMED.
Motion efficiency	Taylor and Gilbreth	Adopted rapidly by Ford
Work cells, cellular organization	H. L. Gantt described factory layout strategies to reduce transportation distances (1911 or earlier). In use at Ford's Highland Park plant by 1915.	
Continual improvement (kaizen)	Ford	Masaaki Imai (*kaizen, gemba kaizen*)
Visual controls	Ford	Gilbreth (1911) discusses the use of color
Supply chain management	Ford	Ford identified the need for this and he also performed supplier development
JIT and inventory reduction	Ford	Taiichi Ohno, Toyota production system.
Concept of inventory as waste	Ford	
Continuous flow, dock-to-factory-floor	Ford	
Theory of constraints, synchronous flow manufacturing	Goldratt	Ford originated the idea that a factory should run like a clock. Basset (1919) describes the placement of an inventory buffer at a bottleneck (constraint) but not the rest of the pull system.

Table 1-1. Origin of Leading-Edge Management Techniques, *continued*

General principles	Origin	Major exponents and modern examples
Quality and productivity		
Benchmarking (learning from competitor's products)	Ford	
Design for manufacture and design for assembly (DFM, DFA)	Ford	
Poka-yoke or error proofing, and self-check systems	Ford	Shigeo Shingo
Best practice deployment, standardization of the "one best way"	Taylor, Ford	Harry & Schroeder, *Six Sigma* (2000)
Waste reduction	Ford	Elimination of *muda* (waste) and *muri* (strain): Masaaki Imai
Statistics and related issues		
Statistical process control (SPC)	Shewhart	
Design of experiments (DOE)	(various)	Taylor (1911) attempted a controlled experiment to improve a metalworking operation; the requisite statistical techniques did not exist.
Reduction of variation	Ford	
Gage calibration	Ford	
Quality auditing	Ford	ISO 9000

Name references	
Gilbreth	Frank Gilbreth, inventor of motion study
Goldratt	Eliyahu Goldratt, author with Jeff Cox of *The Goal*. Originator of the theory of constraints and synchronous flow manufacturing
Masaaki Imai	Author of *Kaizen*, *Gemba Kaizen*
Taiichi Ohno	The father of the Toyota production system
Tom Peters	Author or coauthor of *In Search of Excellence*, *Thriving on Chaos*, other books
Shewhart	Walter Shewhart, the inventor of statistical process control
Shigeo Shingo	Commonly associated with *poka-yoke*, SMED
Taylor	Frederick Winslow Taylor, author of *The Principles of Scientific Management* (1911)

Shigeo Shingo, who is best known for error proofing (poka-yoke) and single-minute exchange of die (SMED), obtained a copy of Frederick Taylor's *Principles of Scientific Management* in 1931. Taylor's assertion that high-wage workers could produce low-cost goods fascinated Dr. Shingo, who did not sleep until he had read the entire book. "At that point I resolved to devote my life to scientific management" (Shingo, 1987, xv–xvi).

Bank official Yukinori Hoshino published a translation of *Principles of Scientific Management* with Taylor's permission in 1913. The Japanese were also reading Frank Gilbreth's *Motion Study* and Taylor's *Shop Management* (1911a) as well (Tsutsui, 1998, 19). The latter could well have inspired SMED, as shown by Figure 1-1.

Suzaki (1987, 10) acknowledges Ford's influence on Japanese management science. "As early as the 1920s Henry Ford was concerned with the problem of waste. He discussed it specifically in his book *Today and Tomorrow*, which Toyota people diligently studied later. To put it in simple terms, 'If it doesn't add value, it's waste.'"

Ford implemented design for manufacture (DFM) and design for assembly (DFA):

Start with an article that suits and then study to find some way of eliminating the entirely useless parts. This applies to everything—a shoe, a dress, a house, a piece of machinery, a railroad, a steamship, an airplane. As we cut out useless parts and simplify necessary ones, we also cut down the cost of making (Ford, 1922, 14).

But also it is to be remembered that all the parts are designed so that they can be most easily made (Ford, 1922, 90).

Ford also identified concepts that we now associate with Six Sigma process capability—the ability to machine parts to tolerances of a tenth of a mil (0.0001inch, 2.54 microns) instead of two or three mils. He introduced gage control and calibration systems to achieve ever-tighter tolerances. He hired Carl Johansson, the Swedish maker of the famous precision gage

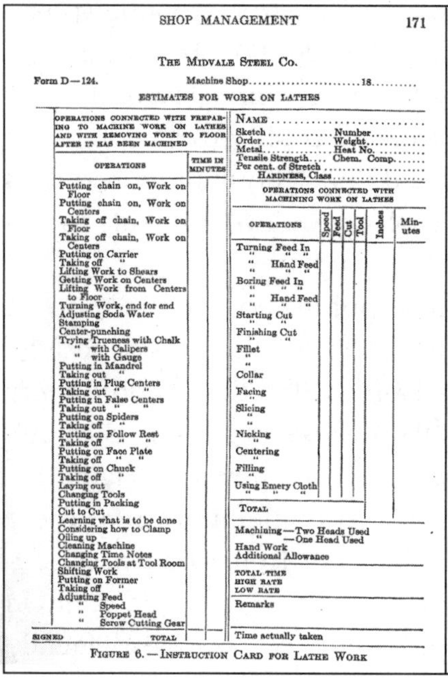

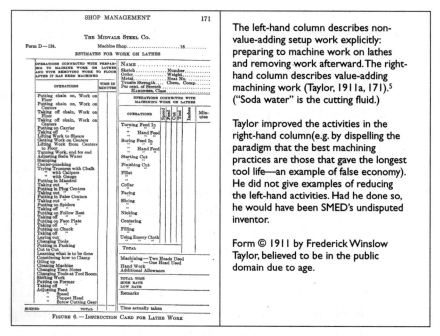

SHOP MANAGEMENT 171

THE MIDVALE STEEL CO.

Form D—124. Machine Shop........................18..........

ESTIMATES FOR WORK ON LATHES

OPERATIONS CONNECTED WITH PREPARING TO MACHINE WORK ON LATHES AND WITH REMOVING WORK TO FLOOR AFTER IT HAS BEEN MACHINED

OPERATIONS	TIME IN MINUTES
Putting chain on, Work on Floor	
Putting chain on, Work on Centers	
Taking off chain, Work on Floor	
Taking off chain, Work on Centers	
Putting on Carrier	
Taking off "	
Lifting Work to Shears	
Getting Work on Centers	
Lifting Work from Centers to Floor	
Turning Work, end for end	
Adjusting Soda Water	
Stamping	
Center-punching	
Trying Trueness with Chalk	
" with Calipers	
" with Gauge	
Putting in Mandrel	
Taking out "	
Putting in Plug Centers	
Taking out " "	
Putting in False Centers	
Taking out " "	
Putting on Spiders	
Taking off "	
Putting on Follow Rest	
Taking off " "	
Putting on Face Plate	
Taking off " "	
Putting on Chuck	
Taking off "	
Laying out	
Changing Tools	
Putting in Packing	
Cut to Cut	
Learning what is to be done	
Considering how to Clamp	
Oiling up	
Cleaning Machine	
Changing Time Notes	
Changing Tools at Tool Room	
Shifting Work	
Putting on Former	
Taking off "	
Adjusting Feed	
" Speed	
" Poppet Head	
" Screw Cutting Gear	
SIGNED TOTAL	

NAME ....

Sketch .... Number............

Order.............. Weight............

Metal.............. Heat No. ....

Tensile Strength.... Chem. Comp.......

Per cent. of Stretch ....

HARDNESS, Class ....

OPERATIONS CONNECTED WITH MACHINING WORK ON LATHES

OPERATIONS	Speed	Feed	Cut	Tool	Inches	Minutes
Turning Feed In						
" " "						
" Hand Feed						
" " "						
Boring Feed In						
" " "						
" Hand Feed						
" " "						
Starting Cut						
" "						
Finishing Cut						
" "						
Fillet						
"						
"						
Collar						
"						
Facing						
"						
Slicing						
"						
"						
Nicking						
"						
Centering						
"						
Filling						
"						
Using Emery Cloth						
" " "						
TOTAL						

Machining—Two Heads Used
" —One Head Used
Hand Work
Additional Allowance

TOTAL TIME
HIGH RATE
LOW RATE

Remarks

Time actually taken

FIGURE 6.—INSTRUCTION CARD FOR LATHE WORK

The left-hand column describes non-value-adding setup work explicitly: preparing to machine work on lathes and removing work afterward. The right-hand column describes value-adding machining work (Taylor, 1911a, 171).[5] ("Soda water" is the cutting fluid.)

Taylor improved the activities in the right-hand column(e.g. by dispelling the paradigm that the best machining practices are those that gave the longest tool life—an example of false economy). He did not give examples of reducing the left-hand activities. Had he done so, he would have been SMED's undisputed inventor.

Form © 1911 by Frederick Winslow Taylor, believed to be in the public domain due to age.

Figure 1-1. Nineteenth Century Instruction Card from Taylor's *Shop Management*

blocks or Jo blocks, whom he described as "the one man in the world who had made a business of absolute accuracy" (Ford, 1926, 84). He then bought the American manufacturing rights for Johansson gages, and Johansson's plant in Poughkeepsie, New York, for good measure.

Ford also recognized that natural variation prevents the manufacture of any part to exactly its nominal specification, and he selected equipment and processes to suppress this variation. It fell to Walter Shewhart, however, to develop statistical process control (SPC) .

Flat and Porous Organizational Structure

Ford introduced the flat organization that Tom Peters promoted much later.

> We made that cut [from 15 to 9 workers per car per day] by applying the rule that everything and everybody must produce or get out.

We cut our office forces in halves and offered the office workers better jobs in the shops. We abolished every order blank and every form of statistics that did not directly aid in the production of a car.

... We formerly had a foreman for every five men; now we have a foreman for every twenty men. The other foremen are working on machines (Ford, 1922, 174).

W. Edwards Deming and Tom Peters both advise their readers to break down organizational barriers. Ford was doing this by 1922. There were no work rules that limited an employee's role. Nobody said, "it's not my job," if he could do it.[6]

And so the Ford factories and enterprises have no organization, no specific duties attaching to any position, no line of succession or authority, very few titles, and no conferences. We have only the clerical help that is absolutely required; we have no elaborate records of any kind, and consequently no red tape...

Because there are no titles and no limits of authority, there is no question of red tape or going over a man's head...

The health of any organization depends on every member—whatever his place—feeling that everything that happens to come to his notice relating to the welfare of the business is his own job (Ford, 1922, 92–94).

Ford and the Toyota Production System

Ohno (1988) devotes an entire chapter to the comparison of the Ford and Toyota systems. Small lot sizes and rapid tooling changeovers apparently comprise the key difference. Where the Ford system would make long production runs of a single car model, Toyota could (and preferred to) produce Coronas and Carinas in alternating sequence. Single-minute exchange of die (SMED) makes this possible.

The Japanese did not, however, start out by trying to make a wide variety of automobiles. They first gained market share through an approach they knew worked: one very similar to Ford's, "You can have any color you want, as long as it's black!"

They [Japanese firms] got to be giants not by catering to consumer whims but by producing a few models very well, often in market segments that were being ignored by other companies. Low-cost, high-quality production leads to growth in market share (Henry Ford's credo) (Schonberger, 1982, 12).

The Ford Motor Company, meanwhile, learned to make diverse products in single production lines. Open and closed bodies had required different sets of ovens (presumably for hardening or drying enamel or paint), conveyors, flow stations, sash enclosures, and suction systems at the Highland Park plant. The new River Rouge plant's ovens could process either body type, and this reduced production costs enormously (Ford, 1930, 188).

Ohno says the Toyota system is the opposite of the Ford system because the latter ". . . promotes large lot sizes, handles vast quantities, and produces lots of inventory." Ford, however, defined inventory as waste and said he did not own a single warehouse.

Clockwork and synchronization were the models for Ford's production control system; he had, as a boy, repaired watches. This suggests that all operations worked at exactly the right rate to supply enough parts for finished vehicles. (This is the concept of takt time, or time-per-unit, which smoothes production flow to a steady pace.) The Toyota system uses kanban, or cards that downstream operations use to authorize production at upstream ones. In summary, then, there are only two obvious differences between the Ford and Toyota systems:

- The Toyota system uses rapid tool changeovers to allow small-lot production of different products. The Ford system made only one product at first but it later became more flexible.
- The Ford production control system was designed to run like a clock. The Toyota system uses a pull system in which kanban from downstream operations authorize production by upstream ones.

The following are key considerations in both systems:

- Avoidance of inventory accumulation.
- Short distances between workstations, because transportation is waste.
- Elimination of strenuous or unnecessary motions by workers.

It should now be obvious where the Japanese learned to make those cars with which they captured a large share of the American market during the 1970s and 1980s. The next section is a synopsis of Ford's basic principles, which appear throughout the rest of the book.

FORD'S BASIC PRINCIPLES

Anyone who is unfamiliar with Henry Ford's books will be amazed as they proceed through this book and discover a steady stream of so-called modern or leading edge management, quality, and productivity methods that Ford introduced more than three-quarters of a century ago. He also described them in plain language without the trappings of academic theory. The best place to start is the beginning, with Ford's basic principles and values. Here is a very condensed overview of Ford's two paramount principles for the *human* and *operational* aspects of any enterprise.

- Natural law, the set of fundamental principles behind all human and organizational behavior, is the foundation of successful human relations. Management-labor and supplier-customer relationships endure and prosper under natural law. Natural law requires a square deal for all participants in any business, economic, social, or personal relationship. It is a prerequisite for commitment, or willingness of an organization's members to place its welfare above their own. Ford wrote of natural law,

    The advantage of what we call moral is that it is natural; it represents the way life must go if it is to go at all. The good is natural. Morality is part of good management. The good manager may resent the word as applied to his work, he may retort that it is only common sense. But that is morality—the plain, practical development of life according to its nature.

The social effect of this morality finds expression in devoting business to the service of the whole people instead of to service of the few. The expression, "spirit of service," sounds idealistic. The spirit of service is just a knowledge that no man can survive, no industry can survive, no government can survive, no system of civilization can survive which does not continually give service to the greatest possible number (Ford, 1926, 273).

- Elimination of all forms of waste is the foundation of operational success. It is, in fact, the single underlying concept behind the lean enterprise. Every lean manufacturing technique suppresses or eliminates some form of waste. Today's lean manufacturing practitioners will recognize the Japanese terms *muda* (waste) and *muri* (strain), but the Ford Motor Company literally wrote the book(s)—specifically by Ford and Crowther—on this subject. We must recognize the waste before we can eliminate it, and Ford's ability to do this was among his principal success secrets.

Chapter 2 begins the exploration of Ford's principles in detail, with a discussion of natural law. It also treats continuous improvement not only in business but also in life itself. The latter is a recurring theme in the Japanese way of life, so the idea of applying Ford's ideas to business may have had a special appeal in Japan.

Notes

1. On the night of the birth of Alexander the Great, for example, lightning struck and destroyed the temple of Artemis in Ephesus in Asia Minor. When the Persian Magi saw this, "They 'ran about beating their

faces and crying aloud that woe and great calamity for Asia had that day been born,' a firebrand that was destined to destroy the entire East" (Green, 1991, 35).

The destruction of the World Trade Center on September 11, 2001 underscored the significance of another card, the Tower. This card, which shows a tower being struck by lightning, means, "Unforeseen catastrophe, disruption of one's style of life or way of thinking which may be followed by enlightenment" (*Aquarian Tarot*, 1975). This accurately describes the event's effects on American thinking, and the 1941 attack on Pearl Harbor had the same significance: a sudden and violent wake-up call.

2. Yamamoto was the admiral who bombed Pearl Harbor, and then ran the Japanese Navy until his death during the war.

3. "The tendency has been for women to go up to men's scales of wages, as indeed they should when they are producing work of equal value" (Ford, 1922a, 234–235). Ford was, however, against the idea of married women working because he believed that many did so only to buy frivolous luxuries. He believed that a family should be able to live on one income and his company's high minimum wage made this possible. Ford's paternalism would not be acceptable by today's standards but it probably was by contemporary ones.

4. Lacey (1986, 222-223) writes that Ford hired Blacks, with equal pay for equal work, during the 1920s—a time when discrimination was legally and socially acceptable.

5. Taylor's *Shop Management* (1911a, opposite 166) also includes a fold-out sheet for timing metalworking operations. The form, "Observations of Hand-Work on Machine Tools, Figure 5," includes sections on setting the work, setting the tool (including adjustments for feed rate and speed), and removing the work.

6. There is a widely-circulated story about four people: Somebody, Everybody, Anybody, and Nobody. Anybody could have done a certain job. Everybody thought Somebody would do it, but Nobody did it.

TWO

Ford's Principles: The Foundation

The introduction to *My Life and Work* is not typical of a book on industrial engineering and operations management. It is discourse on the laws of human behavior that westerners call natural law, Hindus call dharma, and Chinese call Tao or the Way.[1] This is not merely of historical and academic interest—modern change agents and managers must apply these behavioral laws to transform their own organizations into top performers. Ford treats the soft sciences as well as any modern school of labor relations.

This chapter shows other Zen, Buddhist, and Hindu aspects of Henry Ford's philosophy. The Asian nature of Ford's thinking may have helped his ideas gain enthusiastic acceptance in Japan. We begin, however, by quoting Ford's four business principles, which he repeats twice in *My Life and Work* and cites as "the basis of all our work." We then discuss natural law, which is the foundation of all successful human enterprises, social organizations, and nations. The four business principles are (Ford, 1922, 19–20):

- An absence of fear of the future or of veneration for the past. One who fears the future, who fears failure, limits his activities. Failure is only the opportunity more intelligently to begin again. There is no disgrace in honest failure; there is disgrace in fearing to fail. What is past is useful only as it suggests ways and means for progress.
- A disregard of competition. Whoever does a thing best ought to be the one to do it. It is criminal to try to get business away from another man—criminal

because one is then trying to lower for personal gain the condition of one's fellow men, to rule by force instead of by intelligence. [Manufacturers should instead try to gain business by elevating their own condition (i.e. by offering a better product or service). This principle almost certainly refers to such destructive—if not illegal—business practices as the coalition of automakers that tried to put Ford out of business. They invoked the Selden patent, which supposedly covered all "road locomotives" and for whose rights they, but not Ford, had licenses. They claimed that Ford's automobiles fell under its scope.]

- The putting of service before profit. Without a profit, business cannot extend. There is nothing inherently wrong about making a profit. Well-conducted business enterprises cannot fail to return a profit but profit must and inevitably will come as a reward for good service. It cannot be the basis—it must be the result of service.
- Manufacturing is not buying low and selling high. It is the process of buying materials fairly and, with the smallest possible addition of cost, transforming those materials into a consumable product and distributing it to the consumer. Gambling, speculating, and sharp dealing tend only to clog this progression.

The next section describes natural law. As Ford did many decades ago, organizational leaders must understand and apply this material if they hope to achieve outstanding results. Natural law must also become part of the organizational culture, that is, "the way we do things around here."

NATURAL LAW

Natural law is a universal set of principles that governs all human behavior, and it stretches back to the dawn of recorded history. It governs the relationship between employer and employee, and between supplier and customer. It is the foundation of success in any organization from a business, sports team, or civic group to an army or nation. Dr. Stephen Covey (1991, 18–19) provides an excellent summary of natural law:

> Our effectiveness is predicated upon certain inviolate principles—natural laws in the human dimension that are just as real, just as unchanging, as laws such as gravity are in the physical dimension. These principles are woven into the fabric of every civilized society and constitute the roots of every family and institution that has endured and prospered.
>
> Principles are not invented by us or by society; they are the laws of the universe that pertain to human relationships and human organizations. They are part of the human condition, consciousness, and conscience.
>
> . . . The lesson of history is that to the degree people and civilizations have operated in harmony with correct principles, they have prospered. At the root of societal declines are foolish practices that represent violations of correct principles. How many economic disasters, intercultural conflicts, political revolutions, and civil wars could have been avoided had there been greater social commitment to correct principles?

Going against natural law in India results in bad karma. Perpetrators and even innocent bystanders can suffer for more than one lifetime, and even gods are not immune to karma's law. Violations of natural law are the seeds of most Greek and Shakespearean tragedies.[2]

Natural Law Is Self-Evident and Self-Enforcing

Natural law actually provides an objective definition of good and evil. Whatever supports or conforms to natural law is good, anything that violates it is evil. Ford defines stealing not as merely a crime but as bad karma!

> The moral fundamental is man's right to his labour. . . . When a man has earned his bread, he has a right to that bread. If another steals it, he does more than steal bread; he invades a sacred human right (Ford, 1922, 9).

The statement about bad karma is not tongue-in-cheek. Ford described violations of natural law exactly as a Hindu might discuss a violation of dharma:

> There is still a higher law which gets all without exception—it is *the moral law.* You may violate man-made law, and no one be the wiser and, apparently, no one the worse. You may violate economic law and still be carried through by the momentum of society's economic soundness. But the moral law you can never evade. *You cannot even break it!*
>
> ... The law stands there in its eternal integrity. You have not broken it, but you have broken something in yourself against it.[3] In conflict with the moral law all that we can break is ourselves. If we steal, we break some bulwark of self-respect within us—inevitably break it. If we lie, we break some tissue of integrity within us. . . .
>
> Every virtue we practice is a battery filling us with power . . . And everything that is not virtuous, but indirect, unclean, and shifty, takes power from the eye and confidence from the voice and steadiness from the purpose. . .[4]
>
> Many men have escaped man-made law, they have escaped economic law—so far, at least (nobody need be too cocksure about this, for the end of the test has not come), but no man ever lived without receiving sentence in himself upon every violation of the moral law. It gets us all, for sentence or reward. High or low, none escape. It is godlike in its impartial operation. It cannot be postponed, nor fought to a higher court, nor bribed. . . . It has the final word, and its word is final (Ford, 1922a, 230).

This last paragraph is an exact description of karma's operation: "It gets us all, for sentence or reward." This applies not only to individuals but to organizations and even nations. Organizations and countries that conform to natural law thrive, those that go against it perish.

Natural law is not the creation of any government, it is self-evident like the law of gravity. The United States Declaration of Independence says this up front: "We hold these truths to be self-evident, that all men are created equal, that they are endowed by their Creator with certain unalienable Rights, that among these are Life, Liberty and the pursuit of Happiness."

The *Tao Te Ching* says, "Man models himself on earth,/ Earth on heaven,/ Heaven on the way,/ And the way on that which is naturally so." Tao, or the Way, is Hinduism's dharma, an ideal so important that Hindus personify Dharma as a god. The key phrase is, "that which is naturally so." Ford introduces this idea up front:

> I am now most interested in fully demonstrating that the ideas we have put into practice are capable of the largest application—that they have nothing peculiarly to do with motor cars or tractors but form something in the nature of a universal code. I am quite certain that it is the natural code and I want to demonstrate it so thoroughly that it will be accepted, not as a new idea, but as a natural code.
> The natural thing to do is work—to recognize that prosperity and happiness can be obtained only through honest effort. Human ills flow largely from attempting to escape from this natural course. I have no suggestion which goes beyond accepting in its fullest this principle of nature. I take it for granted that we must work (Ford, 1922, 3).
> ... when one regards the moral law as merely the law of right action or truth it becomes quite different from "trying to be good." The universe is set in a certain direction, and when you go along with it, that is "goodness" (Ford, 1929, 33).

Good and evil in this context are therefore not matters of opinion or subjective judgment. Whatever supports or obeys natural law is good, whatever violates or undermines it is evil.

A Universal Code of Human and Organizational Behavior

This universal code, as Ford calls it, is the foundation of all major religions and all successful societies:

> Tai Gong Wong lived around 3100 years ago and, at that time, wrote the first military text in the world. His philosophy

was adopted by countless Chinese military strategists; even the highly acclaimed *Art of War* by Sun Tzu was based on his work. His military strategy was based not solely on maneuvering and placing the troop formations, but rather on the understanding of human nature. Through his personal observations and studies of human behavior, he discovered that there existed unwritten laws mandating the principles of utility and mutual benefit that ordinary human beings unconsciously followed (Chu, 1992, 191).

These "unwritten laws" are the foundation of human behavior. We may clothe them in modern terminology, but we neglect them at our peril. Hinduism says that those who protect and honor dharma gain its protection while dharma destroys those who violate it.

The "principles of utility and mutual benefit" align perfectly with Ford's statement that business transactions must serve both parties. A relationship that profits one at the other's expense cannot endure. "The American idea of business is based on economic science and social morality—that is, it recognizes that all economic activity is under the check of natural law ..." (Ford, 1926, 20).

Natural law ties in with organizational, social, or national culture. Bottorff reinforces Covey's, Ford's, and Chu's discussions of its nature and role.

> Aquinas and Kant[5] referred to culture as "natural law" that exists independent of human authority but nonetheless governs human behavior. The ancient philosophers also recognized that the efficiency, or utility, of the social system improved when man's law more closely approached natural law.
>
> ... Ethicists describe cultures as complex and diverse people systems that seek the same universal principles of utility, relevance, internal consistency, mutual sympathy, cooperation, justice and greater good. This holds true for all organizations, from the smallest business to the largest of nations (Bottorff, 2001).

We again see a set of unwritten laws that are universal to all organizations and that guide all human behavior.

Natural Law Is the Foundation of Government

Ford makes it clear that societies and governments must stand on the foundation of natural law, and that this is the basis of the United States Constitution. Natural law is the universe's constitution.

> So, while the people are indeed supreme over the written Constitution, the spiritual constitution is supreme over them. The French Revolutionists wrote constitutions too— every drunken writer among them tossed off a constitution. Where are they? All vanished. Why? Because they were not in harmony with the constitution of the universe. The power of the Constitution is not dependent on any Government, but on its inherent rightness and practicability (Ford, 1922a, 248).

The next section shows the correlation between Ford's philosophies, including those regarding natural law, and Eastern thought. This alignment may have helped Ford's operational and technological methods appeal to the Japanese.

FORD AND EASTERN PHILOSOPHY: THE JAPANESE CONNECTION

Henry Ford's books never mention Asian philosophy, but there is a fascinating parallel between his principles and Eastern thought. His attitude toward life and work—". . . when a man is sure of what he has to do, he should go ahead full speed. To be right means mainly to be in tune with destiny and willing to obey" (Ford, 1929, 75–76)— answers a Zen *koan* (riddle) that he had probably never seen. (A subsequent section provides the details.) His ideal of placing service before profit, whereupon the profits will take care of themselves, could have come straight from the Hindu *Bhagavad Gita*.

Japan was importing Henry Ford's ideas during the 1930s. The results of his technological and operations management methods spoke for themselves. Ford's ideas probably had added appeal, however, because his views of leadership and life itself resembled those of the Japanese. Asian Indians and Chinese also could relate to Ford's writings, which described the underlying principles of enlightenment—the goal of Zen and Buddhism—in everyday terms.

Ford's Karma or Destiny

The idea of personal destiny or duty, or what Hindus and Japanese call an individual's karma, appears in Virgil's *Aeneid*. This story influenced Penn State football coach Joe Paterno when he was in high school. Paterno explains that the Latin word *fatum* does not mean fate but a divine word or calling.

> Destiny, the fatum, the divine word, the inner voice, whatever you want to call it, tells you where you have to wind up and what you're destined to do, but it doesn't tell you how to get there or how to do it. . . . Through years of hardship and peril, Aeneas reluctantly but relentlessly heeds his fata until he founds Rome (Paterno, 1989, 43–45).

Ford recognized the same concept: "The whole secret of a successful life is to find out what it is one's destiny to do, and then do it" (1929, 75). Furthermore,

> The appointed task may be less to your likes than you expected. A man's real work is not always what he would have chosen to do. A man's real work is what he is chosen to do. There is all the difference between *choosing* and *being chosen*. Sometimes our choices are our destruction (Ford, 1922a, 292).

Ford reinforces the idea of personal duty or destiny even further:

> Faith is the sixth sense that completes all the others and it shows itself chiefly in loyalty to Duty, for Duty sums up all the creative work we do. Our career is our duty, and our duty is our contribution to life. Creative work is not a fine and pleasant frenzy; it is often doing what we would not choose to do, for we are chosen oftener than we choose. A man plodding along at what he knows to

be his duty is an agent of the universe, in his right place (Ford, 1922a, 307).

Ford capitalizes Duty as a Hindu might personify Dharma as a god. The phrase "agent of the universe" underscores this point even further. There is no discernable difference between Ford's concept of a personal duty, or role in the world, and the Indo-Japanese concept.

The *Bhagavad Gita* is the Hindu story of the hero Arjuna's internal struggle over his duty to fight a war in which his cousins and revered teachers are on the other side. Krishna, the avatar of the god Vishnu, tells Arjuna, "And do thy duty, even if it be humble, rather than another's, even if it be great. To die in one's duty is life: to live in another's is death" (Mascaró, 1962, 59). Krishna's role is to help Arjuna through this psychological struggle to an acceptance of his destiny. Ford (1922a, 292) could be describing this scene: "The loneliness comes when a man settles within himself whether he is to be a mere form following a conventional routine, or whether he is to listen [to] and obey the voice of a changeful life. It is lonely for him while he is deciding. If he decides to do what duty bids him, then he is no longer lonely; he comes at once into the fellowship of all liberated souls. The only liberated souls are those dedicated to perpetuate [sic] obedience."

Henry Ford Answers a Zen Riddle

A *koan* is a Zen riddle for stimulating intuitive thought. When the Mongols invaded Japan in 1268, a Zen priest, Bukko, advised the Japanese general Hojo Tokimune, "Dash straight forward and don't look around!" (Newman, 1989, 78). Part of the koan is, "What is the meaning of the general's (Tokimune's) dashing straight forward?" Ford probably never saw this *koan*, but he wrote, ". . . when a man is sure of what he has to do, he should go ahead full speed. To be right means mainly to be in tune with destiny and willing to obey" (1929, 75–76).[6] This approach to life and work doubtlessly appealed to the Japanese when they began to introduce Ford's ideas during the 1930s, for the idea of a personal destiny or karma is a deep part of Japanese culture.[7]

The next section introduces kaizen or continuous improvement, which the Japanese apply to every aspect of life.

CONTINUOUS IMPROVEMENT: KAIZEN

The Japanese view life itself as "a battle to achieve continuous improvement" (Peters, 1987, 272), and only a dead person has nothing left to learn. Ford describes people who stop looking for ways to improve their work as "half-alive." "Life, as I see it, is not a location, but a journey" (1922, 43). The idea that one has arrived at a final goal, and can therefore stop advancing and progressing, is the beginning of the end for an individual or a business. The word *success* should be reserved for a tombstone.

> The man receives his last advancement—and usually it is his *last*—with the feeling that at length he has arrived. . . . We want to write the word 'success' too soon. It should be kept for the epitaph. Any man who thinks he is a success, has come to his terminal. He is about ready to get off (Ford, 1922a, 34–35).

The idea of continuous improvement even applies to holding off the effects of advancing age. Modern researchers have, in fact, identified a connection between mental activity and delaying the onset of Alzheimer's disease. Continuous learning promotes mental health that, in turn, influences physical well being.

> Anyone who stops learning is old—whether this happens at twenty or eighty. Anyone who keeps on learning not only remains young but becomes constantly more valuable—regardless of physical capacity. . . . Anyone who is satisfied with the progress that he is making or is inclined to be thankful for having arrived at his present position is old (Ford, 1930, 89–90).

This principle applies not only to individuals but also to organizations and nations. Lawrence Miller's *Barbarians to Bureaucrats* shows how an organization's wealth and physical power lag behind its vitality.

The cycle of the seasons is an excellent model. Suppose the hours of sunlight in a day reflect vitality and the temperature measures wealth and power. The summer solstice is the longest day of the year, and it is analogous to the height of an organization's vitality. The solstice is not, however, the height of summer but only its beginning. The days will grow warmer, as the organization's power will continue to grow, but the days have already begun to get shorter.

This model shows how an organization's (or a nation's) wealth and power lag its vitality. This is a lesson that the United States must consider very carefully, especially given the steady efflux of its manufacturing base.

Ford expands further:

> Success is the enemy. It is the only enemy that can overcome men who are invincible to failure. Men who cannot be beaten though they fail a score of times, men who cannot be discouraged by an army of difficulties, sometimes go tumbling down as the result of a little success. More men are failures on account of success, than on account of failure (Ford, 1922a, 27).[8]

The word for first degree black belt, *sho dan*, means first step, not expert. No one ever becomes a master of a martial art or other activity, in the sense that a master has nothing left to learn. Ford says, "... no one ever considers himself expert if he really knows his job. A man who knows a job sees so much more to be done than he has done, that he is always pressing forward and never gives up an instant of thought to how good and how efficient he is" (1922) What some might call success, Ford calls a first step: *sho dan*. "What he [the successful manager] has done he regards as a beginning—maybe a mighty good beginning, but only a beginning after all" (1922a, 28).

Beware of Complacency

The rot has begun to set in when an organization's members start to say, "We've always done it that way." Ford warns,

> Men fall into the half-alive habit. Seldom does the cobbler take up with the new-fangled way of soling shoes, and seldom does the artisan willingly take up with new methods in his trade. Habit conduces to a certain inertia, and any disturbance of it affects the mind like trouble. . . . Business men go down with their businesses because they like the old way so well they cannot bring themselves to change. One sees them all about—men who do not know that yesterday is past, and who woke up this morning with last year's ideas (Ford, 1922, 43).

Ford discusses more warning signs further on:

> When a business becomes congested with bad methods; when a business becomes ill through lack of attention to one or more of its functions; when executives sit comfortably back in their chairs as if the plans they inaugurated are going to keep them going forever; when business becomes a mere plantation on which to live, and not a big work which one has to do—then you may expect trouble (Ford, 1922, 159).

Charles Sorensen (1956, 51) adds that incompetent people seldom destroy an organization because they rarely rise to sufficiently high positions to do so. The people who have actually done things but then want to coast on their achievements are the real danger. He calls for businesses to be "kept in perpetual ferment" to preserve their vitality, and he adds Napoleon's comment, "The art of government is not to let men go stale."[9]

Sorensen (1956, 217–218) blamed the Model T's eighteen-year success for killing the company's initiative. Sales declined as competitors introduced new models, but Henry Ford was unwilling to accept the idea that the Model T's day was over. It took half a year of persuasion from his son Edsel and others to get him to introduce a new car, the Model A. This is an object lesson for any organization that thinks, "It can't happen to us." If it happened to Henry Ford, who *knew* the danger of a long run of success, it can happen to us very easily.

Miller (1989) defines the roles people take at the various stages in the rise and fall of a business or a nation in Table 2-1.

Table 2-1. Organizational Phases and Their Leaders

Growth: the morning	
1. The Prophet	Someone with an organizational vision, a mental picture of where he or she wants to go
2. The Barbarian	A dynamic and aggressive leader who can make the Prophet's vision reality. The Barbarian can lead an organization through its rapid growth phase.
3. The Builder and the Explorer	These leaders have the skills necessary to build the organization and explore new opportunities. They develop specialized skills and structures that support growth. Leadership focus shifts from command to collaboration.
Plateau: noon	
4. The Administrator	This leader installs the organizational controls that are necessary to run a large organization. The Administrator can build integrating systems and structures. Leadership focus shifts from expansion to security.
Decline: afternoon, twilight, and nightfall	
5. The Bureaucrat	The Bureaucrat is more interested in pushing paper (non-value-adding) and serving the system, as opposed to making the system serve the organization's stakeholders. Think of "meeting engineers" and departments whose function is to show each other colorful overhead transparencies. Prophets and Barbarians are unwelcome in this environment.
6. The Aristocrat	To the Aristocrat the organization is, in Ford's words, "a mere plantation on which to live."

He goes on to describe the Synergist as someone who seems to be the ideal, combining the functions of Prophet, Barbarian, Explorer, Builder, and Administrator. These five roles are necessary and constructive. (The Bureaucrat is not necessary and is indeed a form of waste.) Ford's own weakness was, in fact, that he was Prophet, Barbarian, Builder, and Explorer but had little patience for administration or organizational structures.[10] Fortunately the Ford Motor Company had an able administrator in its early years in James Couzens, whom Sorensen describes as "a dragon at the cash box." Couzens also played a major role in driving sales, service, advertising, and dealer relationships.

Another problem Ford had with complacency was that he could not imagine a successor to himself (Sorensen, 1956). Miller (1989, 46) cites H. G. Wells's comments about Alexander the Great: "The idea that the world would have to go on after Alexander, engaged in any employment other than the discussion of his magnificence, seems to have been outside his mental range." Like Alexander, who left his empire to "the strongest," Ford gave little attention to an orderly succession of power. Edsel Ford, his obvious successor, predeceased him. This was a major reason for the subsequent decline in the company's fortunes.

Ford's weaknesses were only relative. The Peter Principle says that most people eventually rise to their level of incompetence, a position for which their past achievements do not equip them to succeed. Ford's level happened to be the apex of the greatest industrial empire that the world had ever seen. Not only that, his leadership deficiencies only became apparent when he was in his seventies and had suffered a stroke.

Ford encompassed the first three leadership aspects: Prophet, Barbarian, and Builder and Explorer. He provided the vision statement for an affordable car and then he made it happen. He built the physical infrastructure, a vertically-integrated enterprise, to make the product in huge quantities. As an Explorer he put his hand successfully to other enterprises like railroading, lumber, mining, shipping, and health care.

Ford's disinterest in administration may have been a weakness during the late 1920s. Alfred Sloan's introduction of organizational structure at General Motors may have given GM a competitive advantage over Ford, but remember that organizational structure can lead to productivity-inhibiting barriers. Administration is necessary, especially in large enterprises, but do not allow it to progress to bureaucracy or aristocracy.

Find a Way or Make One

"What I can't touch doesn't exist," was a memorable line from Orson Welles in his role of Bayan of the Hundred Eyes in *The Black Rose*. Kublai Khan's general was proud of his "practical" lack of imagination. Bayan's remark provides a useful contrast to the culture at Ford, as stated repeatedly by Charles Sorensen: "The only thing we can't make is something we can't think about."

The following discussion outlines one of this book's most important concepts: Don't take any aspect of the job—its tools, materials, methods, or anything else—for granted. This is the key to greatness—literal greatness, as achieved by Alexander of Macedonia and Henry Ford, and mythical greatness, as achieved by Hercules.

The legend of Hercules changed the world by teaching Alexander the Great how to overcome seemingly impossible obstacles: by not taking any aspect of a job or task as a given. Alexander knew the Hercules stories, and he regarded the mythical hero as a personal role model. Macedonian coins later depicted Alexander in a lion skin, in imitation of Hercules. Many people think of Hercules as a Bronze Age version of Superman who used his strength to rescue people and right wrongs. Few recall that he had a mercurial temper and sometimes killed friends and other bystanders in fits of rage (as did Alexander). Table 2-2 shows, however, that Hercules had to rely on innovative solutions as much as on his strength.

Alexander used the same principle to conquer most of the known world.

This is also how Henry Ford thought. He was reluctant to hire experts to do anything because experts often knew why something couldn't be done. "No operation is ever directed by a [technical expert], for always he knows far too many things that can't be done. Our invariable reply to 'it can't be done' is, 'go do it'" (Ford, 1926, 53).

Table 2-2. Work smarter, not harder. *Don't take any part of the job as a given.*

Hercules	Alexander the Great
Hercules' lion skin might not seem unusual because Greek hunters were quite capable of killing lions. Hercules', however, belonged to the Nemean Lion and it was impenetrable. Most people would have given up and concluded that the lion could not be killed. (Anyone who says it can't be done is right— as far as he or she is concerned.) Hercules realized that the skin, while impenetrable, had to be flexible or the lion could not have moved. He slew the lion by strangling it and then, by experimentation, discovered that its claws would cut its skin. Hercules had to clean out the Augean Stables, a job that had been long neglected. Frederick Winslow Taylor realized that shoveling was a science, and that workers should use different shovels for different loads: small ones for iron ore and large ones for rice coal and ash. This is an example of seeing an inefficiency has been built into the job (another key principle) *but even Taylor took the shovel itself as a given.* Taylor's first inclination might have been to show Hercules how to shovel more efficiently while providing a shovel to take a Hercules-sized load: more than the 21.5 pounds (9.8 kg) that he found optimal for mortal workers. Hercules did not take the shovel as a given, at least not for moving manure. He may have used one when he diverted two rivers through the stables, thus finishing the job quickly and keeping his hands relatively clean.	There was a prophecy that whoever unraveled the Gordian Knot would rule Asia Minor. The knot was very complex and its ends were buried deep inside it. Many people had tried and failed to untie it. The obstacle was mental, not physical. Everyone took as a given that the knot had to be untied. Alexander didn't; nowhere did the rules say that he had to *untie* the Gordian Knot. He drew his sword and cut it. The fortress city of Tyre was on an island and it was thus unapproachable by infantry. Alexander may have remembered Hercules' alteration of geography when he had his engineers build an isthmus from the mainland to the island. He thus captured a fortress that many people thought was invincible. The famous horse Bucephalus threw everyone who tried to mount him. Instead of trying to force him to obey (a losing proposition, as a horse is far stronger than a man), Alexander observed him and discovered that he was afraid of his own shadow. When Alexander turned him so he could no longer see his shadow, Bucephalus allowed Alexander to ride him.

Ford continues by citing the example of the manufacture of plate glass in a continuous ribbon, without any hand work. The world's glass experts said it could not be done. Ford employed workers who had never been in a glass plant and, although they had to surmount all the expected problems and some unexpected ones, they succeeded. The new plant at Highland Park:

- occupied half as much space as Ford's older plant at Glassmere, which relied on the traditional method of making glass in clay pots.

- produced almost twice as much glass.
- required a third as many employees.

This was no small accomplishment. Furnaces had to be charged every fifteen minutes with sand, soda ash, and other chemicals. The molten glass flowed out in a continuous stream onto a revolving iron drum and continued under a roller that gave it the correct thickness. The sheet passed from the roller into an annealing furnace, or lehr, at 50 inches (127 cm) a minute. The lehr was 442 feet (135 meters) long, which is longer than an American football field. The lehr annealed the glass under gradually diminishing heat. The operation had to be controlled closely to avoid distortion from thermal shock. It turned out that PPG Industries was working on this problem at the same time (1922–1924), and the two companies solved it independently (Shreve and Brink, 1977, 187–188). Sorensen (1956, 172–173) adds that Ford's venture into glassmaking had profound effects on the entire industry. It compelled American glassmakers to improve their facilities and practices, and all because the Ford Motor Company refused to accept the prevailing methods as givens.

Aluminum casting was another so-called impossibility. Sand molds are traditional in casting operations because air can escape through the sand. When liquid metal enters solid molds or metal dies, air bubbles form and create "blows" in the casting. Ford and his people cut this industrial Gordian Knot quite nicely:

> Then the secret of feeding the molten metal into the dies from underneath was discovered.
>
> The die is placed directly above the pot containing the molten metal. In fact, it takes the place of a lid. When a cast is to be made, the operator turns the air pressure into the hot metal. The pressure forces the metal up through a feeder into the die. As the metal goes in, the air is forced out through miniature vents. As the top of the die is filled first, the cast naturally solidifies from that point downward. The air is forced out by the first rush of molten metal on the top of the mould, and as metal can enter only by the

feeder, all danger of air bubbles is eliminated, and the cast is perfect (Ford, 1926, 71).

The results of the company's venture into steel-making speak for themselves. After the company built a steel mill at the River Rouge plant, both Charles Schwab of Bethlehem Steel and Bill Irwin of United States Steel wanted to buy it. They offered to meet Ford's steel requirements at guaranteed prices and volumes. Charles Sorensen told them they could have it only if they bought the entire Ford Motor Company with it (Sorensen, 1956, 174).

Ford was reluctant to keep records of experiments because records of failures might discourage others from trying. I do not agree with this. Good records, even of failures, can avoid the waste of resources on approaches that were proven unsuccessful. Records of partial successes can facilitate subsequent progress.

The people who use the records should, however, do what Hannibal said the Carthaginians would do about the passage of the Alps: "We will find a way or make one." The innovative Carthaginians dealt with a road-blocking rockslide by felling trees and building a bonfire next to the boulders. When the rocks were red-hot, a douche of water (or possibly sour wine) cracked them by thermal shock; it was then easy to break them apart with pick-axes (Bradford, 1981, 69–70). This is how Ford wanted his workers to think.

> ... no one ever considers himself expert if he really knows his job. ... Thinking always ahead, thinking always of trying to do more, brings a state of mind in which nothing is impossible. The moment one gets into the 'expert' state of mind a great number of things become impossible. ...
>
> Most technical training and the average of that which we call experience, provide a record of previous failures and, instead of these failures being taken for what they are worth, they are taken as absolute bars to progress (Ford, 1922, 86–87).

The person who knows it can't be done is always right—as far as he or she is concerned. The phrase "everybody knows..."

should be a bright warning flag. Ford points out that Columbus would not have set sail had he believed what everybody else knew about geography: "Columbus did not study geography; he made it" (1922a, 146).

Mass Production Requires Continuous Improvement

Ford warned explicitly that mass production is not rigid production. Successful mass production requires continuous improvement.

> Rigid machine production of the kind known as mass production quickly comes to an end, for it violates the first principle of large-scale production—which is that the makers must constantly improve the design and quality of the goods turned out.... [The products] were bought because they could always be depended upon to be first-class, but they were first-class only because they were constantly improved—although possibly the improvements were seldom mentioned. But if, after the reputation of the articles had become assured, and those who had built the reputation rested, or were followed by men who were content to take the product as they found it and depend on the fine reputation, then dry rot set in and the product steadily slipped back and another product took its place (Ford, 1930, 27–28).

Another way of saying this is, "only God can rest on the day after creation. All others must keep working." No flaw in Henry Ford's legacy allowed foreign competitors, especially the Japanese, to supersede American mass producers. One must look for the fault in that legacy's application, or lack thereof.

Price Reductions and Continuous Improvement

A company's decision to reduce its prices while increasing its wages, even when competitive pressures do not force it to do so, drives continuous improvement. Ford cites the story of a German immigrant who came to work for him. The German described his experience as part of a crew that was installing electrical wiring in a German castle. The crew had to break holes in the thick stone walls to do this, and it took three and a half days to make a hole in a four foot (1.2 meter) thick cellar wall. He complained to the leader, who was one of the company's best, that a tool should be designed to make this job easier. The leader answered that the job had always been done that way and that a better tool might put them out of work. (The next section discusses the paradigm that workers must soldier, or limit productivity, to keep their jobs.)

The Germans earned only two to three dollars a week and the leader got four. The German who told this story emigrated to the United States and went to work at Ford, and he described his experiences there:

> I saw new machinery, new processes, new methods constantly being introduced. I heard of price reductions and wage increases, but I never heard anybody say: "We always made the holes in this manner; we always got them through—the old method is all right, why try to change it?" I never heard this sentiment in America.
>
> Even I, though I am not a millionaire, can today afford my own car, because there were some people who said, "Let us make those holes a little faster," and thus brought down the cost of cars, of houses, radios, washing machines, etc. so far that even the worker can afford them.
>
> So I have learned from my work, that the American people are prosperous and receive high wages, not because they won the war, but because they are always looking for better and faster methods to do their work instead of pinning their hopes for better living on political strifes and machinations (Ford, 1930, 170–171).

This story is also another example of never taking the job as a given, or accepting that it's right because "we've always done it that way."

The next section discusses the principle that management and labor are not adversaries but partners. This is a simple extension of natural law and the idea that any arrangement must benefit all its stakeholders. The company that achieves this spirit of cooperation gains a decisive advantage over its competitors.

BRINGING WIN-WIN TO THE WORKPLACE

Dr. Stephen Covey (1991) describes the scarcity mentality that often limits organizational performance. The scarcity mentality is the assumption of a win-lose situation where participants must divide some finite resource. If one person gets more, someone else must get less. Ford defined it outright: "For hundreds of years men have been talking about the lack of opportunity and the pressing need to divide up things already in existence" (1926, 2). Then he broke this self-limiting paradigm:

> . . . we already have enough tested ideas which, put into practice, would take the world out of its sloughs and banish poverty by providing livings for all who will work. Only the old, outworn notions stand in the way of these new ideas. The world shackles itself, blinds its eyes, and then wonders why it cannot run! (Ford, 1926, 2)

The scarcity mentality resulted in soldiering, the workers' practice of deliberately limiting production to preserve jobs.[11] The practice was so widespread that other countries developed their own names for it: "hanging it out" in England and "ca canae" in Scotland. The workers believed that, if employee productivity increased, the company would need fewer employees. They expected mechanization to have the same effect. The Luddites of the early nineteenth century even sabotaged machinery. Because the budget for wages was presumably limited, any increase in per-worker productivity would go unrewarded anyway. Taylor recognized that some companies reinforced the latter perception by cutting piece rates as workers became more productive:

> . . . after a workman has had the price per piece of the work he is doing lowered two or three times as a result of his having worked harder and increased his output, he is likely entirely to lose sight of his employer's side of the case and become imbued with a grim determination to have no more cuts if soldiering can prevent it (Taylor, 1911, 8).

Henry Ford said essentially the same thing:

The theory that efficiency and better methods make for unemployment is pernicious, but it is widespread. . . . It all goes on the theory that there is only so much work in the world to do and it must be strung out. . . . The fallacy of this has been proved over and over again and nowhere more effectively than in our own industries (Ford, 1926, 157).

Henry Ford and Frederick Winslow Taylor played major roles in overturning the scarcity mentality in the workplace. Higher productivity allowed the employer to pay higher wages while enjoying a lower per-piece labor cost.

Scientific management . . . has for its very foundation the firm conviction that the true interests of the two [employers and employees] are one and the same; that prosperity for the employer cannot exist through a long term of years unless it is accompanied by prosperity for the employee, and vice versa; and that it is possible to give the workman what he wants—high wages—and the employer what he wants—a low labor cost—for his manufactures (Taylor, 1911, 1).

Implications for Lean Manufacturing

Womack and Jones (1996) stress this principle repeatedly in conjunction with lean manufacturing. The introduction of lean techniques and methods can yield phenomenal productivity gains. Some employers might be tempted to discharge workers who become unnecessary. If they prove the soldierers and Luddites correct, they will get exactly what they deserve (Figure 2-1).

Disgruntled workers do not have to resort to overt sabotage as the Luddites did. Sabotage means literally "to clatter shoes," a French expression for working clumsily or soldiering, as opposed to vandalism. Doing exactly and only what they are told and refusing to exercise any judgment or initiative are sufficient. This is sometimes known as a *white mutiny*, a mutiny that relies on dogmatic compliance with orders. *Malicious compliance* is another term.

There are three alleged origins of "Luddite": (1) a real person named Ned Lud (per the *American Heritage Dictionary*), who destroyed stocking frames during the late 18th century, (2) incidents of machine-smashing in Lud, England, and (3) a mythical labor leader, Good King Lud.

Figure 2-1. Don't cut jobs when productivity rises

Lean manufacturing and its close relative, the kaizen blitz (lightening continuous improvement), rely on the intimacy of frontline workers with their jobs.[12] These workers must be more than acquiescent; they must be enthusiastic about making lean manufacturing work. Job security and the delivery of higher wages in exchange for productivity improvements are the ways to foster such enthusiasm.

Taiichi Ohno, the father of the Toyota production system, reinforces this point:

> Hiring people when business is good and production is high just to lay them off or recruiting early retirees [encouraging people to take early retirement] when recession hits are bad practices. Managers should use them with care. On the other hand, eliminating wasteful and meaningless jobs enhances the value of work for workers (Ohno, 1988, 20).

What should the employer do with the now-excess workers? Assign the better ones (the reassignment should be a reward, not a penalty or a sinecure) to improvement teams whose job is to drive further productivity improvements. More work fosters higher productivity, which in turn usually results in bringing in even more work.

The Luddites were afraid that textile machinery would put them out of work but Crow (1943) describes how mechanization actually affected this industry. Americans of the colonial era lived in abject poverty. Ninety out of 100 people were farmers, and many farm families lived in single-room houses. They had to make most of what they needed, including clothing. Store-bought clothing was a luxury, homespun was common. "No farmer could hope to earn enough money to buy clothing for his family and they were all dressed in homespun or skins or not at all" (Crow, 1943, 16).

A worker could separate five pounds of cotton a day from the unusable seed; Eli Whitney's first crude cotton gin could process fifty. The price of cotton fell from a dollar to thirty cents a pound, and other textile machinery made cloth even cheaper. Textile workers of 1812 were 200 times more productive than those of a few generations earlier (Crow, 1943, 37). This is what the Luddites feared, that one worker could take the jobs of 200.

What actually happened, though, was that clothing became far more affordable. People who would have otherwise worn homespun garments, rags, or animal skins now bought cotton shirts. The shirts sold for much less but, because each worker was now far more productive, he sold far more shirts. Whitney's other great achievement, the introduction of interchangeable parts, made it far easier to produce other goods. Crow (1943, 51–52) concludes:

> Most of all, this American system of manufacturing which was universally adopted was of great benefit to the consumer—to the customers who were later to buy the never ending and always increasing products of American factories. . . . The mass production of the assembly line meant the production of cheaper and better merchandise of standard quality. By the employment of workmen of varying degrees of skill he spread employment over a wider range and so created more customers for the products of the American factories that were to follow.

Europe Steps Backward[13]

TANSTAAFL is the acronym for "There Ain't No Such Thing As A Free Lunch." France seems to think, however, that there is a free lunch.

> As a law it's unique in Europe. As of February 1st, 14 million workers in France are having to work less while receiving the same paycheck ... The government expects that the 35-hour week will create 450 thousand new jobs. But critics say that instead of creating new jobs the regulation could actually lead to jobs being cut. Companies might simply invest in new equipment to eliminate higher labour costs ("France Launches the 35-Hour-Week," 2000).

This quote will appear again later but it is worth mentioning now:

> The demand of the disorderly element is practically that everybody be requested to raise fewer potatoes, and yet that everybody be given more potatoes.... If everybody does less work and everybody gets more of the product of work, how long can it last? (Ford, 1922a, 177).

The only way the French can have shorter hours without cutting wages is, of course, to increase productivity; this is how Ford gave the world the 40-hour workweek. Distributing the work of seven among eight is simply a variant of soldiering.

Edmondson and Johnston (1997) say that French employers are trying to improve productivity by, for example, having employees work 45-hour weeks during peak production periods and 20-hour weeks during slack periods. Ford himself had a vision of workers moving between factory and farm according to the season but, because his own tractors have reduced farm employment to a small fraction of the population, this is no longer realistic. Meanwhile,

> In Germany, shorter workweeks have killed rather than created jobs. There, union IG Metall secured a 35-hour workweek in 1995 for some 3.5 million industrial workers. But hundreds of thousands of manufacturing jobs a year

continue to vanish. . . . In 1994, VW [Volkswagen] reduced hours at its main German assembly plants from 36 to 28.5 to avoid laying off 30,000 excess workers. Now, wage costs are 8 percent higher than at several VW plants where employees work 35 hours per week or more (Edmondson and Johnston, 1997).

BusinessWeek Online, (May 3, 1999)[14] adds that the effect of the French law has not been to reduce unemployment but to raise it. Higher labor costs encourage investors to create jobs in other countries.

TANSTAAFL is worth remembering, and we will look at it in more detail later. For now, the French and German examples underscore this principle. The only way for everyone to get more potatoes for less effort is to raise the potatoes more efficiently— and Ford's methods make this possible.

Natural Law and Labor Relations

We have already seen that Henry Ford recognized and applied the principles of natural law to his business. The absolute sovereignty of natural law in organizational behavior appears in Confucius' *Analects* and again in Sun Tzu's *The Art of War.* Sun Tzu defined moral law, moral influence, or Tao as one of the five key factors in organizational success. Confucius wrote:

> He who rules by moral force is like the pole-star, which remains in its place[15] while all the lesser stars do homage to it. . . . Govern the people by regulations, keep order among them by chastisements, and they will flee from you, and lose all self-respect. Govern them by moral force, keep order among them by ritual and they will keep their self-respect and come to you of their own accord (1938, 88).

Ford echoes Confucius, as follows:

> You can show your authority till doomsday and make people fear it too; but you will never make them respect it. . . . Handling men, giving them leave to act upon their own goodwill and not under compulsion, emancipating

them from all fear and anxiety and insecurity in their thoughts of the shop and the job—this is the secret of goodwill in production (Ford, 1922a, 59–60).

We have already seen that, when a business pays its workers as little as it can, soldiering and other dysfunctional behavior often result. The workers flee from their employer—in the sense of limiting their production or otherwise doing as little as possible—and lose the self-respect that comes from doing a job well. When managers lead in accordance with natural law, or moral force, there is no need to watch the employees to make sure they work. They will come to the employer, in the sense of doing as much as they can, on their own. The organizational behavior term is *commitment*, the willingness to sacrifice comfort and ease on an organization's behalf.

Commitment isn't just a feel-good word, it affects the bottom line. Shellenbarger (2000) cites Watson Wyatt Worldwide's study that shows, "Companies where employees trusted top executives posted shareholder returns 42 percentage points higher than companies where distrust was the rule."

The concept of the leader as the organization's servant ties in with commitment, and the next section discusses it.

SERVICE

A leader exists to serve his or her followers, not the other way around. The idea of the leader as the servant of his or her followers pervades many cultures.[16] Ford defined the essence of what Covey and other sources call servant leadership. An employer "cannot say, 'I have so many thousand men working for me.' The fact of the matter is that so many thousand men have him working for them . . ." (Ford, 1922, 120–121). Ford also advocates profit-sharing on these pages.

A business similarly exists to serve its stakeholders—employees, owners, and customers—not the other way around. Ford applied this idea to business explicitly:

The leaders of business are as responsible for the welfare of the people as the generals of an army are responsible for the welfare of the soldiers. . . . They are servants, else their tenure is very short. Their responsibility has to do with continually seeing to it that their activities are beneficial to the people as a whole. A big business never becomes big by being a narrow society looking after only the interests of its organization and stockholders (Ford, 1930, 64–65).

Tribus repeats this idea more than sixty years later while discussing the principles of W. Edwards Deming:

The CEO believes that the company is the people. The CEO takes as the purpose of the company to remain in business forever, to provide meaningful employment for the people, useful services and goods for the public and a fair return to the shareholders, in that order of priority (Tribus, 1992, 30).

Ford said that a business holds its profits in trust for the customers who provided those profits, and that management and labor are partners and not rivals. He disliked bankers and stockholders who put money into a business only for the sake of harvesting interest or dividends. Ford (1930, 2) uses the word service to encompass his basic principles of business:

Only disaster can result when the fundamental principles of business are disregarded and what looks like the easiest way is taken. These fundamentals, as I see them, are:
1. To make an ever-increasingly large quantity of goods of the best possible quality, to make them in the best and most economical fashion, and to force them out on the market.
2. To strive always for higher quality and lower prices as well as lower costs.
3. To raise wages gradually but continuously—and never to cut them.
4. To get the goods to the consumer in the most economical manner so that the benefits of low-cost production may reach him.
5. These fundamentals are all summed up in the single word service . . .

Serve and the Profits Will Take Care of Themselves

Ford wrote that one should go into a business to serve customers and society in general, not to make money:

> The producer depends for his prosperity upon serving the people. He may get by for a while serving himself, but, if he does, it will be purely accidental, and when the people wake up to the fact that they are not being served, the end of that producer is in sight. . . . Being greedy for money is the surest way not to get it, but when one serves for the sake of service—for the satisfaction of doing that which one believes to be right—then money abundantly takes care of itself (Ford, 1922, 12–13).[17]

This could have come straight from the Bhagavad Gita:

> Set thy heart upon they work, but never on its reward. Work not for a reward; but never cease to do thy work. Do thy work in the peace of Yoga and, free from selfish desires, be not moved in success or in failure. . . . Work done for a reward is much lower than work done in the Yoga of wisdom. Seek salvation in the wisdom of reason. How poor those who work for a reward!" (Mascaró, 1962, 52).

Work for personal satisfaction is more rewarding spiritually than work for money, but Ford—the world's first self-made billionaire—does not make a virtue of poverty. Work for the task's own sake is likely to be performed well, and the financial rewards then come naturally.[18] Charles Sorensen wrote of the early Ford culture that work was play, the task of growing the company was its own reward. Money came along naturally; the organization's participants did not have to look for it.

Service includes not merely a square deal but a synergistic or win-win deal, and natural law plays a key role. The thought of bad karma in an unfair transaction is evident in the phrase, "you upset the world" in the following quote:

> If a man is not better off for buying than he would be if he had kept his money in his pocket, there is something wrong. Buyer and seller must both be wealthier in some

way as a result of a transaction, else the balance is broken. Pile up these breaks long enough, and you upset the world. We have yet to learn the anti-social nature of every business transaction that is not just and profitable all around (Ford, 1926, 40).[19]

Ford pointed out the decline of the service ethic in "Change Is Not Always Progress," an editorial in the *Dearborn Independent*:

Industrial leaders have been poisoned to the extent that some of them look on their industries as "money makers," instead of plow-makers, or chair-makers, or clothing-makers. That is the new code: "Get the money." If you can get the money quicker by destroying the business, then destroy the business!

Professional life has also been infected with the same idea. Lawyers once had clients and doctors patients: now they have "customers."

... In industry, the man who still takes pride in his day's work, who really looks for satisfaction in the labor of his hands, is rated by his fellows as a "boob." He is a "back number" (Ford, 1922a, 277).

This is as true today as it was then, if not more so. Health management organizations (HMOs) make money from covered populations instead of by treating patients. If HMO administrators provided an element of scientific management to health care they might add value, as shown in Chapter 6. Most, however, apparently try to ration care and cut corners so they can make as much money as possible. They care for money instead of patients, but their executive offices give them a social status that is probably not accorded to the registered nurses who have their hands on the actual work.

Manufacturing, the backbone of national prosperity and security, has oft been perceived as being a low-class, dirty occupation. Finance and marketing have glamorous reputations, and supposedly only those who can't make it in these occupations go into manufacturing. But the plain truth is that there would be nothing to finance, and nothing to market, without manufacturing!

Service Includes Quality and Reliability

The inhabitants of Huxley's *Brave New World* receive psychological conditioning that encourages them to consume and discard products. Hypnopedia, or sleep learning, teaches them, "Ending is better than mending." Planned obsolescence keeps the factories going.

This idea would have appalled the deity of Huxley's future world. Ford wanted his cars to run forever and give trouble-free service. "It is my ambition to have every piece of machinery, or other non-consumable product that I turn out, so strong and so well-made that no one ought ever to have to buy a second one" (Ford, 1922, 57). He also recognized that quality sells itself by word of mouth, and vice versa.

> If the machine does not give service, then it is better for the manufacturer if he never had the introduction, for he will have the worst of all advertisements—a dissatisfied customer. . . . A man who bought one of our cars was in my opinion entitled to the use of that car, and therefore if he had a breakdown of any kind it was our duty to see that his machine was put into shape again at the earliest possible moment (Ford, 1922, 41).

Ford also attacks changes in clothing styles as a form of planned obsolescence:

> The purpose is that a man shall buy several hats a year—four or five. It is not planned that any of them shall last over the year. In case, however, the *quality* does outlast the year, the *style* is changed, and that, of course, with people who are easily influenced, puts a perfectly good hat out of commission. . . .
>
> So that the basis of more than one line of business, involving vast quantities of material and human energy, is built not upon the durability of that material and the serviceability of that labor, but only upon the decree of some interested parties that this is "old" and that is "new."
>
> Next to the fiction that gold is wealth, this fiction of "style" is one of the most potent devices for robbing the public purse (Ford, 1922a, 276).

Clothing manufacturers, especially designer brands, keep coming out with new styles even today. They, not Henry Ford, promote the idea, "Ending is better than mending." Ford's own ideal was to manufacture the product so it would not even require mending. As for changing styles, he even resisted the introduction of a successor to the Model T until competition forced him to do so. This competition involved not mere differences in appearance but improvements in performance.

SUMMARY

Dr. Stephen Covey's *Principle-Centered Leadership* is among the best books on natural law and its importance in human organizations. This chapter has shown that Henry Ford was applying natural law during the early twentieth century, and the next chapter discusses it specifically in relation to labor relations.

Notes

1. Japan's Do [long o] is the same as Tao. Karate-do is the empty-handed Way, bushido is the Way of the Warrior.
2. The theft of the Rhinegold and Wotan's agreement to a bargain that he can't keep begins four complete Wagnerian operas (*das Rheingold, die Walküre, Siegfried,* and *Götterdämmerung,* [Twilight of the Gods]) that end with the destruction of the gods themselves. The Judeo-Christian concept of original sin, meanwhile, stretches the ill effects of wrongful conduct over human history.
3. Stephen Covey quotes Cecil B. DeMille to emphasize this idea. "It is impossible for us to break the law. We can only break ourselves against the law" (Covey, 1991, 94).
4. This idea comes straight from Trine's (1899) chapter on "Fullness of Life—Bodily Health and Vigor."
5. Probably the famous philosophers Thomas Aquinas and Immanuel Kant.
6. General Patton said, "The time to take counsel of your fears is before you make an important battle decision. That's the time to listen to every fear you can imagine! When you have collected all of the facts

and fears and made your decision, turn off all your fears and go ahead!" (Williamson, 1979, 78).

7. At the end of James Clavell's *Shogun*, Yoshi Toranaga (the historical Tokugawa Ieyasu) meditates on his karma. Personal destiny is an unstoppable force that compels Aeneas to found Rome, and Toranaga to make himself ruler of all Japan.

8. In the motion picture version of the Asian Indian epic, *Mahabharata*, the god Dharma asks his son Yudhisthira for an example of defeat. Yudhisthira replies, "Victory."

> Brigadier General S. L. A. Marshall warns in *Men Against Fire*, "Success is disarming. Tension is the normal state of mind and body in combat. When the tension suddenly relaxes through the winning of a first objective, troops are apt to be pervaded by a sense of extreme well-being and there is apt to ensue laxness in all of its forms and with all of its dangers" (1947, per Tsouras, 1992, 412).

9. The government of Cordwainer Smith's science fiction world was the Instrumentality of Mankind, and its principal function was to *assure the ongoing vitality of the human race*. Smith was actually a psychologist, Dr. Paul Myron Anthony Linebarger. He served as a psychological warfare officer during the Second World War and Korean War, and he wrote nonfiction books on Sinology and psychological warfare.

10. Per Lacey (1986, 75–76), one of James Couzen's clerks, Frank L. Klingensmith, was searching for a lost invoice during the early 1900s. He found enough pending correspondence, including bills and checks, on Henry Ford's desk to fill two wastepaper baskets. Klingensmith found it hard to get Ford to pay attention to more than one short letter at a time; he preferred to spend time in the company's design laboratories.

11. Taylor (1911a) provides a clue to the origin of "soldiering" by using it in connection with "marking time." Parade ground drills were more important in Taylor's time than in ours because soldiers actually fought in formations. Drills often required the soldiers to mark time, or march in place without going anywhere, to maintain the synchronization and rhythm that allowed them to maneuver in formation. The idea of going through motions without doing anything may have carried over as a term for limiting production in the workplace.

12. Cox and Blackstone (1998) state that *kaizen* blitz is a service mark.

13. References in this section were found by searching the Internet for the French 35-hour workweek.
14. http://www.businessweek.com/1999/99_18/b3627193.htm
15. Shakespeare's Julius Caesar describes himself as "constant as the northern star."
16. King Frederick II of Prussia said that the prince is the first servant of the State.
17. Basset (1919, 71) says, "Neither employer nor employee can get the maximum service unless the minds of both are centered upon the single object of service instead of upon the nearest dollar."
18. *Intrinsic motivation* means the task is its own reward. It is much more effective in sustaining continued and intense efforts than extrinsic motivation, which includes pay, working conditions, and recognition. The fence-whitewashing story in Mark Twain's Tom Sawyer is a perfect, if tongue-in-cheek, example. Tom could not pay the other boys enough to whitewash his aunt's fence but, when he described it as an important job with which only he (Tom) could be trusted, the other boys paid him for the privilege of doing it.
19. Basset (1919, 34-35) cites exactly the same principle.

THREE

Ford on Labor Relations

Students spend thousands of dollars in tuition and four years of their lives to earn bachelor's degrees in the science of labor relations. Henry Ford's books can teach them its common-sense principles in a few hours. Here is the basic premise:

> You may talk about material and efficiency and profits from now until the end of the world, but if you omit the human equation, all your plans are due for a fall some day.... if we are held up anywhere, it is in a lack of spirit of partnership between those who plan and those who execute the work of a great business (Ford, 1922a, 159).

A single sentence describes the management-labor relationship: "Management furnishes the method, labor furnishes the medium; both together spell service; service is the basis of reward; and upon the basis of honest reward, prosperity is built" (Ford, 1922a, 196). This summarizes the foundation of labor relations, although modern practitioners recognize the frontline worker's role in providing the method as well. Anyone who understands this and everything it implies—and the rest of this chapter expands on this—knows as much about labor relations as any professor of that science. Some coursework in organizational psychology is helpful in understanding workplace morale, motivation, and teamwork, but Ford teaches his readers everything they need to know about earning and keeping their workers' loyalty and commitment.

The next section covers a key principle of both Ford and Frederick Winslow Taylor. A viable business enterprise does not consist of factions—labor, management, customers, and stock-holders—with conflicting interests in a zero-sum game, or one in which one party's gains must be balanced by other parties' losses. They are partners, each of whom must get a square deal if all are to have long-term prosperity.

MANAGEMENT AND LABOR AS PARTNERS

Say "we," "us," and "ours" when you're talking, instead of "you fellows" and "I."

—Rudyard Kipling, *Norman and Saxon*[1]

You see, the man at the head can no longer say MY business, but all of them together can say OUR business, and when this is the spirit, and it is practiced all the way through, the very best kind of a partnership exists. There is too much of the 'my' and too little of 'our,' both in the shops and the head office (Ford, 1922a, 42).

Management and labor are not entities with conflicting goals. The act of hiring anyone, even for the most menial job, creates a partnership, and Ford defines in one sentence the labor relations prerequisite for organizational success as a lean enterprise.

It ought to be the employer's ambition, as leader, to pay better wages than any similar line of business, and it ought to be the workman's ambition to make this possible (Ford, 1922, 117).

Ford continues by pointing out the employer's and employees' interdependence.

The moment a man calls in assistance in his business, even though the assistant be but a boy, that moment he has taken a partner. He may himself be sole owner of the resources of the business, sole director of its operations, but only as he remains sole manager and sole producer can he retain the title of "independent" (Ford, 1922a, 157).

The employee cannot make a sophisticated product or deliver a valuable service without the employer's resources and guidance. The employer cannot use these resources without the workers' aid.

Ford places equal blame on unions and management for poor labor relations:

> The only true labour leader is the one who leads labour to work and to wages, and not the leader who leads labour to strikes, sabotage, and starvation. . . .
>
> There is a change coming. When the union of 'union leaders' disappears, with it will go the union of blind bosses—bosses who never did a decent thing for their employees until they were compelled. If the blind boss was a disease, the selfish union leader was the antidote. When the union leader became the disease, the blind boss became the antidote. Both are misfits, both are out of place in well-organized society. And they are both disappearing together.
>
> . . . The producers—from the men at the drawing board to the men on the moulding floor—have gotten together in a real union, and they will handle their own affairs forthwith (Ford, 1922, 256-257).

Mutual Trust and Commitment Between Labor and Management

A reporter asked a soldier in General Patton's Third Army if he thought Patton might go elsewhere than Heaven after death. The soldier said, "If General Patton goes to hell, I'd sure like to go along!" Commitment means willingness to make personal sacrifices on a leader's or organization's behalf, and it is something leaders must earn. Rudyard Kipling's *Together—England at War* is worth posting in the boardroom and on the shop floor (Kipling, 1940, 711 and 724–725).

> *When Horse and Rider each can trust the other everywhere,*
> *It takes a fence and more than a fence to pound that*
>   *happy pair;*
> *For the one will do what the other demands, although he is*
>   *beaten and blown,*

And when it is done, they can live through a run that neither
could face alone.

When Crew and Captain understand each other to the core,
It takes a gale and more than a gale to put their ship ashore;
For the one will do what the other commands, although they
are chilled to the bone,
And both together can live through weather that neither could
face alone.

When King and People understand each other past a doubt,
It takes a foe and more than a foe to knock that
country out;
For the one will do what the other requires as soon as the
need is shown;
And hand in hand they can make a stand which neither
could make alone!

This wisdom had Elizabeth and all her subjects too,
For she was theirs and they were hers, as well the
Spaniard knew;
For when his grim Armada came to conquer the Nation and
Throne,
Why, back to back they met an attack that neither could
face alone!

It is not wealth, nor talk, nor trade, nor schools, nor even
the Vote,
Will save your land when the enemy's hand is tightening
round your throat.
But a King and a People who thoroughly trust each other in
all that is done
Can sleep on their bed without any dread—for the world will
leave 'em alone!

Ford's customers could rely on him to lower the price of his cars when cost reductions made this possible. His employees trusted him to share the benefits of productivity improvements by raising wages instead of taking all the profits for himself. Ford could, in turn, rely on his employees to look for ways to improve productivity and quality. This realized the principle, "The business man's ambition ought to be to pay the best wages the business can carry, and the workman's ambition should be to respond to make the best wages possible" (Ford, 1922a, 41). This is what mutual commitment, the backbone of a first-rate organization, is all about.[2] It is the soft science prerequisite for a successful transition to lean manufacturing.

Industrial Justice

The concept of what Ford calls *industrial justice* is key in earning and keeping workers' commitment and loyalty:

> All this can be arrived at with great friendliness and common sense between employers and employes [sic] if they only seek the higher unity and not their own limited interests. And if so be an employer, having been once a workingman himself, sees the need of adjustments and makes them before his men ask him, so much the better—his act means a great increase in confidence and a new feeling that the world still has a square deal left in it (Ford, 1922a, 179).

Henry Ford was not, however, the first prominent American to adopt the idea of paying workers as much as possible, or to point out the beneficial perspective of an employer who had once been an employee. Paul Revere paid his copper mill employees two dollars a day in an era when farmhands got two dollars a week. The two-dollar wage was

> ... much more daring and liberal than the five dollar wage announced by Henry Ford more than a hundred years later. ... Having been a workman himself [Revere] had a lively sympathy for workmen. There were few labor troubles in America when the industries were run by former workmen who were in daily personal contact with their men. Disputes began when financiers gained control of industries others had founded (Crow, 1943, 97).

Ford disliked financiers and did not want them to have any part of running his business.

He also had, like Revere, the perspective that comes with having been an ordinary working person. Henry Ford came from a moderately prosperous but by no means wealthy farm family. He began his career as a mechanic and he worked his way up to chief engineer at the Detroit Electric Company (to which he later refers as the Detroit Edison Company). Charles Sorensen, who played one of the most important roles in Ford's success, began work by making patterns for iron casting molds at three dollars a day. Frederick Winslow Taylor (1911a, 185), despite his college education, took pride in saying that he had worked as an apprentice, laborer, machinist, and gang boss.

Ford's principles of industrial justice apply to prices as well as wages. Shortsighted businesses cannot see beyond the apparent benefit of paying workers as little as possible while charging customers as much as possible.

> The right price is not what the traffic will bear. The right wage is not the lowest sum a man will work for. The right price is the lowest price an article can steadily be sold for. The right wage is the highest wage the employer can steadily pay (Ford, 1926, 155).

High wages can make your own employees your best customers. Low prices turn luxuries into commodities and necessities, and this translates into higher sales. Everybody wins.

> There can be no true prosperity until the worker upon an ordinary commodity can buy what he makes. Your own employees are part of your public. The same ought to be true everywhere, but one of the difficulties in Europe is that the workman is not expected to buy what he makes. A part of Europe's trouble is that so much of its goods has gone abroad in the past that there is little thought of really having a home market (Ford, 1926, 135–136).

Lacey (1986, 130) adds, "Wage earners were also wage spenders, and, twenty years before Keynes, Henry Ford demonstrated the importance of consumption in fueling economic growth."

Think "Employment," Not "Employer and Employee"

Employment is the process through which a business enterprise serves its customers and earns income, and employment cannot exist without both the employer and the employees. Every member of a business should take Ford's statement that "Employment is Greater Than 'Employer' or 'Employee'" to heart.

> When two men are in mid-lake in a boat, their common interest, no matter what their personal differences may be, is in the integrity of that boat. They may differ and argue and contend as much as they please regarding what seat each ought to occupy, but if they break the boat or swamp it, the seat question ceases to exist—and possibly the men too.
>
> It will not make much difference how we decide to divide the golden egg, if during the squabble we destroy the goose that lays it (Ford, 1922a, 179-183).

Parsimony Is Not Economy

The employer realizes additional benefits by paying workers as much as possible. This is especially true in modern factories that use expensive and sophisticated equipment.

> Good workmanship has to be paid for, and good workmanship is cheap at almost any price. It is simply a waste of time and money to erect elaborate manufacturing equipment and then expect that it can be run by low-paid men.
>
> There is nothing sentimental about wages. Hiring men because they are cheap will ruin a business as quickly as buying material because it is cheap (Ford, 1930, 53).

Frederick Winslow Taylor spoke of running a business with "high-priced men," or workers whose qualifications allowed them to demand—and earn—high wages. Basset (1919, 64) adds the following:

> We all know that cheap labor is not cheap . . . In any operation in which the material costs are high as compared with the labor costs, the highest possible pay is the cheapest if it

results in savings of material, or in a fine product, or in both. In the grades of production where labor is the big factor, high wages are economical if the wastes of human power can be cut to a minimum.

Ford also realized that the crew's pay is a very small part of a ship's operating cost. The ship's time is the investment's most important aspect. Ford could count on the best sailors that money could hire to keep the ship's equipment in good shape so there would be no breakdowns. A "high-priced crew," to use Taylor's words, would get the most use out of the ship, and that was the idea. Ford avoided a problem that is common among many purchasing departments today: looking for the best bargains, not the best quality materials or the most reliable suppliers.

Communication Between Management and Labor

Ford blames labor problems on poor communications between management and workers. He places most of the responsibility for a harmonious workplace where it belongs, with the leaders:

> The employer who knows his job never lets a bad condition come to a head any more than an engineer who knows his job allows his engine to break down before he repairs it.
> The employer who knows his job does not permit bad conditions to remain a day after they are discovered, any more than an aviator would allow a leak in his gas tank to run longer than was required to fix it.
> When an improving eye is kept constantly on the business, when an employer knows all that his men know about the business, when a spirit of partnership reigns so that both parties feel free to communicate one with the other, then the matters which tend to grow big and demand big conferences to settle them, are nipped in the bud and never allowed to work harm either to the conditions of the business or the relations between the men engaged in it (Ford, 1922a, 165).

This avoids the problems that come with unionization:

Things have come to a pretty pass when workmen can only speak to their employer through the medium of a government committee, and when employers can only speak to their men through the medium of agents whose entire interest—financial, professional, and social—is bound up in the continuance of a quarrel and the fomenting of misunderstanding (Ford, 1922a, 165).

This is industrial and labor relations in simple, common-sense language.

No One Wins a Strike

Ford realized that effective communication among all stakeholders is important in averting strikes.

A strike is war. War is unnecessary. War is an irrecoverable loss to both winner and loser. Let us delay both war and strikes and use the simpler and more effective means of meeting man face to face, as fellow-laborers who desire to find the right basis. For it is only the right basis that can continue. Anything that is not right, whether it temporarily favors the employes [sic] or the employers, cannot last—because it is not right (Ford, 1922a, 218).

All forms of waste offended Ford, and strikes were offenses to nature and natural law. A farmers' strike wasted the growing season. A farmer who struck was, to use Ford's words, "a traitor to Nature. The shining sun, the falling shower would rebuke him. Seedtime without seed would denounce him, and harvest-time without harvest would curse him" (Ford, 1922a, 217). Ford then applies this principle to other occupations:

Has any other man who handles the fruits of the soil the right to do what the farmer has no right to do?

Has the miner the right to refuse coal that the wheat may be baked into bread? Has the spinner a right to refuse labor that the cotton and wool might be spun into clothing? Has the railroad man a right to refuse his skill that food and clothing and the means of living might be transported to those who need them? Clearly, if the farmer has no right to withhold, the others may not. Ford (1922a), 217

Ford does not let management off the hook either:

Let it be said right here that labor has a right to high wages, a right to proper hours, a right to proper conditions, a right to a share in the profits, a right to a voice in the conduct of industry. These are moral rights; they are inherent. Whether they are acknowledged or not, they still remain rights, because they are fundamentally human rights—they are just, they are good, they are humane, they are practicable, they produce social good and prosperity (Ford, 1922a, 217).

The influence of natural law is apparent: moral rights are inherent or self-evident. Ford continues by saying that an employer who does not understand this is "not fit to direct his workplace." The UPS strike of 1997 is a perfect example of any strike's wasteful nature. Perishable shipments rotted. Workers and employers who had nothing to do with UPS's labor dispute suffered when they could not get materials or ship finished goods. UPS proved that it could damage large segments of the country's economy. Neither its workers nor its managers won any friends by doing this. Today's businesses would run far more smoothly if management, labor, and stockholders understood the next section's message: TANSTAAFL, There Ain't No Such Thing As A Free Lunch.

NO FREE LUNCH: A KEY CONCEPT

Be brave, then, for your captain is brave and vows reformation. There shall be in England seven halfpenny loaves sold for a penny, the three-hooped pot shall have ten hoops, and I will make it felony to drink small [weak] beer.[3] All the realm shall be in common, and in Cheapside shall my palfrey go to grass. And when I am king, as king I will be . . . there shall be no money. All shall eat and drink on my score, and I will apparel them all in one livery that they may agree like brothers, and worship me their lord.

—Jack Cade in King Henry VI, Act IV, Scene 2

The demand of the disorderly element is practically that everybody be requested to raise fewer potatoes, and yet that everybody be given more potatoes.... If everybody does less work and everybody gets more of the product of work, how long can it last? (Ford, 1922a, 177)

Jack Cade symbolizes the "disorderly element" quite well. The Cade rebellion was, in fact, the violent prelude to the internecine bloodletting known as the Wars of the Roses. This is what one gets by empowering someone who promises a free lunch.

Engineers and scientists know the principle of mass conservation: input minus output equals accumulation. If output exceeds input, the accumulation is negative and the system goes empty sooner or later. The same principle applies to wealth; no business entity can deliver more than it produces. "Certainly no business can stand an outgo that exceeds its income. When you pump water out of a well at a faster rate than the water runs in, your well goes dry" (Ford, 1922a, 181).

Many conflicts between business stakeholders arise because people refuse to recognize TANSTAAFL. For example:

- For workers who demand fewer hours and higher pay: how is the business system going to deliver more pay if its employees produce less?
- For stockholders who want higher dividends: how is the business going to generate the wealth with which to pay those dividends?

Ford offers the only possible answer to these questions: The only way for everyone to get a bigger piece of the pie is to make the pie bigger. As simple a concept as this is, the history of friction between management, labor, and stockholders shows that many people do not understand it. Management must improve the system in which employees work so the system can produce more wealth per unit of resources: labor, material, and capital. Ford and Taylor both recognized the worker's role in identifying and implementing these improvements; this is worker empowerment.

Managers and Workers Must Grow the Business

The illusion of a free lunch is the root cause of most stakeholder conflicts. Ford summarizes the thought that must be paramount among every participant in a business enterprise.

> Instead, therefore, of men saying that the 'employer' ought to do thus-and-so, the expression ought to be changed to, 'the business ought to be stimulated and managed so it can do thus-and-so.'
>   ... It will be infinitely better if both [management and labor] turn their eyes upon the business and ask, 'how can this industry be made safe and profitable, so that it will be able to provide a sure and comfortable living for all of us? (Ford, 1922a, 182)

HUMAN RESOURCE PRACTICES

The Ford Motor Company had three production classifications: A, B, and C, with C requiring the least skill. All new employees, no matter what their background, started at the bottom. It was expected that education or a trade skill would allow its possessor to move up from that initial classification. Workers in class A jobs could move into toolmaking or supervision. This approach was probably more workable back then because very few people went to college, and many did not even complete high school. The production jobs did not require much education, nor did they usually rely on trade skills like blacksmithing.

A criminal record did not disqualify a person from employment. Ford believed, in fact, that a person who had been in jail would make a special effort to avoid going back, and most former convicts worked out well.

Although the company did not place workers on the basis of their trade, it kept a skills inventory. For example, Ford wanted a Swiss watchmaker, and the skills inventory revealed that one was running a drill press. The Heat Treat department found a skilled firebrick layer who also was running a drill press. That employee later became a general inspector. The skills inventory or training matrix supports ISO 9001:1994 section 4.18 (ISO 9000:2000 6.2.2), Training.

No Restrictive Work Rules

Union shop work rules that restrict employees to certain trades or occupations are a form of systematic soldiering. In some shops, for example, salaried workers are forbidden to touch, repair, or operate certain machines. Only a cleaner can pick up a broom or a wastebasket, only a drill press operator can touch a drill press, and so on. If the drill press operator has no work he or she stands idle. He cannot, for example, operate a lathe even if he is trained on it. Rules of this nature are a suicide pact in today's competitive economic environment, and Ford stressed this concept more than seventy-five years ago.

> ... often a man will remain idle unless work in his partic-
> ular line shows up. No man in our employment considers
> himself as fixed in any line of work; he is ready, whenever
> the necessity arises, to take on some sort of work he may
> never have heard of before. It is not good for the country
> to have men regard themselves exclusively as miners, engi-
> neers, or machinists (Ford, 1926, 172).

This benefit is not just for the employer. Multiskilled workers are more valuable and have better job security; as Ford put it, "Every man is the better for having several strings to his bow" (Ford, 1926, 172). Lean-thinking employers must assure job security not only to prevent soldiering and Ludditism, but also to enable employees to move from jobs made obsolete by lean manufacturing improvements to value-adding work that will probably be more interesting and possibly better paying.

The Role of Handicapped Workers

Ford was decades ahead of the Americans with Disabilities Act in employing handicapped workers. He had all the jobs in his factory classified with the following results. Of 7,882 different jobs (tasks or operations, not job classifications or titles):

- 949 (12.0%) were heavy work that required strong and able-bodied men.
- 3,338 (42.3%) required ordinary strength.
- 3,595 (45.6%) required no physical exertion and could conceivably have been performed by older children.

The company reclassified these light jobs according to the kinds of people who could do them.

- Legless workers could perform 670 of them.
- One-legged workers could do 2,637.
- Armless workers could perform 2.
- One-armed workers could do 715.
- Blind workers could do 10.

The assessment identified 4,034 out of 7,882 jobs, or slightly more than half, that disabled workers could perform.

The job designs apparently allowed the handicapped workers to perform at, or even above, the levels of able-bodied ones. Ford cites the example of a blind man whose job was to count bolts and nuts for shipment to branch departments. Two sighted men also were in this department. A couple of days after the blind worker started the foreman released the sighted men to other assignments because he no longer needed them. Ford does not explain why; we can speculate that the blind worker had developed other abilities, such as the ability to count objects by touch, to compensate for his lack of sight.

Ford also performed an interesting experiment with bedridden workers who could sit up:

We put black oilcloth covers or aprons over the beds and set the men to work screwing nuts on small bolts. This is a job that has to be done by hand and on which fifteen or twenty men are kept busy in the Magneto Department. The men in the hospital could do it just as well as the men in the shop and they were able to receive their regular wages. In fact, their production was about 20 percent, I believe, above the usual shop production. No man had to do the work unless he wanted to. But they all wanted to. It kept time from hanging on their hands. They slept and ate better and recovered more rapidly (Ford, 1922, 109–110).

Deaf and mute employees could apparently perform any job at Ford. The company also had about 1,000 tubercular workers in the material salvage department. Contagious ones worked in a quarantined shed. Most of this work was outdoors because this was considered beneficial for tuberculosis patients. Norwood (1931, 47–48) adds that the River Rouge plant even had reserved parking for handicapped employees.

The Role of Older Workers

Many companies try to reduce costs by encouraging higher-paid workers in their early 60s and even late 50s to retire. Ford exposes such early retirement incentives as another example of the false economy of running high-priced equipment with low-priced people. "It is absolutely necessary, in order to get the work through, to have a solid framework of older and more experienced men who know exactly what they are doing" (1930, 92–93). Older workers serve as a repository of experience and organizational knowledge. Normal attrition through retirement is not a serious problem, but the sudden departure of many experienced employees through a retirement incentive is often harmful to organizational well-being.

Braun (2000) concurs with Ford's view in an editorial about the role of older workers in the high-technology semiconductor industry. He suggests the use of retired engineers to make up the shortage of skilled semiconductor professionals. "Industry's disregard of such a pool, especially when viewed against the background of alleged need, is indeed puzzling." Younger engineers' college degrees are more current, but older ones have more experience, and the basics haven't changed: ". . . a Fourier transform is the same today as it was thirty years ago." In addition, government statistics show that older workers miss fewer workdays.

EMPLOYEE HOUSING AND STORES

Ford recognized that concentration of too much industry in an area drove up local housing prices and encouraged exploitation of workers. In an era when many people walked to work, landlords near a big factory could charge inflated rents. Even today, construction of a large plant causes local real estate prices to rise. Exorbitant real estate prices in certain industrialized parts of California prevent even many professionals from living there.

Consider the dynamics of the Gold Rush. Most people who got rich from the discovery of gold in California in 1849, and from a later discovery in Alaska, did not get their money from mines. They followed the miners and prospectors and sold them equipment—probably with high markups. Others built boomtowns that eventually became ghost towns when the gold ran out. The same dynamics show up today when a large company moves in—and when it downsizes or closes.

If real estate developers raise prices and landlords increase rents in response to industrial growth, the employer must pay higher wages and salaries to attract and retain employees. This doesn't help either the employer or the workers because the extra money flows into the pockets of middlemen, retailers, and other non-value-adding entities.

When Ford bought the Imperial Mine at Michigamme, the local housing was very bad. He did not particularly want to be in the housing business, but he realized that he would need to house miners and lumberjacks—he was also buying coal mines and timber. The company erected single-room dormitories for single men and portable houses for couples. Cottages later replaced the portable houses (Ford, 1926, 48).

Modern advisors say that people should not spend more than twenty-five percent of their income on housing. The cottages rented for twelve dollars a month. This was two days' wages at six dollars a day, or about ten percent of a month's pay. The company also built a school and a store that sold its goods at cost.

Employee Commissaries

Bryan (1997, 223) begins a story that one might expect to lead to spiraling wage-and-price inflation. "In 1919, following World War I, Ford saw his workers' wages eroded by the high inflationary prices being charged for the household goods they purchased." Today's expected reactionwould be for the workers to agitate for higher wages. Union leaders might point out the eminent reasonableness of a cost-of-living increase.

However, Ford did not have to tolerate this any more than he had to put up with pricey and often substandard housing for his workers. He did not see why he should pay higher wages so retailers and other non-value-adding middlemen could increase their profits. A worker who took home seven dollars a day instead of six, but who then had to spend an extra dollar on groceries and clothing because of rising prices, was no better off than a worker who got six dollars a day to spend at stable prices. (He or she would be worse off under today's progressive income tax system.) Bryan continues, "His solution to his employees' situation was to operate high-volume outlets where they could buy high-quality commodities at rock-bottom prices." "The Ford Clothes Shop: Saves you the Retailer's Profits," read a 1921 advertisement in *Ford News*.

Ford actually introduced the ancestor of today's member warehouse stores. The Ford Commissaries purchased merchandise in bulk and sold it at cost. They offered not only food, clothing, and household goods but coal for heating and fertilizer for farming. Terms were cash-and-carry so the commissaries did not have to worry about processing credit. The stores became so popular that Ford finally had to allow only his employees to shop in them.

Bryan (1997, 221) cites a summary from Dry Goods Reporter.[4] Here are the key principles.

- Place the store outside the downtown district.
- The store layout should minimize waste motion by employees.
- Aisles should be wide to accommodate crowds.
- Don't install expensive fixtures for "atmosphere."
- Pay attention to how goods get from delivery trucks to the store counters. (Remember that transportation and waiting add no value.)
- Prepackage goods to save the sales clerks' time.
- Buy just-in-time and cut out non-value-adding middlemen.
- Offer minimal services. (Department stores of that era offered tea rooms, and playrooms for children.)
- Simplify the stock by not carrying duplicate brands or expensive novelties.
- Do not sell small quantities.

Sam's Club and similar member warehouse stores follow most of these criteria. Ford used the company store to give his employees genuine value instead of more money, which would have simply been taken by non-value-adding retailers and other merchants.

Michigan later enacted a law, Public Act 271 of 1941, that forbade employers to sell their workers products they did not produce or handle. Bryan (1997, 224) explains, "Employee pay was increasing and employer paternalism was being frowned upon by unions demanding more substantial cash benefits." The unions, of course, should have followed Ford's lead in questioning whether cash and wealth are the same thing. Bryan concludes, "All in all, Henry Ford's attempts to help his employees receive maximum benefit from their hard-earned wages was very much appreciated by the majority of his workers during that era."

Employee Credit Unions

Employees at Ford's Highland Park plant could invest up to $2.00 per month in a "private membership association." The association advanced money at the rate of ten cents for the use of $5.00 for one to thirteen days.

This makes the membership borrower his own loan-shark, as the profits from advances go wholly to the association subscribers. Of course, the fore-handed subscriber who never asks advances is the greater gainer, but it is far better for the man who is forced to solicit a loan to apply to an association of which he himself is a member than to go to an outside [usurer] for assistance (Arnold and Faurote, 1915, 44).

SUMMARY

This chapter has discussed Henry Ford's extremely progressive and enlightened views on labor relations. Although he was writing from the perspective of an owner and a manager, he emphasized that labor and management are both responsible for achieving a cooperative work environment. Furthermore, the primary responsibility for achieving such cooperation rests with management. The next chapter discusses personal and organizational characteristics that are prerequisites for the outstanding success that Ford achieved.

Notes

1. Ford and Kipling were both Freemasons. I have not been able to discover whether Ford ever spoke directly with Kipling. Ford visited England during Kipling's lifetime, and it is possible that he used the opportunity to visit another prominent Mason.
2. Harris Semiconductor's plant in Mountaintop, Pennsylvania, applied this principle to union-management relations. "The best way to secure union jobs is to strengthen the business. All company stakeholders have the same long-term interests" (Bishop, in Levinson, 1998, 30-31).

3. A three-hooped pot held one quart, or about one liter. Cade was there-fore promising three and a third quarts for the price of one.
4. "Henry Ford: Retailer," in *Dry Goods Reporter*, April 23, 1927, and May 7, 1927.

FOUR

Principles for Organizational and Personal Success

Our strong arms be our conscience, swords our law.
March on; join bravely, let us to it pell-mell
If not to heaven, then hand in hand to hell.
—*King Richard III*, Act V, Scene 3

This chapter covers Henry Ford's principles for individual and organizational success. They are, to paraphrase Dr. Stephen Covey's well-known book title, the habits and characteristics of highly successful people and organizations. It will begin with self-reliance and *virtù*, or vitality. These are indispensable characteristics of successful people, business enterprises, and nations. It will then cover other characteristics like persistence, judgment, and initiative.

Self-reliance, or internal locus of control, is a key factor in personal or organizational success. It is inseparable from what Niccolò Machiavelli (1965, liv–lvi, 7-8) calls *virtù*: boldness, bravery, resolution, and decisiveness. Although virtù is not always virtuous—the Duke of Gloucester's virtù takes the form of ruthless decisiveness—it is strongest when it accords with natural law:

> *Virtù* may be associated with extreme wickedness and with the pursuit of power and self-aggrandizement and at any price...
>
> But when superior *virtù* is found combined in an individual with pre-eminent *prudenzia* [prudence, wisdom], as in Romulus and Cyrus, dedication to the common good will characterize his behavior. Machiavelli believes that the

strongest motive for altruism is a selfishness directed by intelligence. For the prudent man of virtù will soon recognize that his labor in behalf of the common good will bring him the greatest personal power and security from conspiracy, and will win for him the truest glory (Machiavelli, 1965, lv–lvi,).

Virtù is a characteristic that individuals and organizations develop through conditioning and training. Machiavelli illustrates this idea by citing barbarian tribes like the Gauls, whose cultures were warlike and spirited. These qualities alone, however, do not constitute virtù without conditioning and training. The Gauls could not, despite their warlike spirit, endure a protracted contest because of their lack of discipline. The Romans were not as spirited as the Gauls, but their social as well as military organization, discipline, and conditioning endowed them with superior virtù. This is why, despite the comic book character Asterix the Gaul's[1] string of victories over Rome's lumbering legions, French is almost as Latinized as Spanish and Italian. Asterix's creators can, however, take comfort in the likelihood that their work probably has more modern readers than Caesar's *Gallic Wars*.

Machiavelli (1965, 77) wrote that republics develop more people of virtù than monarchies because republics prize and honor virtù while monarchies fear it. This is because even a monarch of virtù must fear displacement by an ambitious subordinate. Alexander the Great, for example, did not name a successor for fear that whomever he chose would gain the power and ambition to overthrow him. Henry Ford often set his top executives against one another (e.g. Harry Bennett against Charles Sorensen and Edsel Ford). As he grew older, Ford thought people were conspiring to take his company away from him—a characteristic of monarchs whose fear of conspiracies was often justifiable.

Ford does not use the word *virtù* but he summarizes its aspects (Ford, 1922a, 148): "And the texture of a man is his vitality, his energy, his character, his courage and his rock-bottom brain power."

Virtù allows its possessor to defy the whims of Machiavelli's fortuna, or Fortune: "Fortune may place us in particular circumstances, but whether we exert some control over our lives, instead of becoming the plaything of chance, depends upon our virtù." Virtù's opposite, Machiavelli's *ozio*, includes inaction, indolence, and lack of energy. Remember the important psychological concepts and role models to be found in tarot cards:

> The tarot deck includes a card for strength. It means, 'courage, magnanimity, persistence, patience, spiritual power. Able to offset any bad luck in surrounding cards' (Aquarian Tarot, 1975). Its attributes are those of virtù. Like virtù, [the strength card] can offset bad luck or the whims of Fortune. Its reverse means 'weakness, possible loss of honor, and discord.' Thus, we have the two opposites: virtù and ozio (Levinson, 1994, 62-63).

Ozio leads to errors of omission and lost opportunities. Errors of omission—that is, not doing anything—are often worse than errors of commission, or doing the wrong thing. There is something to be said for failing through virtù instead of ozio:

> Thus, Julius Caesar, Alexander of Macedon, and all such men and excellent princes always fought at the head of their own armies, always marched with them on foot, and always carried their own arms; if any of them ever lost his power, he simultaneously lost his life and died with the same virtù which he had displayed while he lived (Machiavelli, 1965, 211).

Machiavelli continues by saying that, although one might condemn some of these role models' taste for aggression and conquest, they are beyond reproach for indolence, soft living, or other aspects of ozio. Richard III meets a well-deserved end at Bosworth, but he holds the audience's attention through the play. Shakespeare's Richard II and Henry VI are, in contrast, almost spectators in the plays that bear their names. Their murders are almost mercy killings—merciful, that is, for readers and audiences who no longer have to hear these pathetic characters mope and whine about their ill fortunes, which, due to their ozio, were largely of their own making.

The virtù of Henry V serves as an excellent contrast to the ozio of his hapless son:

King Henry V, Act IV, Scene 1	*King Henry VI*, Act II, Scene 5
[The night before the Battle of Agincourt: King Henry's soliloquy contrasts the king's duties and responsibilities, for which his only recompense is "ceremony," with the carefree role of a commoner.]	[Watching a battle near York in which his wife, Margaret of Anjou, and his retainer, Lord Clifford, are leading his army! Henry VI is indeed a mere spectator in the plays that bear his name.]
Upon the king! Let us our lives, our souls,	Here on this molehill will I sit me down.
Our debts, our careful wives,	To whom God will, there be the victory.
Our children, and our sins, lay on the king!	For Margaret my queen, and Clifford, too,
We must bear all. O hard condition,	Have chid me from the battle, swearing both
...What infinite heart's ease	They prosper best of all when I am thence.
Must kings neglect that private men enjoy?	Would I were dead, if God's good will were so—
	For what is in this world but grief and woe?
	O God! Methinks it were a happy life
	To be no better than a homely swain.
	To sit upon a hill, as I do now...

The difference between the two men is, of course, the fact that Henry V embraces his leadership role despite its hardships and responsibilities, while his son tries to avoid it. As Clifford lays dying, he places the blame for the Wars of the Roses squarely where it belongs:

Here burns my candle out—ay, here it dies,
Which, whiles it lasted, gave King Henry light.
... And Henry, hadst thou swayed as kings should do,
Or as thy father and his father did,
Giving no ground unto the House of York,
They never then had sprung like summer flies...

—*Henry VI,* Act II, Scene 6

Another lesson here is that the proactive leader, the leader of virtù, does not "give ground" to problems and hope they'll go away.

The opposing characteristics of virtù and ozio recur in major references on business and statesmanship:

- Peters and Waterman (1982) define a bias for action as "a preference for doing something—anything—rather than sending a question through cycles and cycles of analyses and committee reports."
- John Maynard Keynes (1936, 161–162) says, "Our decisions to do something positive, the full consequences of which will be drawn out for many days to come, can only be taken as a result of animal spirits—of a spontaneous urge to action rather than inaction."
- Carl von Clausewitz (1976, Book 3, Ch. 16) describes virtù and ozio in a military context, and he emphasizes the danger of inaction or errors of omission. "Woe to the government which, relying on half-hearted politics and a shackled military policy, meets a foe who, like the untamed elements, knows no law other than his own power! Any defect of action and effort will turn to the advantage of the enemy."
- Hayes, Wheelwright, and Clark (1988, 30) almost paraphrase Clausewitz: "When business becomes too analytical, too concerned with the calculus of costs versus benefits and risks versus returns, it becomes prey to those who seek market share, the dynamics of growth, and a place in the sun."

- The Russian commander Aleksandr V. Suvorov (1729–1800) used the word *unterkunft* (lodging, accommodation, logistics, "under the bed") to refer to missed opportunities. "The Archduke Charles did nothing and spent nearly three months in Unterkunft," Suvorov complained about his Austrian allies during the Italian campaign of 1799 (Longworth, 1965, 265). He chided another Austrian, "Although you were the victor, you stopped and sat down in *Unterkunft* and indecision. Having shot up the enemy, you should have chased him" (Longworth, 1965, 249). Suvorov sometimes invented words, or assigned his own meanings to them, and the meaning of *unterkunft* is clear from its context in his statements.
- General Patton said that a foxhole is a grave because inactivity concedes the initiative to the enemy (in business terms, the competitor).

Ford identified the concept of opportunity cost, or the marginal cost of not acting on an opportunity. In discussing a loss on some inventory he wrote,

> He can take the direct loss on his books and go ahead and do business or he can stop doing business and take the loss of idleness. The loss of not doing business is commonly a loss greater than the actual money involved, for during the period of idleness fear will consume initiative and, if the shutdown is long enough, there will be no energy left over to start up with again (Ford, 1922, 137–138).

Under poor business conditions, the manager should be proactive and try to make his or her product more competitive (using his or her virtù) instead of waiting for the market to improve (relying on Machiavelli's *fortuna*).

Ralph Waldo Trine (1899, 165–166), whose work influenced Ford, describes the importance of an internal locus of control. "When we recognize the fact that a man carries his success or his failure with him, and that it does not depend upon outside conditions, we shall come into the possession of powers that will quickly change outside conditions into agencies that make for success."

The following story summarizes the key principle of internal locus of control, self-reliance, or virtù. A Japanese lord declared his intention to visit the Atago Shrine to pray to the archery god for success in battle. His father replied, "Don't pray to the archery god; if he sides with the enemy, cut him in two!"

The following sections describe the two main characteristics of virtu: persistence and initiative.

PERSISTENCE

> Once more unto the breach, dear friends, once more;
> Or close the wall up with our English dead.
> —*King Henry V*, Act III, Scene I

Ford describes persistence, a key aspect of virtù: "More men are beaten than fail. It is not wisdom they need or money, or brilliance, or 'pull,' but just plain gristle and bone. This rude, simple, primitive power which we call 'stick-to-it-iveness' is the uncrowned king of the world of endeavor" (1922, 220). Ford cites external factors as what a person does not need. "If only I was rich, or if I had the right connections…" is external locus of control, a feeling of dependence on factors outside oneself.

Frederick Winslow Taylor cites the same internal characteristics as leadership qualifications:

> The fact is, that the more attractive qualities of good manners, education, and even special training and skill, which are more apparent on the surface, count for less in an executive position than the grit, determination, and bulldog endurance and tenacity that knows no defeat and comes up smiling to be knocked down over and over again.
>
> The two qualities which count most for success in this kind of executive work are grit and what may be called "constructive imagination"—the faculty which enables a man to use the few facts that are stored in his

mind in getting around the obstacles that oppose him, and in building up something useful in spite of them . . . (Taylor, 1911a, 140).

Ford displayed persistence by fighting the Selden patent lawsuit of 1909. A group of rival automakers had licenses under a very broad patent for "road locomotives," and they claimed that Ford's automobiles fell under the patent's scope. They tried to use the patent to drive him out of business. Ford lost the first court case, but he assured his customers that he would win. He even offered to indemnify them against any harm if the plaintiffs came after them. Ford prevailed in the appeals.

Refusal to quit or give up is an aspect of internal locus of control, or self-reliance; it is virtù. The Prussian field marshal Helmuth von Moltke (1800–1891) described its importance as follows:

> The decision of a battle begins when one side gives up the battle as lost. Many times battles have been won because the enemy believed himself beaten before the victor did, even though he was no less shaken. In case of doubt, one must therefore persist (Hughes, 1993, 132).

Walt Whitman's *An Old-Time Sea Fight*, an account of the battle between the American *Bonhomme Richard* and H.M.S. *Serapis* off Flamborough Head during the Revolutionary War, is a perfect example of Moltke's observation. *Bonhomme Richard* was already down five feet (approximately 1.5 meters) due to flooding when *Serapis* set her on fire, a terrifying contingency in the age of wooden ships. This was when *Bonhomme Richard's* captain, John Paul Jones, told the *Serapis'* commander, "We have not yet begun our part of the fighting." As the contest continued through the next two hours,

> *The leaks gain fast on the pumps, the fire eats toward the*
> *   powder magazine.*
> *One of the pumps has been shot away, it is generally thought*
> *   we are sinking.*
> *Serene stands the little captain,*
> *He is not hurried, his voice is neither high nor low,*

His eyes give more light to us than our battle-lanterns.
Toward twelve there in the beams of the moon they surrender
to us.

Whitman did not take poetic license in exaggerating the Americans' plight, for *Bonhomme Richard* never fought again. *Serapis*, the losing ship, actually sank the victor! The Americans gained possession of the surviving vessel because they did not, unlike their opponents, realize that they had lost. This applies to both individuals and organizations. If you think you're beaten, you're right.

The next section discusses initiative, another aspect of virtù.

INITIATIVE

Employees get ahead by exercising initiative and taking responsibility. On a larger scale, organizations succeed by taking the initiative to meet customer needs. Ford's editorial "No Help Wanted—An Untrue Sign" in the *Dearborn Independent* says,

> You see a shop that says, "No Help Wanted" and you know, of course, that the sign means that the shop needs help before it can give any. Have you an idea that will start another wheel turning? Have you any help to give that shop? Can you open any channel for the outflow of its product? Can you serve as an ignition point in its organization? (Ford, 1922a, 12–15)

Frank Wheatley, a consultant at Fairchild Semiconductor's plant in Mountaintop, Pennsylvania, and the inventor of the insulated gate bipolar transistor (IGBT), recounts a story from his youth during the early 1940s. Stores were not offering work, but he went to a store and offered to scrape all the gum from the floor for twenty dollars. The store owner probably hadn't given the gum a second thought but now he recognized a new need, and he agreed. The job took less than a day, and it earned what many adult workers would have considered two or three days' wages.

Another Ford editorial asks, "Can You Make Your Job Bigger?" Workers who take the initiative to go beyond their job descriptions might make their positions more satisfying and better paying:

> If you say you are too good for your present job, have you ever given any thought to methods by which your present job could be made good enough, or even too good, for you? ... Have you ever studied your own job from the standpoint of making it a worthy life career? (Ford, 1922a, 107–111)

Ford also advises, "Grow along with the business."

> But you must not think that the factory exists for the express purpose of promoting you. As long as you are there, your business is to promote the business of the factory. Then, as it advances, you go with it.
>
> Every business that is growing is creating new places for capable men. It cannot help but do so. A settled business that is just holding its own, where someone must die or resign before there can be advancements, is necessarily slow in promotions. But growing businesses are not (Ford, 1922a, 205–208).

This is simply the personal-level application of the idea that the only way for every stakeholder to get a bigger piece of pie is to make the pie bigger.

Employers who want their workers to exercise judgment and initiative must create a supportive environment. Rigid job descriptions and hierarchical lines of communication and control stifle initiative. Mechanistic systems (management systems in which rigid rules tell people what to do) encourage and even force people to recite the civilian equivalent of, "I'm a private, they don't pay me to think." Committees discourage anyone from taking responsibility for anything; the buck passes around and around but stops nowhere. This is discussed in the following section.

Committees and Experts Stifle Initiative and Progress

Ford was wary of experts, especially those who were expert in explaining why something couldn't be done.

All the wise people demonstrated conclusively that the [internal combustion] engine could not compete with steam. They never thought that it might carve out a career for itself. That is the way with wise people—they are so wise and practical that they always know to a dot just why something cannot be done; they always know the limitations. That is why I never employ an expert in full bloom. If ever I wanted to kill opposition by unfair means I would endow the opposition with experts. They would have so much good advice that I could be sure they would do little work (Ford, 1922, 28).

Dr. Shigeo Shingo recognized the same problem. He heaped "scorn on what he calls *nyet* engineers (*nyet* is Russian for 'no'), who use their experience and position to reject—smugly and without hesitation—useful changes." For National Cash Register's John Patterson, ". . . the words 'it can't be done' were grounds for dismissal" (Robinson, 1990, 14). Yoshiki Iwata used the term *concrete heads* (Womack and Jones, 1996, 128–129), and this reference also cites *anchor draggers*. I will admit to thinking of a former coworker as "Mr. But, Can't, and Won't."

Moltke also described exactly why "nothing ever gets done around here" in civilian as well as military activities. There is always an expert who knows why something won't work. The experts never counsel, much less carry out, anything positive, so success cannot prove them wrong. "The negation remains in the right, and everyone agrees to do nothing" (Hughes, 1993, 77). This leads back to the principle that errors of omission—everyone agrees to do nothing—are often worse than errors of commission—doing the wrong thing.

BREAKING DOWN ORGANIZATIONAL BARRIERS

W. Edwards Deming advised his readers to get rid of departmental barriers in the workplace. Tom Peters recommends making an organization porous to its employees, customers, and suppliers.

There were few job classifications under Ford, and they were absolutely not restrictive. No one said, "It's not my job" if he or she could do it.

> The divisions of work among the men were abolished; an engineer can now be found cleaning an engine or a car or even working in the repair shop. The crossing tenders act as track walkers for their districts, the station agents sometimes paint and repair their own stations. The idea is that a group of men have been assigned to run a railroad, and among them they can, if they are willing, do all the work. If a specialist has some of his special work on hand he does it; if he has no such work he does labourer's work or whatever there may be to do (Ford, 1926, 200).

This idea ties in with synchronous flow manufacturing (SFM).[2] SFM practitioners recognize that people often make unusable inventory because they want to keep themselves and their equipment busy and productive. But manufacturing workers do not have to make unusable parts to stay busy. If they have been cross-trained, they can perform other tasks when they are not making parts. They can do preventive maintenance or cleaning, and they can even look for ways to improve the process.

Although he encouraged cross-training, Ford did not, admittedly, introduce frequent cross-functional communication. He subscribed to the Tayloristic view that the people who planned the work should make sure that different departments worked in harmony (1922, 92). Departments were, however, self-contained enough to perform a complete task. (Chapter 8, "Ford's Factory," will show that Ford adopted a cellular manufacturing approach in which each department had all the tools and equipment it needed to make an entire part. There were no separate departments for heat-treatment, brazing, drilling, milling, and so on.) The D.T. & I. example shows that there were not separate departments for train operators, repairers, and car cleaners that had to communicate with each other. A single department apparently contained all the people and all the skills it needed to perform its mission. Departments therefore did not have to talk with one another frequently.

Flattening the Organization

The idea of breaking down organizational barriers goes with the lean or flat organization. Fewer layers of hierarchy make the organization more porous. When the D.T. & I. Railroad's legal department was abolished, legal costs fell from $18,000 to $1,200 a year. The railroad's executives occupied only two rooms, and the accounting department fit into a small building. The pre-Ford D.T. & I had 2,700 employees. It fell to 1,500 under Ford, and then rose to 2,390, but these 2,390 employees handled twice the tonnage of the old railroad. The Flat Rock headlight factory had 500 employees, of whom only two were managerial or office workers.

Ford warned specifically against letting too much bureaucracy and red tape into an organization. This leads to buck-passing and the reluctance of anyone to take responsibility for doing anything.

> To my mind there is no bent of mind more dangerous than that which is sometimes described as 'the genius for organization.' This usually results in the birth of a great big chart showing, after the fashion of a family tree, how authority ramifies.... If a straw boss wants to say something to the general superintendent, his message has to go through the sub-foreman, the foreman, the department head, and all the assistant superintendents, before, in the course of time, it reaches the general superintendent. Probably by that time what he wanted to talk about is already history (Ford, 1922, 91).[3]

Mechanistic and Organic Management Systems

The dichotomy of mechanistic and organic management systems is an important subject of modern management theory that apparently originated during the 1960s.[4] It ties in with the removal of organizational barriers because flat and porous organizations are compatible with organic systems. Charles Sorensen identified this dichotomy explicitly in 1956, and he was writing about events that took place decades earlier (Sorensen, 1956, 41). He contrasted a "rigid system, in which rules tend to be paramount," (i.e., a mechanistic system) against a "flexible method," (i.e., an organic system) whose purpose was to get the job done. He defined the two management practices as "diametrically opposed." Supervisors should not occupy themselves with paperwork, they should go to the production line (Masaaki Imai's *gemba*) and see for themselves what was happening.

Henry Ford identified what Joseph Juran calls "the law of the situation." This means that one person does not give orders to another person; both take their orders from the job or the task at hand. "The work and the work alone controls us" (Ford, 1922, 93). One of his three key principles for managing a workplace is, "Do the job in the most direct fashion without bothering with red tape or any of the ordinary divisions of authority" (Ford, 1926, 199–200). "The job, not convention, rules."

The next section reveals the corporate culture that prevailed at Ford during its phenomenal growth phase. Corporate culture, "the way we do things around here," suggests collective habits, values, and behavior. As with individual characteristics, corporate culture must develop through behavior that becomes ingrained and habitual.

CORPORATE CULTURE AT THE FORD MOTOR COMPANY

We few, we happy few, we band of brothers.
—*King Henry V*, Act IV, Scene III

The people who built the Ford Motor Company—James Couzens, C. Harold Wills, Walter Flanders, Charles Sorensen, and others— did not always remain happy or behave like brothers. They often fell out with Henry Ford and each other. Sorensen (1956, 32) even accused the Dodge Brothers of sending the same rejected parts back to Ford six times—and said he had the records to prove it. Sorensen (1956, 8) adds, ". . . not all the people working at Ford were perfect little gentlemen who remembered their Sunday-school lessons..."

For a time, however, the group that led the Ford Motor Company achieved what Napoleon Hill's *The Law of Success*— which drew on Henry Ford's life as its primary source—calls the Master Mind. This is "... a mind that is developed through the harmonious co-operation of two or more people who ally themselves for the purpose of accomplishing any given task" (Hill, 1928, 23). Furthermore, "... the individual minds become blended into a 'Master Mind,' by which is meant that the chemistry of the individual minds is modified in such a manner that these minds blend and function as one" (Hill, 1928, 59). Some of Hill's material savors of metaphysics, but his Master Mind is an accurate description of the group dynamics at Ford in those early days.

Groupthink, a dysfunctional behavior in which everyone places the group's harmony above all other considerations, did not become a problem. Organizational success, not group harmony, was the Ford leadership group's paramount consideration. The members argued and quarreled, but a common goal provided unity.

The Champion's Companion

Charles Sorensen himself played a critical role that often appears in anthropology and mythology. The leader or champion often has the help of one special companion. The critical characteristics of such a relationship are:

1. The companion is a friend who advises and helps the champion but does not wish to supplant or succeed him, as shown in the following examples:
   - This was a typical role of a tribal shaman or medicine man. His position was not in line of succession to the tribal chief's. The chief could therefore trust the shaman's or medicine man's advice without having to worry about an ulterior motive.

- The companion is emphatically not a yes-man. Charlemagne had an English monk, Alcuin of York, as his personal advisor. Alcuin often argued with the king openly. A court jester's position often allowed him to criticize or disagree with the king because bystanders could interpret the criticism as a joke and the king would not lose face. Shakespeare illustrates this relationship in *King Lear*.
- Yoshi Toranaga (the historical Tokugawa Ieyasu) in James Clavell's Shogun, on his relationship with the Englishman John Blackthorne: "I need one friend." Blackthorne, a non-Japanese, could not have possibly supplanted Toranaga but he had knowledge and perspectives that the future Shogun lacked.[5]

2. The companion is emphatically not a lesser version of the champion (i.e., a sidekick or apprentice). The companion is loyal to the champion but does not hesitate to disagree with him or her. He or she has skills and talents that the champion lacks. They have a synergistic relationship that makes their whole greater than the sum of their parts.

3. There is often a special rapport between the champion and the companion.

Sorensen describes himself as "Henry Ford's man." He states that he never had any desire to supplant or succeed Ford, and this fulfills the first aspect of the special companion. As for the second aspect,

> I helped make him; he made me . . .
>
> We had a business relationship closer than even his family had with him, and in many ways I knew him better than did members of his family. It was useless to try to understand Henry Ford. One had to sense him (Sorensen, 1956, 6).

Sorensen was "Henry Ford's man" but was emphatically not his yes-man, a role he ascribed to Harry Bennett. History provides examples of a dysfunctional relationship in which the champion's companion is indeed a sidekick or yes-man. Alexander the Great's relationship with Hephestion is a perfect example. There is a legend that, when a Persian noblewoman met Alexander and his entourage, she addressed Hephestion as Alexander. When she realized her mistake Alexander said, "Don't worry about it, he is Alexander too." Hephestion was simply an extension of Alexander and he would agree with whatever Alexander said.

This is not surprising because the Greek hero Achilles was one of Alexander's role models. In Homer's *Iliad*, the Greek hero Patroclus is essentially Achilles' sidekick. When Patroclus insists on fighting the Trojans by himself, Achilles tells him not to pursue them too far lest he get hurt—or win too much fame while Achilles sulks in his tent. As he grew older, Ford also began to resent people who took publicity away from him.

Sorensen says that Henry Ford's greatest failure was his relationship with his son Edsel. The elder Ford saw his son as an extension of himself, he wanted Edsel to be exactly like him. Harry Bennett (1951, 40–41) supports this assertion and adds that, when Edsel took on a project that his father didn't like, his father would undermine it. Edsel could never fulfill the companion role not only because his father saw him as an extension of himself but because he was his father's heir—and, again like Alexander, the elder Ford could not imagine a time when the world would have to get along without him.[6]

Two important myths underscore the proper relationship of champion and companion. In the Asian Indian *Bhagavad Gita*, the warrior Arjuna is the achiever-hero and Krishna is his spiritual guide. In the Sumerian *Epic of Gilgamesh*, a wild man, Enkidu, becomes the companion of King Gilgamesh.

The third aspect of this relationship is a special rapport or understanding in the champion and companion role pair. Longworth (1965, 317) describes the relationship between Field Marshal Aleksandr V. Suvorov (1729–1800) and his disciples. ". . . with men like Bagration, Kutuzov, and Miloradovich the rapport was complete. Of Kutuzov, Suvorov once said he had to 'order one, hint to another; but there's no need even to speak to Kutuzov—he understands it all by himself.'" Sorensen wrote that he could often sense what Ford, who could not draw a blueprint, wanted. He could convert Ford's desire into a three-dimensional object.

Having been such a companion, Sorensen provides a valuable perspective on what the Ford Motor Company was like during the early twentieth century in his book, *My Forty Years with Ford* (1956). Two chapters, "What Made the Ford Organization Tick?" and "Work was Play" focus specifically on the culture that prevailed before the Model T's introduction in 1908; these are discussed in the following sections.

Sorensen: "What Made the Ford Organization Tick?"

Although Ford had very rigid rules (standardization of the prevailing "one best way") for specific jobs, management was organic instead of mechanistic. In a mechanistic system rules are paramount. Organic systems are flexible and the objective is the master. The situation or job is the real boss, its authority is absolute over everyone, and a true leader is one who evokes prompt and immediate responses to it (Sorensen, 1956, 43). The idea is to get the job done.

Masaaki Imai discusses *gemba* managers, managers who spend time in the value-adding workplace (*gemba*) instead of offices. Ford did not bother with a private office. He did much of his work in a combined office and drafting room when he wasn't walking around the plant. Supervisors watched the production lines so they could see anything that might go wrong, instead of waiting to read a report about it. Sorensen adds,

> These superintendents and their assistants were not of the sitdown type. I did not permit the top men to hold down a chair in an office. My formula for them was "You've got to get around" (Sorensen, 1956, 179).

He also demanded plant cleanliness and attention to anything that might make the work easier. We will see later that cleanliness and organization (now aspects of 5S-CANDO) played major roles in Ford's operations. Suppression of friction was, meanwhile, central to the company's business approach.

Sorensen: "Work was Play"

We had a sense of achievement by association, by teamwork.
—Sorensen, *My Forty Years with Ford*

Sorensen's next chapter, "Work was Play," describes the company leaders' behavior during the pre-Model T days. It's easily reminiscent of the culture that author Tom Peters describes for vital, growing, and innovative companies. Samuel Crowther, who did much of the actual writing of Ford's books, saw the leaders at work.

> He [Crowther] discovered that the "motive" came from a close-knit group of men who lived on the job and that there were ideas in every corner of the shop.
> With this group, work was play. If it had not been play, it would have killed them. They were as men possessed. They often forgot to eat. They drove themselves much harder than they drove anyone else (Sorensen, 1956, 54).

Harry Bennett and his writer Paul Marcus confirm Ford's own habit of, to use management expert Tom Peters' expression, "managing by wandering around."

> Henry Ford loved machinery. He was never in his office. He circulated through the plant observing with an expert eye—encouraging with the useful suggestion. . . . At all times he knew what was happening in every department (Bennett, 1951, 22).

Furthermore,

> Ford was not only a "hands on" leader. He was daring and ambitious, he had apparently inexhaustible energy, and he was a man of amazing vision (Bennett, 1951, 27).

Everyone focused on continuous improvement. Sorensen reinforces Ford's point that no good innovator ever considers himself an expert. The best results often came from people who had no previous knowledge of what they were trying to do. Therefore they did not know why it couldn't be done. Anyone who knows that something can't be done is always right, as far as he or she is concerned.

The members of the core group were always sure they could improve on whatever they were doing. They often amazed the people on the shop floor. For example, when Charlie Morgana gave toolmakers specifications for a machine that was to make hundreds of pieces per hour, the toolmakers were sure he meant pieces per day. It wasn't a mistake, the machine could really deliver the specified output. Arnold and Faurote (1915, 307) tell the same story or a related one: the Ford people really meant 200 pieces an hour, not 200 pieces a day. An unnamed eastern U.S. manufacturer said, "You can't do it. There is no machine built that will do it." The Ford people showed him the machine, and it was indeed doing it.

Henry Ford's Personal Leadership

A character study of Henry Ford provides valuable insight into his leadership style.

> He has no sense of personal importance, meets his factory heads on terms of absolute and even deferential comradeship, and because he had, up to about his thirty-fifth year, an intimate personal knowledge of day-wage life, his strong natural impulse is to aid his workmen …without waiting to be stimulated by demand from others for such action on his part.
>
> Mr. Ford is by nature a comrade; and this, together with his sense of humor, leads him to smile often and much and to enjoy a laugh at his own expense, and he is rather inclined to under-rate his own abilities and his own achievements.
>
> … He follows his own self-imposed tasks without one thought of looking back, unconscious of obstacles in his chosen path and careless of reward at the end of his

labors, so that he but follow his ideal and reach the goal he has set for himself.

... Henry Ford is an inventor, a creator, a master mind with a vivid imagination whose dictates he follows relentlessly; a generous comrade, making strong friends and willing servants of those whom he takes into his confidence, quick to praise the young men who are his factory aids and who are constantly encouraged by him in their strongly individualized and highly successful efforts towards bringing the Highland Park plant to that condition of Ideal Efficiency which is the never-to-be-fully-attained ambition of the competent factory manager at large.

... [He] listens willingly to others, decides quickly, and of two mechanical devices chooses intuitively that which best suits the desired end, be it of his own suggestion or another's.

... He has thus built up about himself not so much an organization as a staff of aids—all ranking as equals, none in command of any one department, all ranking any titular department head, each eager both to meet any suggestion Ford advances or to volunteer suggestions for his decision, each as likely as the other to be put in charge of any shop-betterment idea Ford may conceive, because he observes no discrimination in lines of service. This alone makes the Ford establishment unusual, to say the least, in his direction. It also makes the establishment his own absolutely throughout, though, as he said, leisurely looking out of his office window, "I have no job here—nothing to do" (Arnold and Faurote, 1915, 16–20).

Sorensen said that Ford knew everyone on the payroll, often by first name. A true leader earns a reputation for wisdom and fairness, and true leadership evokes enthusiastic participation and voluntary effort. The boss and the workers must know and respect one another (Sorensen, 1956, 51). Harry Bennett adds,[7]

Although self-taught and self-made, he was excellent at judging men and technical aptitude. His very success attracted the cream of managers and designers and he was generous in rewarding new ideas (Bennett, 1951, 13).

HOW THE FORD MOTOR COMPANY
LOST ITS CULTURE

The sudden loss of an organization's core leadership can be fatal, as shown in James Clavell's[8] introduction to *The Art of War* (Sun Tzu, 1983, 6).

> So Sun Tzu became a general for the King of Wu. For almost two decades the armies of Wu were victorious over their hereditary enemies, the Kingdom of Yueh and Ch'u. Sometime within this period Sun Tzu died and his patron, the King of Wu, was killed in a battle. For a few years his descendents followed the precepts of Sun Tzu and continued to be victorious. And then they forgot.
>
> In 473 B.C. the armies of Wu were defeated and the kingdom made extinct.

This section examines similar events at Ford during the late 1930s and early 1940s.

2001: Ford Rediscovers Its Own Heritage

The Ford Motor Company invented or at least implemented all the so-called Japanese productivity improvement techniques. Why then did James Padilla, the group vice-president in charge of global manufacturing, have to learn these techniques from Mazda in the late 1980s (Shirouzu, 2001)? Not only that, the article states:

> Here, and throughout Ford's global operations, Mr. Padilla is trying to entice assembly workers and engineers to abandon nearly all they know about the mass manufacturing system that Henry Ford brought to life about 90 years ago.

Study of the article shows, however, that Mr. Padilla was actually reintroducing that system the way the company's founder meant it to work! He was teaching kaizen, one of Henry Ford's paramount principles, and standardization.

A cynic might argue that terms like kaizen and poka-yoke (error-proofing) help sell these American-developed concepts to

Americans. While restaurants can easily sell sushi for a dollar an ounce, few patrons will order "raw fish" even if it is free. Meanwhile, someone posted an apparently humorous commentary on America's fixation on Japanese quality techniques in an Internet newsgroup, misc.industry.quality. The posting declared a familiarity with kaizen, poka-yoke, and so on, and then asked if anyone had heard of seppuku or knew when it should be used. It drew a couple of serious inquiries about what readers thought was another Japanese quality or productivity method. Seppuku is actually ritual suicide.

The Shirouzu article says that Toyota developed lean manufacturing during the late 1950s; we have already seen that Toyota learned it from Ford. It goes on to say, "Standardization refers to the goal of finding the absolutely most efficient way of accomplishing a task, rather than following tradition or workers' preferences." The idea of finding the "one best way" obviously did not come from Toyota during the late 1950s; Frederick Winslow Taylor described it explicitly in 1911. Ford combined standardization with kaizen by emphasizing that a standard was only *today's* "one best way" that could, and should, be superseded by a better one tomorrow.

Shirouzu (2001) adds that workers resisted a team leader who tried to redesign jobs to eliminate unnecessary motions. "One co-worker swore at Mr. [Tony] Tallarita when he tried to consolidate two trunk hinge assembly stations into a single station and save the other employee some 2,000 unnecessary steps each shift. 'Don't bother,' the man said. 'I like walking.'" One of Henry Ford's cardinal job design principles was that no worker should have to take more than one step in any direction; pedestrianism does not pay very well. The team leader did exactly what the company's founder would have done, but he apparently didn't know it.

Why were Ford executives taken similarly by surprise when Japanese executives showed them *My Life and Work* in 1982 (Stuelpnagel 1993, 91)? An educated guess points to the loss of key personnel during the mid-1940s.

The Collapse of the Original Ford Organization, 1943

Taylor quoted a highly successful American manufacturer, whom he does not name, on the value of a good management team.

> If I had to choose now between abandoning my present organization and burning down all of my plants which have cost me millions, I should choose the latter. My plants could be rebuilt in a short while with borrowed money, but I could hardly replace my organization in a generation (Taylor, 1911a, 63).

There is strong evidence that this is exactly what happened to the Ford Motor Company during the Second World War. Sorensen (1956) describes how, after Henry Ford suffered a stroke during the 1930s, he began to have paranoid delusions. It wasn't complete paranoia; Ford had spent a good part of the 1930s fighting union organizers. Nonetheless, Ford began to take out his anger on innocent bystanders. He fired A. M. Wibel, who began work as a machinist in 1912 and succeeded Fred Diehl as head of purchasing. Wibel had been a capable and loyal worker, and Ford had never found any fault with him before he suddenly announced, "Wibel is through" (Sorensen, 1956, 322).

Edsel Ford, one of the company's most effective leaders, was under enormous stress because of his dysfunctional relationship with his father. This stress may have even hastened Edsel's death at 49 in 1943. Henry Ford, who was then eighty, took over as president, but he no longer had the physical or mental capacity to perform in that capacity. Bennett (1951, 298–299) confirms Sorensen's statement that, after Sorensen's retirement in 1944, Ford often asked his chauffeur to take him to the plant to "see Charlie." He added (1951, 307) that Ford was in "a constantly confused state" by 1945. "The picture was clear; the team was breaking up. The captain was a sick man, unable to call the plays. The line coaches were gone. Anyone who made a brilliant play was called out" (Sorensen, 1956, 329).

Sorensen himself also had had enough, and he retired after Henry Ford Jr. assumed the presidency. Bennett, who did not always get along with him, said of his departure:

> Sorensen had been the plaster that held the plant together. When word came through that he was leaving, real panic swept through the Rouge. When Sorensen left, the Rouge lost its soul (Bennett, 1951, 298).

One of Sorensen's friends asked him why he never developed a real successor to Ford. Sorensen reprinted his answer to his friend's question, a letter that could well serve as the epitaph of the original Ford organization. "Mr. Ford, like many men of his kind, never had a successor, they just can't acknowledge that such a thing is possible" (Sorensen, 1956, 333).

In summary, the company lost the following key personnel in the space of a few years:

- Henry Ford, largely incapacitated by ill health
- A. M. Wibel (and others), fired or resigned
- Edsel Ford, died
- Charles Sorensen, retired

The rest of the key players had departed long ago. A key lesson is that, while most organizations can survive the gradual attrition of their senior members, the sudden loss of their core people can damage them badly.

After the war ended and the company's founders were long gone, the company hired the so-called Whiz Kids who had impressed the Air Corps with analytical management methods, to implement a management system:

> In the decade following World War II, Ford's Whiz Kids created a corporate culture based on a financial paradigm, in which virtually every business decision was a function only of profitability (Hoyer, 2001).

Financial controls took precedence over marketing, manufacturing, and engineering (Standard and Davis, 1999, 32). The bean counters now had their hands on the tiller, and it is no surprise that the Ford Motor Company forgot the principles that had created it.

Unionization at Ford

This chapter raises another question: why, given Henry Ford's insistence on a square deal for all organizational participants, did his workers unionize? Upton Sinclair suggests that the root cause was the company's abandonment of its own principles. His *The Flivver King* comes across as a fairly impartial history of the Ford Motor Company in which Sinclair suggests that Ford lost touch with his own company, an organization that had grown far beyond a single person's ability to manage.

> But now the world had changed. Henry's plant was ten times as big, and Henry himself was old; he left his troubles to others, and avoided knowing what they were doing (Sinclair, 1937, 76).

By this time the company was violating the previously discussed maxim that lean manufacturing must not destroy jobs if *the* company is to retain its workers' loyalty and commitment.

> Twenty men who had been making a certain part would see a new machine brought in and set up [at the River Rouge plant], and one of them would be taught to operate it and do the work of the twenty. The other nineteen wouldn't be fired right away—there appeared to be a rule against that. The foreman would put them at other work, and presently he would start to "ride" them, and the men would know exactly what that meant (Sinclair, 1937, 81).

The reference adds that managers now discharged excess workers on the most trivial pretexts. Safety, one of Ford's paramount considerations, also fell by the wayside because the speed-up department kept overruling the safety department. The company did not deteriorate because of any defect in its founder's principles but because of its failure to adhere to those principles.

Notes

1. http://www.asterix.tm.fr/english/
2. See Murphy and Saxena in Levinson, 1998, Levinson and Rerick, 2002, and Goldratt, 1992, for information about SFM and the Theory of Constraints.
3. Carl von Clausewitz (1976, Book 5, ch. 5) says, "First, an order progressively loses in speed, vigor, and precision the longer the chain of command it has to travel. . . . Every additional link in the chain of command reduces the effect of an order in two ways: by the process of being transferred, and by the additional time needed to pass it on. It follows that the number of subdivisions with equal status should be as large as possible, and the chain of command as short as possible." Field Marshal Helmuth von Moltke (1800-1891) said essentially the same thing.
4. http://web.cba.neu.edu/~ewertheim/introd/history.htm, http://llanes.panam.edu/edul6384/organizationaltimeline, http://www.colostate.edu/Depts/DSA/HE676/history.htm, sites at Northeastern University, University of Texas Pan American, and Colorado State as of 12/29/01. Klein and Ritti (1984, 115–116) cite two references, one from 1961 and one from 1969, with respect to organic and mechanistic systems.
5. Clavell may have modeled Blackthorne on the historical Will Adams.
6. Bennett (1951, 149–151) speculates that an argument over Henry Ford's will damaged Ford's relationship with his son. Clifford Longley wanted to change Ford's will to avoid the inheritance tax. Edsel agreed that most of his father's property should be put into escrow to avoid the tax. Henry Sr. believed the change was a plot to get his money away from him. At one point, he became so angry and paranoid that he vowed to spend everything he had before he died. Since Ford lacked an extensive formal education, it's conceivable that he did not understand what Longley was trying to do.
7. The long italicized sections of *Ford: We Never Called Him Henry* appear to be the commentary of ghostwriter Paul Marcus.
8. Clavell is better known as the author of *Shogun*, *King Rat*, and *Tai-Pan*.

FIVE

Perceiving Genuine Value

This chapter provides valuable supporting information for change management and transformation of organizations to a lean culture. It begins by emphasizing manufacturing's importance to national prosperity. Change agents can use this information to promote morale in manufacturing organizations. The chapter goes on to assess the value of supply chain elements like intermediaries and retailers.

Two activities are the foundations of all human wealth: extractive industries, or getting raw materials from nature, and manufacturing, or adding value to the raw materials by transforming them into goods. No other activities create wealth. A third activity, transportation, adds no value. Manufacturing and distribution of products cannot, however, happen without it.

> The primary functions are agriculture [to which we can add mining, lumbering, and other extractive industries: getting materials from Nature], manufacture, and transportation. Community life is impossible without them. They hold the world together. . . .
>
> The foundations of society are the men and means to *grow* things, to *make* things, and to *carry* things. As long as agriculture, manufacture, and transportation survive, the world can survive any economic or social change (Ford, 1922, 6–7).

Even the Communists agreed with Henry Ford—about the role of manufacturing and agriculture in national prosperity, as shown by their hammer and sickle. The problem was that they let their government and political ideologues try to manage these activities. This is why abundant food and consumer goods could usually be found in Five-Year Plans but nowhere else.

Robert Thurston Kent, editor of *Industrial Engineering*, said the same thing in his introduction to Frank B. Gilbreth's *Motion Study*.

> The actual wealth of the nation is in what it takes from the ground in the shape of crops or minerals plus the value added to these products by processes of manufacture. If by reducing the number of motions in any of these processes we can increase many fold the output of the worker, we have increased by that amount the wealth of the world; we have taken a long step in bringing the cost of living to a point where it will no longer be a burden to all but the very wealthy; and we have benefited mankind in untold ways (Gilbreth, 1911).

A WARNING TO THE UNITED STATES

This chapter should already be sounding alarms throughout the United States where manufacturing's share of the gross domestic product (GDP) has been declining for the past few decades. Service jobs and positions in dot-com companies, neither of which grow, make, or carry anything, are replacing manufacturing jobs. (See Figure 5-1.[1]) Recent bankruptcies of many dot-coms reinforces the idea that these business built themselves on a foundation of sand. While internet businesses do reduce the waste that is inherent in retailing, *they must still have something to sell.* This section describes the problem and underscores the need to readopt Henry Ford's principles.

Some non-wealth-producing activities like health care are essential. It's discomforting to find, however, that the retail and wholesale trade portions of the GDP together equal the manufacturing percentage. This suggests that half a manufactured item's price consists of non-value-adding overhead and profit for intermediaries. This half does not include transportation, the cost of getting the item from the manufacturer to the customer.

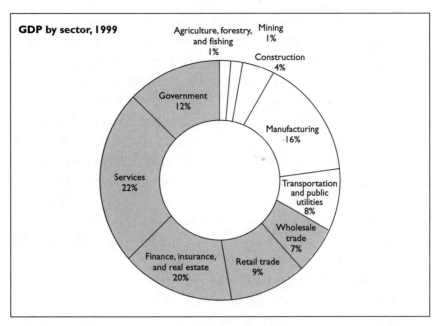

GDP by sector, 1999

- Agriculture, forestry, and fishing 1%
- Mining 1%
- Construction 4%
- Manufacturing 16%
- Transportation and public utilities 8%
- Wholesale trade 7%
- Retail trade 9%
- Finance, insurance, and real estate 20%
- Services 22%
- Government 12%

Figure 5-1. Percentage of U.S. gross domestic product, 1999 (wealth producing activities are light, non-wealth-producing activities are dark

Quality magazine's former editor Tom Williams warns,

Japan has been manufacturing while the U.S. has been producing 'dot com' companies and jobs at Wal-Mart . . . For most of history, manufacturing has been a solid part of the U.S. economy and identity. Those who would have us build the economy without emphasizing manufacturing are placing this country on a foundation of sand (Williams, Feb. 2000, 6).

Williams later (April 2000, 6) cites a business book that names Dell Computer, Wal-Mart, and Amazon.com as excellent models for customer satisfaction, revenue growth, and market share growth. The problem is that none of these companies actually makes anything; even Dell outsources its assembly operations. Williams compares marketing and sales to a circus sideshow attraction that has somehow made its way under the big top. "We are to suspend our disbelief and buy into the notion that having no core competency—for example, being only a marketing company—is really having a core competency." Real manufacturing companies ". . . produce a tangible product. They don't ask us to believe they've created something where nothing exists."[2]

The ash heap of history is full of countries that allowed the fundamental activities of manufacturing, mining and agriculture, and transportation to decline. Levinson and Tumbelty (1997, 3–5) describe how gold from the New World ruined Spain and Portugal. The Spanish and Portuguese confused gold with wealth, when true wealth lies in the ability to manufacture and transport goods. Spain and Portugal ruined their own manufacturing industries by spending their gold on manufactured goods from England and Holland. The English and Dutch built merchant ships to carry the raw materials that their craftspeople needed to make goods for Spain and Portugal; they increased their ability to carry things. Then they built powerful navies to protect the merchant ships, and the technologically superior English Navy wrecked the Spanish Armada at Gravelines in 1588. Captain Alfred Thayer Mahan (1980, 46) explained what had happened. "The tendency to trade, including of necessity the production of something to trade with, is the national characteristic most important to the development of sea power."

Manufacturing: The British Had Good Thing and They Knew It

England then maintained its dominant position through manufacturing (making things) and transportation (carrying things). The controversial Navigation Acts of the late eighteenth century were, in fact, designed to monopolize sea transportation by English shipping. England also passed laws to protect domestic industries by prohibiting manufacturing in the American colonies. "The English prohibition against colonial manufacture had been a constant irritant and eventually became one of the causes of [the Revolutionary] war" (Crow, 1943, 24).

Crow (1943, 26–30) adds that parts of England had monopolies on certain products. British wool merchants agitated for and got a ban on calico, a cotton cloth from Calicut in India. They also obtained a ban on the manufacture of cotton cloth. Textile mill owners in Manchester, England, got Parliament to prohibit the export of spinning jennies and improved looms. Another law forbade emigration of the skilled textile workers who operated this equipment.

The infant United States wanted to acquire manufacturing technology, and it was not above using industrial espionage. Pennsylvania offered a £100 reward for the invention of a carding machine, and the legislature was not particular as to the intellectual property's actual ownership or the manner in which it was "invented." Any Englishman who brought the design of one of the Birmingham machines would have received the money.

Samuel Slater, who completed his apprenticeship as a cloth maker around 1789, memorized the machine's design and posed as a farmhand so he could get out of England. He arrived in the United States and built a factory in Rehemoth, Massachusetts, in 1801. He is often called the father of American manufacturing. Per Crow (1943, 20), another American obtained an English textile machine by sawing it into small pieces and shipping it to France disguised as plate glass—presumably inside protective, and concealing, packaging. He then sent it to America for reassembly and duplication. The subterfuge was necessary because the Royal Navy intercepted ships on the high seas to retrieve such cargo. When we consider the lengths to which early Americans went to build manufacturing industries, the gross folly of allowing their loss today becomes even more manifest. The decline of manufacturing in the United States should be nothing short of alarming. The United States must reverse this trend to avoid joining the list of nations whose former greatness resides only in history books.

Manufacturing: China Knows a Good Thing When It Sees It

Acquisition of manufacturing capability is a key priority for China. Briscoe (2001) quotes Generalists Inc.'s president, Buck Crouch: "There's no question they endeavor to become an economic superpower.... It was like they were trying to sell their resources to us—they would like to see a huge shift of manufacturing to China." Thirty-five percent of China's gross domestic product, versus 16 percent of the United States', comes from manufacturing. Instead of declining as it is in the United States, manufacturing has an annual 9 percent growth rate in China. This trend is extremely dangerous because manufacturing, the backbone of military power, has malicious as well as beneficial uses. The uses to which the current Chinese government might put its growing industrial power are causes for concern given its behavior toward its Asian neighbors, its own people (e.g. Tiananman Square), and the American airplane crew it held hostage in April 2001.

Another reference makes China's manufacturing focus even clearer. The Chinese government requires companies that import raw materials to pay a large deposit. The government refunds most of the deposit if the importer can show that the raw materials went into manufactured goods for export ("Too Tempting? Smuggling Makes a Comeback in China," 2001). This is not to say we should begrudge Chinese workers the benefits of industrialization, which Ford said removes the root causes of poverty and even war. The expansion of Chinese manufacturing at the expense of American manufacturing is, however, totally unacceptable. Lean manufacturing, an outgrowth of Taylor's scientific management and Ford's methods, is the answer to the lure of cheap offshore labor.

On a final note, the Briscoe article reveals China's lack of consideration for its workers' well being. Chinese machines often lack safety guards, a feature that Ford required during the early twentieth century. Workplace lighting is often poor and Chinese workers often lack hearing protection. Observers also saw huge inefficiencies in Chinese plants such as poor layouts that required excessive transportation.

Manufacturing's Low Prestige

Ford recognized the root of the problem. "Too many people believe that Success consists of getting your bread and butter by dickering or talking instead of by producing" (Ford, 1922a, 132). Furthermore, "There is a class of men who regard the white collar as a sign of emancipation from work. An idea like that, if true, would soon bring the white collar into disgrace" (Ford, 1922a, 198). Too many modern business schools perpetuate the idea that the best MBAs go into glamorous occupations like finance and marketing, while those who can't make it in those areas go into manufacturing. Finance and marketing are nothing without manufacturing! A company that does not make a product, and a good one, has nothing to market and nothing to finance.

Ford did his best to eliminate jobs that did not relate directly to production. He also stressed the pivotal role of the skilled production worker and manufacturing engineer:

> The requirement for skill is constantly increasing in the shops so that today a man in a shop is usually better off than a man in an office. Workers at machines need a higher grade of skill then the routine men in the office, while tool makers must have a very high grade of skill indeed. This is gradually but surely destroying the advantage of the white collar, and soon we shall have our brightest young men seeking the shops rather than the office. Brains are becoming so necessary in shops that it is considered good business to pay very highly for them, and there will no longer be social distinctions between the man who works at a desk and the man who works at a machine (Ford, 1930, 56).

If our business schools emphasized this idea, American business would be far more profitable and the country would be much wealthier.

Other So-called Industries Cannot Replace Manufacturing

Hayes, Wheelwright, and Clark (1988, 15–17) asked a business manager, "How's business?" He answered, "Oh, business would be fine if only we didn't have to make the stuff." The reference continues,

Making the stuff was the dirty part; it involved the grubby details of coaxing products out of recalcitrant machines and uncaring workers. . . . It was the last hurdle—more often the last roadblock—to bringing all their beautiful product designs, all their careful marketing plans, all their precise financial calculations, to fruition.

This executive attitude reflects itself in its treatment of manufacturing operations. Hayes et. al. describe how plants get fewer corporate resources because "making the stuff" is the dirty and unimportant part of the business. Equipment, morale, and performance deteriorate, and the best employees leave.

The executive attitude becomes a self-fulfilling prophecy. "Suddenly someone at corporate headquarters does an analysis and says, 'Let's close this place down and go somewhere else.' So the company builds a new plant in a new location—far away from those tired managers and hostile workers." Corporate headquarters' attitude has not changed; however, the executives (or their successors) find themselves with the same situation 20 or 25 years later.

The prestigious product designers, marketing analysts, and financial planners must ask themselves, "What would we sell if someone didn't 'make the stuff?' Do we want to be at the economic mercy of those who do 'make the stuff?'"

Historian Ellsworth Grant says that Hartford, Connecticut, was once the wealthiest city in the United States. Mark Twain apparently saw Hartford as such a symbol of industrial ingenuity and manufacturing prowess that his fictional Connecticut Yankee was the superintendent of the Colt Armory before a blow on his head sent him back to Arthurian England. Hartford was also the home of Pratt & Whitney, and were more than 60 factories within the city's borders. Then the rot set in:

Since the turn of the century, though, Hartford has plummeted from that level to become one of the ten poorest cities in the country, set back by natural disasters, residential flight and city planning fiascoes. As service-oriented jobs began to outstrip those in manufacturing, Hartford also suffered two major floods, in 1938 and 1955...

"I think 1960 was really a watershed year for Hartford," says Grant, "because that was the year the service industry took over as the major employer..." (Marciano, 1999).

Banking and insurance are now two of Hartford's major so-called industries. "Would you like fries with that loan or insurance policy?" It's time to bring back Mark Twain's Connecticut Yankee and his real-world intellectual heirs.

Factories Create Jobs Outside Their Walls

Ford (1930, 74) points out how manufacturing creates jobs in other sectors. "...the chief usefulness of industry to our economic situation is that it is not a whirlpool sucking all into itself, but a geyser constantly giving out; it has created more jobs outside industry than it has inside.... Our products have made at least ten or twenty times as much employment outside of our company as they have in it ..." This is how the Ford Motor Company made the United States the wealthiest and most powerful nation on earth. The automobile industry is still among the biggest customers for other manufactured products. The automobile itself creates other jobs through its demand for roads and service stations.

Ford (1930, 177) later enumerates the Model T's exact contribution to national wealth and prosperity during nineteen years of production. This figure did not include the wealth contributed by railway workers, rubber workers, oil workers, and others for whom the Model T created jobs. Nonetheless, it was more than the estimated wealth of thirty-five of the country's forty-eight states. Ford concludes, "Those figures show what a single idea will do to the wealth and income of the world—and how footless it is to look back to schemes for redistributing wealth when we can look forward to creating wealth."

There is a very misguided impression today that high-tech service jobs are superior replacements for manufacturing jobs. The problem is that few of those information system, dot-com, or software development jobs would exist unless they either helped manufacture something or supported a manufactured product. No one needs a statistical process control (SPC) software package unless he or she has a manufacturing process to control. No one needs an online store or e-commerce unless they have something (a physical product) to sell. Ford's original product, the automobile, creates a market for mapping and trip planning software, and also for global positioning system (GPS) units.

Henry Towne, a past president of the American Society of Manufacturing Engineers, showed in 1911 why lean manufacturing overcomes the attraction of inexpensive offshore labor. Nothing has happened during the past ninety years to change this.

> We are justly proud of the high wage rates which prevail throughout our country, and jealous of any interference with them by the products of the cheaper labor of other countries. To maintain this condition, to strengthen our control of home markets, and, above all, to broaden our opportunities in foreign markets where we must compete with the products of other industrial nations, we should welcome and encourage every influence tending to increase the efficiency of our productive processes (Foreword to Taylor, 1911a).

Taylor cites a related principle:

> ... the one element more than any other which differentiates civilized from uncivilized countries—prosperous from poverty-stricken peoples—is that the average man in the one is five or six times as productive as the other (1911, 75).

The next sections examine the foundation of lean manufacturing (or lean service): everything must add value. Value means something for which a customer is willing to pay. Identification and elimination of non-value-adding activities yields more profit for the supplier and a lower price for the customer.

EVERYTHING MUST ADD VALUE

One of Ford's overarching principles was that everything in a business must add value to the product or service. This is the same principle underlying today's lean organization:

> We will not put into our establishment anything that is useless. We will not put up elaborate buildings as monuments to our success. The interest on the investment and the cost of their upkeep only serve to add uselessly to the cost of what is produced—so these monuments of success are apt to end as tombs (Ford, 1922, 147–148).

Recall that some of the world's oldest monuments of success, the Egyptian pyramids, are in fact tombs.

The principle sounds obvious: don't put anything into the business that doesn't add value. Chapter 7 shows, however, that it is often very difficult to see the waste. The ability to do so, and to teach others to do it, may well have been Ford's principal success secret.

The next section examines middlemen and intermediaries, who are often built-in waste in any supply chain. Recall that non-value-adding retail and wholesale activities equaled manufacturing in a recent assessment of the United States' gross domestic product.

MIDDLEMEN DO NOT ADD VALUE

Middlemen and distributors counteract efficient and cost-effective manufacturing: "There is no point in economizing in manufacturing if at the same time the suppliers and distributors charge all that the traffic will bear" (Ford, 1930, 18). Furthermore, "The greater the spread between the supply and the need, the more middlemen squeezed in between production and use, the heavier is the drag on the nation's prosperity" (Ford, 1930, 107).

Ford predicted, "If their [capitalists'] money goes to complicating distribution—to raising barriers between the producer and the consumer—then they are evil capitalists and they will pass away when money is better adjusted to work . . ." (1922, 10). The Internet is creating a frictionless marketplace (Gates, 1995) in which producer and consumer have no barriers between them. This is leaving retailers and distributors—even those who once played a legitimate role in commerce—to suffer the fate Ford predicted. Taylor and Jerome (May 1999, p. 87) discuss how economic Darwinism will cull middlemen from commerce: "Travel agents are toast." "Car dealers are cadavers." "Insurance salesmen are an endangered species." "Full-service brokers are knocking on Death's door." "Bankers are about to buy the farm." Specifically, they cite Priceline.com as an online competitor for travel agents and Intuit's Cash Finder as a way to shop around for the best loan rates without the help of a banker.

Anyone Want a Used Shopping Mall?

> Retailers are desperately aware that the Internet is cannibalizing—not augmenting—their sales. According to Jupiter [Communications], 94 percent of online sales in 1999 were hijacked from conventional channels. In the coming months, many retailers will jump at the chance to shutter their pricey storefronts, slash their overhead, and do business entirely on the Net.
>
> . . . The sunglasses you'll pay $200 for at the boutique cost $40 on the Web . . . You won't be paying a store owner's rent ("Top 10 Reasons to Shop on the Internet— Now!" 1999).

Shopping mall owners' desperate reaction to these developments is proof that they take the Internet seriously.

> The Saint Louis Galleria informed its 170 retail tenants in a letter last week of a new policy prohibiting any in-store "signs, insignias, decals or other advertising or display devices which promote and encourage the purchase of merchandise via e-commerce."
>
> . . . In an era when many retailers brandish their Internet addresses on their shopping bags, an e-commerce

ban is a harsh move. But the Galleria's owner, Hycel Partners 1 LP of St. Louis, says the new policy addresses a deep concern of mall owners everywhere—the possibility of losing rental income to online sales (Coleman and Gumbel, 1999, B1).

The mall should, however, heed Bombay Co. President Carmie Mehrlander's warning in the same article: one does not improve business by putting obstacles in the customer's path.

Clothing retailers and even catalog outlets will not be immune to the Internet's effects either. Robinson (1990, 8) says the trend toward lower inventories would lead to a situation where "a shirt ordered over the telephone would be manufactured and mailed within forty-eight hours, instead of retrieved and mailed in the same time frame." The ancestor of the computer punch card was invented during the early nineteenth century to control the Jacquard loom, so the idea of a computer weaving clothing to order should be obvious—and this might be a way to retrieve our textile industry from offshore manufacturers.

Textile/Clothing Technology Corp. (TC²) was actually integrating this idea with garment customization by 1994:

> With this device [a body scanner], a shopper would enter a store, slip into a bodysuit and be measured three-dimensionally from head to toe. Then the customer could select a shirt, pants or a dress from the racks or from digitized images of clothing on a kiosk or television screen. Using the body scan as an electronic paper doll, shoppers could superimpose garments onto their bodies to see how they look (Lee 1994).

The reference adds that the scan could be stored for future use, and that a manufacturer could make a custom-cut garment.

Standard and Davis (1999, 20) cite Custom Foot, a shoe manufacturer that takes the customer's exact foot measurements and makes shoes to order. The orders are emailed to Florence, Italy, and Custom Foot delivers the shoes within three weeks. The price is about 20 percent of that of traditional handmade shoes.

Car Dealers' Showrooms Add No Value

The Ford Motor Company did not sell through dealers during its first five years (about 1903 to 1908). "We sold for cash, we did not borrow money, and we sold directly to the purchaser" (Ford, 1922, 59). Ford later introduced dealerships whose main purpose was apparently to service the cars. The sales representatives were on good salaries, and Ford does not mention commissions.

Car dealers' behavior has changed a lot since then. Dealerships often try to pack expensive but nonfunctional options into every deal. Dealers try to sell environmental protection packages (rust-proofing) of dubious value, while a $100 "fabric treatment" might consist of a spraying from a $5.00 can of fabric protector. The dealer gets hundreds or even thousands of dollars for nothing more than filling the customer's order and taking delivery of the car from the car carrier.

Levinson (1994, 204–206) says that the automobile dealer adds cost but no value to a car purchase, and recommends just-in-time factory ordering. Levinson (1998, 296) cites the effect of the Internet; a buyer saved $4,000 off a car's list price by using Auto-By-Tel. Sisodia and Sheth (1999) also point out that the car dealership represents wasteful inventory:

> Auto retailing is a marketing dinosaur. It is the last refuge of the old-fashioned hard sell, a 'push oriented' model devised under the theory that a loaded dealer is a motivated dealer. While most manufacturers have moved to just-in-time production, the car industry still practices what we call just-in-case marketing. The average dealer has a huge 60- to 70-day inventory.

Inventory has significant carrying costs that add no value for the customer or the manufacturer.

> A rule-of-thumb carrying cost for a unit of product is commonly about one quarter of the product's value per year, with some arguing that the estimate should be much higher. Thus, for example, the direct cost of holding a car worth $15,000 will be about $3,750 per year (Robinson 1990, 19).

The dealer does not, of course, absorb this cost by himself, if at all. He adds to it his own profit on the transaction—a profit he gets for simply happening to be between the customer and the manufacturer. The customer must therefore pay more and the manufacturer must take less. Ford himself recognized the problem with carrying even a thirty-day inventory.

> We make cars to sell, not to store, and a month's unsold production would turn into a sum the interest on which alone would be enormous. . . . We can no more afford to carry large stocks of finished [goods] than we can of raw material. Everything has to move in and move out (Ford, 1922, 167).

Ford (1930, 9) also describes the problem with end-of-model-year sales and incentives—which did not exist in his time. The use of prices to entice customers hands over control of a business to its customers. Car buyers know that unsold inventory is a burden on the dealer, inventory that becomes much harder to sell when the model year changes. Many people wait until the model year is almost over to buy a car because the bargaining advantage passes from the dealer to the customer. Another strong argument for making cars to order is that it frees the manufacturer from the pressure at the end of the model year.

The second part of Figure 5-2, in which cars are made to order on a just-in-time basis, is absolutely realistic. Toyota established seven-day lead times for car orders a long time ago (Womack and Jones, 1996, 82).

Most car buyers are probably willing to wait a week—or perhaps ten days in the United States where transportation distances are much greater than in Japan—to avoid paying for the waste that appears in the first part of Figure 5-2. This waste includes the salesperson, who is basically an order-taker who doesn't really do anything a computer can't, the cost of owning the elaborate showroom, and the carrying costs of inventory that no one may even want. The manufacturer wins too because every car that leaves the factory has a buyer. The manufacturer makes more on each sale,

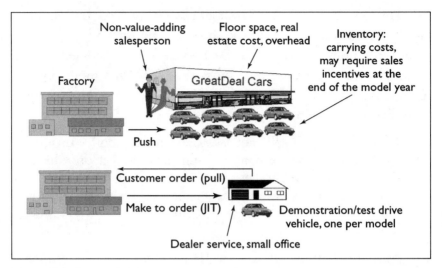

Figure 5-2. Two models for automotive retailing

even at a lower customer price, because no one has to carry the cost of the showroom and its inventory.

Microsoft CEO Bill Gates supports the idea of making cars to order:

> You can imagine the day that a customer in a dealer's showroom or at home uses a PC to order over the Internet exactly the car and options he or she wants and then gets delivery within a few days. 'Build to order,' which has become increasingly popular in the PC industry, is bound to become a major part of other manufacturing industries, from cars to clothing to furniture (Gates, 1999, 290).

Ford's own former CEO, Jacques Nasser, proposed a similar approach:

> Ford CEO Jacques Nasser, in linking up with Carpoint, argued that changes triggered by the online world could alter the way his company makes cars. In his vision, a consumer should be able to go online and configure a car just the way he or she wants it . . . That information should go to the factory and even to suppliers, like the companies that make brakes or seats. Nasser foresees huge savings

because Ford wouldn't have to build inventory that sits on dealers' lots. It would build only cars individual customers want, the same way Dell and Gateway now make PCs (Holstein, 1999).

At this point, who needs the car dealership's expensive showroom and lot full of inventory? Car dealerships' service departments will still be useful although any qualified auto shop can perform warranty repairs. There must also be a place to deliver factory-ordered vehicles. The car dealership of the twenty-first century might be a much smaller organization that serves as a depot for deliveries and as a warranty service shop. It also might keep a sample of each model for test drives.

Although car manufacturers have resorted to drastic price cuts and interest-free financing to move inventory during the economic downturn that began in 2001, they may eventually be forced to adopt this new business model. Cars are durable goods, and 2001's sales will cut into future orders, making this a temporary fix at best.

A New Model for the Recording Industry

Recent controversies about Napster and online sharing of music recordings may mask the true fear of the recording industry: a business model that would remove it from the value chain. Music compact discs (CDs) retail from $13 to $19. Recordable CDs with jewel cases sell in lots of 25 for about $1.10 apiece. The rest, except for artist royalties and production costs, is waste: retailer overhead and profit for the recording industry, distributors, and retailers.

Online stores already allow customers to listen to segments of individual songs. Soon they will be able to select the ones they want and purchase a CD with those selections. Customization and make-to-order, plus elimination of retailers' and distributors' overhead and profit, might allow CDs to sell for half their current prices with artists getting twice their current royalties.

ADVERTISING AS WASTE

Product quality is to selling a product what the edge of a chisel is to splitting an object. A worker needed to apply excessive and wasteful force—the "hard sell"—to a dull chisel to make it cut but a light tap on a sharp one would do the job.

> The cutting edge of merchandising is the point where the product touches the consumer. An unsatisfactory product is one that has a dull cutting edge. A lot of waste effort is needed to put it through. The cutting edge of a factory is the man and the machine on the job. If the man is not right the machine cannot be; if the machine is not right the man cannot be. For any one to be required to use more force than is absolutely necessary for the job in hand is waste (Ford, 1922, 19).

Quality and value sell themselves. Ford (1930, 9) says that sales result primarily from good manufacturing and not publicity. He continues, "First-class goods and commodities can always be sold—at a price" (1930, 16). Ford realized what many people did not until close to the end of the twentieth century: good quality sells itself, and bad quality that dissatisfies a customer is the worst possible form of advertising.

Advertising does not add any value to a company's product or service. Customers who see elaborate and high-volume ads, especially on television, should realize that those ads' costs are built into the product's price. In 1987 I refused to buy a car from a dealer that added a $75.00 advertising fee to the price because the dealer's advertisements gave me no value. (The same dealer tried to pack a costly rustproofing package into the price, with the result that he did not sell me anything at all.)

There is a saying that a fishing lure has done its job when it has caught the fisherman. Whether it catches any fish afterward is largely irrelevant to the vendor. Manufacturers should ask, "Do advertisements sell products to customers, or do advertising agencies sell ads to manufacturers?" (Ford identified a similar problem with many stocks. The company's stock, not its goods or services, was the principal "product.")

How many adults truly pay attention to television ads? How many people throw away the Sunday paper's advertising section unread unless they want to buy something from the classified section? How many people discard bulk mail unopened and unread? People who sell e-mail address lists don't care if the buyers lose their email accounts for spamming (sending unsolicited commercial bulk email, which violates most service providers' terms of service).

Internet advertisers once charged by impressions, or the number of times an advertising banner was displayed. Displays do not necessarily mean sales. Many vendors now pay commissions only for actual sales that result from click-throughs on Internet advertising banners. This is a way of paying the lure's seller by the number of fish it catches, or at least for the number of nibbles.

The Benefits of Continuous Price Reduction

> During one year our profits were so much larger than we expected them to be that we voluntarily returned fifty dollars to each purchaser of a car. We felt that unwittingly we had overcharged the purchaser by that much (Ford, 1922, 161).

A business can rely on continuous price reductions (through lean manufacturing, for example) instead of advertising to increase sales. "If what has been thought to be a luxury can be manufactured in quantities at a low price, then it may become a commodity and a necessity—that is what happened with automobiles" (Ford, 1926, 155). Ford made his cars affordable to the middle class, and this expanded his market (see Figure 5-3).

Ford's supposedly infamous statement, "You can have any color you want, as long as it's black," is an example of a quote that was taken out of context. It sounds like the attitude of an arrogant supplier who has no competition. Here is the context: "If we had permitted any choice of colour or design in Model T, at the very

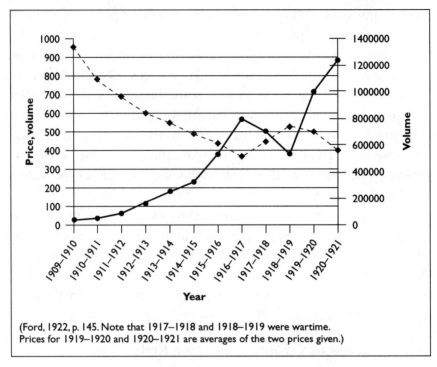

(Ford, 1922, p. 145. Note that 1917–1918 and 1918–1919 were wartime. Prices for 1919–1920 and 1920–1921 are averages of the two prices given.)

Figure 5-3. Price and volume of Ford touring car

beginning, we could not have made the low price at which we intended to sell" (Ford, 1930, 162). As Ford's company gained experience in making cars, it introduced different colors and body designs economically. The reference continues,

> If the production of cars reaches ten thousand a day, then a wider choice of bodies may be made without affecting the economy of manufacturing, for then we have a sufficient production to make use of experience tables as to what body styles and colours customers will ask for . . . We thus gain a flexibility of style for the purchaser without going into manufacturing to order—which would of course be impossible in a product to be sold at a low price.

As discussed in the section on car dealers, "make to order" could actually make cars cheaper today. Ford was writing, of course, sixty or so years before *Internet* was a household word. Ford added that mass-produced subunits or parts can be assembled in different ways to provide the end user with considerable choice. All Model Ts, for example, used the same chassis, but different styles were available. One version even had tracks instead of drive wheels and sleigh runners instead of front wheels. It was a utility vehicle for use in snow.

The price reduction principle applies to modern electronic products. Microwave ovens, which were expensive luxuries during the early 1970s, are commonplace appliances today. As digital cameras become less expensive, more people buy them.

Computer prices have declined slowly despite inflation, while computer performance has increased rapidly. Something that was a fairly expensive luxury in the early 1980s has become almost a commodity. Millions of people can afford personal computers, and the higher sales volume has more than made up for lower prices.

Continuous Improvement Increases
Sales per Customer

Continuous product improvement, in the form of miniaturization, has also expanded the computer market. Many computer owners also buy laptop computers for portability. That is, improvements that make the product less expensive and easier to use often encourage customers to buy more than one. Price reductions and improved portability have done the same thing for compact disk players.

The next section treats a concept that, if an organization's stakeholders all understood it, would prevent many labor disputes. It also would teach stockholders to stop acting like young children who want immediate gratification (i.e. dramatic increases in the quarterly bottom line). Recognition of genuine value includes understanding that no system can deliver more wealth than it produces.

NO FREE LUNCH

Nothing will come from nothing.

—King Lear

This book has introduced the acronym TANSTAAFL, "There ain't no such thing as a free lunch." Much individual, organizational, and national misery results from the mistaken belief that something can come from nothing. No organization or system can disburse more goods and services than it creates.

Ford's books stress the folly of unions, stockholders, and management teams that try to squeeze wealth from a business. Unions that demand higher wages and stockholders who want more dividends must recognize that the business cannot deliver what it does not produce. The only way to reap more benefits for all the stakeholders—labor, management, customers, and stockholders—is to increase productivity.

> It is not good management to take profits out of the workers or the buyers; make management produce the profits. Don't cheapen the product; don't cheapen the wage; don't overcharge the public. Put brains into the method, and more brains, and still more brains—do things better than ever before; and by this means all parties to business are served and benefited (Ford, 1922, 155).

This is how Ford quadrupled his workers' real wages in 20 years while reducing product price and expanding his business.

Putting Finance in Perspective

> I determined absolutely that never would I join a company in which finance came before the work or in which bankers or financiers had a part. And further that, if there were no way to get started in the kind of business that I thought could be managed in the interest of the public, then I simply would not get started at all. . . . it is control by finance that breaks up service because it looks to the immediate dollar (Ford, 1922, 40–42).

Ford disliked bankers and even stockholders, for he perceived that financiers invested in a business only to get money out of a business. Sorensen (1956, 167–168) tells of a visit in 1920 by a New York banker, Joseph Bowers, who thought Ford wanted to borrow money. The banker talked down to Ford, pointed out his inexperience with finance, and mentioned that some Grosse Pointe bankers had described Ford as "erratic and irresponsible." He added that, as a condition of granting a loan, the bank would want a directorship in Ford's company. Sorensen, with Ford's approval, handed Bowers his briefcase with the words, "Here are your papers, you run along and peddle them. Goodbye!"

Ford then reprimanded Klingensmith, the company treasurer, who had invited Bowers or at least suggested that Ford might want credit. Sorensen could not understand why Klingensmith hadn't considered the idea of liquidating inventory to raise cash. "Having a banker's mind, Kling could not see our real resources beyond a financial statement sheet." The professional financier, Ford warned,

> . . . finances for the sake of financing and what he can get out of it in money, without a thought for the welfare of the people. The professional reformer likewise reforms for the sake of reforming and for his own satisfaction, and without a thought of the real welfare of the people.
>
> These two classes are real menaces. The professional financiers wrecked Germany. [Weimar Germany was in the midst of an economic depression in 1926.] The professional reformers wrecked Russia. You can take your choice as to who made the better job of it (Ford, 1926, 26).
>
> Money brokers are seldom good business men. Speculators cannot create values (Ford, 1926, 29).

The American investment community's unhealthy focus on the quarterly bottom line was partly responsible for Japan's inroads into American automobile and electronics markets during the 1970s and 1980s. Japanese investors are far more patient, they seek long-term results, and they get those results. Ford explains exactly what happened:

Money put into a business as a lien on its assets is dead money. When industry operates wholly by the permission of 'dead' money, its main purpose becomes the production of payments for the owners of that money. The service of the public has to be secondary. If quality of goods jeopardizes these payments, then the quality is cut down. If full service cuts into the payments, then service is cut down. . . . Dead money is not a working partner but an idle charge (Ford, 1926, 31).

Businesses also seek to improve short-term profitability by downsizing their workforces and by delaying or canceling capital investments that will improve quality and productivity. This lack of foresight has its natural consequences. This is why most of the audio and video equipment that is sold in the United States comes from Japan. It is why America's highways are full of Toyotas, Mazdas, Nissans, Hondas, and Mitsubishis.

Ford also warns against corporations that do not serve anyone but exist merely to sell their stock. The performance of the stock market during the late twentieth and early twenty-first centuries shows that he was right. Investors bought dot-com stocks in companies that had never earned a penny, simply because dot-com means Internet and the Internet is perceived as an economic cornucopia. Internet stocks sold at price to earnings ratios of more than 100 to 1—if the companies had any earnings against which to divide their prices. The Internet is indeed a frictionless marketplace (Gates, 1995) but, as in any marketplace, you have to have something to sell. Nothing came of nothing, and many investors lost money on dot-com stocks during the early months of 2000.

Don't Let the Cost Accounting System Run the Business

Cost accounting has two, and only two, legitimate purposes: tax accounting and financial statements. Tax laws and Securities and Exchange Commission (SEC) regulations specify procedures for these activities. Ford says, for example, that accounting book values are meaningless. "As for the buildings and machinery, they must be valued in dollars according to the meaningless methods of accounting that are required by law. Actually they are worth only what we can do with them" (Ford, 1930, 25). He goes on to say that his company scraps and replaces entire business divisions routinely to keep up with changing needs. "In these days a plant, no matter how much it costs, is worth only its value in scrap metal, for a complete change in methods may require, almost any day, that it be reduced to scrap" (Ford, 1930, 29).

Apple Computer cofounder Steven Jobs said the same thing about the Macintosh factory. "Because it was designed to last only thirty months, we can tear the line down, sell the metal for scrap, and build a better one."[3] In contrast, some managers try to avoid replacing obsolete equipment that has no book value even if this leaves them at a competitive disadvantage. The manufacture of unusable inventory to dilute per-unit production costs is another dysfunctional effect of cost accounting measurements.

Overhead is a fixed or sunk cost that the factory pays no matter what it does. Accounting systems often treat hourly labor as a variable cost, but it's really a fixed cost because workers are paid for eight hours a day whether they have work or not, Overtime is a genuine variable cost because the business pays it only when it asks people to work beyond their normal shifts. "The foremen and superintendents would only be wasting time were they to keep a check on the costs in their departments. There are certain costs—such as the rate of wages, the overhead, the price of materials, and the like, which they could not in any way control, so they do not bother about them" (Ford, 1922, 98).

Operational decisions, such as what to make and how much to make, should depend only on marginal costs and revenues. What is the extra sale revenue from the next unit, and what is the extra cost to make it? The marginal cost of making another unit does not include overhead, depreciation, or even fixed labor costs. It includes the materials, along with overtime labor if applicable.

(See equation 51: one can play with this model by lowering the unit price to get more sales. See Levinson and Rerick, 2002, for more detail on marginal costs and marginal profits.)

$$\text{Marginal cost} = \frac{d(\text{Cost})}{dn}\bigg]_{n=N} \quad \text{when selling N units}$$

$$\text{Marginal revenue} = \frac{d(\text{Revenue})}{dn}\bigg]_{n=N} = \text{unit price} \qquad \textbf{(Eq. 5-1)}$$

$$\text{Marginal profit} = \frac{d(\text{Profit})}{dn}\bigg]_{n=N} = \frac{d(\text{Revenue-Cost})}{dn}\bigg]_{n=N}$$

The cost accounting system's role is to report what the business has done. Enormous misery often comes from letting it tell the business what to do.

Don't Let Stockholders Pull the Strings

The stockholders, to my way of thinking, ought to be only those who are active in the business and who will regard the company as an instrument of service rather than as a machine for making money (Ford, 1922, 161).

The narrow capitalist and the narrow trades unionist have exactly the same view of business—they differ only on who is to have the loot (Ford, 1926, 237).

The unhealthy focus of the American stockholder on the quarterly report often results in terrible business decisions like:

- Delaying or canceling capital expenditures. This can severely damage the enterprise's long-term competitiveness. The best time to build a new factory is often not when conditions are good and everybody is building, but when conditions are bad. When the market improves, the proactive company that has done this can prosper from its foresight while its competitors scramble to build capacity—in time for the next downturn.
- Laying off employees. Layoffs reduce short-term costs but, when immediate conditions improve, it costs money to

hire and train new workers. Employees who are good enough to pick and choose their employers will not work for a company that hires and fires with every change in the economy's wind.

- Implementing cutbacks in research, development, and employee training. This saves money in the short run but undermines the business's long-term competitiveness. The best time to train employees and run factory experiments is when the factory is not running at full capacity. When the factory is at full capacity, experiments that do not produce marketable product cannot go through the constraint operation without gutting profits. (The constraint is the operation whose capacity limits the factory's capacity. The section on just-in-time manufacturing in Chapter 8 treats this concept further.)
- Creating "phantom" orders. Sales departments sometimes respond to pressure by getting customers to place orders that they know will be cancelled in the next financial period. This wreaks havoc with the production planning system.

Ford's business strategy involved steady reductions in his prices, a strategy that displeased his stockholders until he got rid of them by buying them out.

> This policy does not agree with the general opinion that a business is to be managed to the end that the stockholders can take out the largest possible amount of cash. Therefore I do not want stockholders in the ordinary sense of the term—they do not help forward the ability to serve.
> ... Hence we have no place for the non-working stockholders. The working stockholder is more anxious to increase his opportunity to serve than to bank dividends (Ford, 1922, 162).

Ford's animosity toward stockholders arose from his own experience with them. The Dodge brothers sued Ford in the late

1910s for cutting prices, increasing wages, and reinvesting all the profits. They thought his so-called mismanagement was reducing their dividends. They persuaded a court to compel Ford to pay a dividend. Like the fool who killed the goose to get the golden eggs, they thought only of short-term profit. Ford threatened to have his privately-owned tractor company, Henry Ford & Son, build a new car to compete with the Model T. Then he bought out the minority stockholders so he could pursue his business strategy without their interference.

Sorensen (1956, 166) shows how the minority stockholders made out "in round numbers." The numbers were very round; they had a lot of zeroes after them. Most got $2,500 for every dollar they invested, for a compound annual rate of 63 percent.[4] This was the capital gain only, it does not count the $30 million in dividends that their $33,100 initial investment earned over these 16 years.

Who Should Run the Company?

Finance and marketing MBAs are considered more glamorous than manufacturing-oriented MBAs. Investment banking has the reputation of a glamorous profession. Ford's perspective was, however:

> You will note that the financiers proposed to cure by lending money and not by bettering methods. They did not suggest putting in an engineer; they wanted to put in a treasurer.
>
> And that is the danger of having bankers in business. They think solely in terms of money. They think of a factory as making money, not goods. They want to watch the money, not the efficiency of production.
>
> ... The banker is, as I have noted, by training and because of his position, totally unsuited to the conduct of industry (Ford, 1922, 177).

Manufacturing, agriculture, and related enterprises create wealth. Investment bankers, venture capitalists, and financiers can only deal in wealth that others have created. This assessment extends to government, where most professional politicians can think only in terms of redistributing wealth that they have no idea of how to create.

Mergers and Acquisitions

"You don't get an eagle by merging two turkeys." This principle is attributed to Tom Peters, and Henry Ford held a similar view. Ford acquired businesses like coal mines, railroads, and even South American rubber plantations for a reason: they all provided raw materials for his principal product. Vertical integration made it much easier to manage the supply chain to get the best results. Many companies, however, seem to pursue mergers for their own sake. Of these Ford writes,

> A merger of corporations may be distinctly beneficial in bringing together a number of units that belong together, but it is more usual for weak than for strong corporations to merge. No lamp posts have been provided for weak or overstimulated business to cling to and so they are apt to cling to each other. The embrace is called a merger (Ford, 1930, 21).

This chapter has shown the role of manufacturing in assuring national prosperity and security. It has exposed possible sources of waste in the value stream: intermediaries, retailers, and advertising. It has also shown the dysfunctional effects of finance. The next chapter applies similar considerations to macroeconomics, government, and health care.

Notes

1. http://www.bea.doc.gov/bea/dn2/gposhr.htm#1993-99
2. See also Levinson, 2000. "Lose Manufacturing, Lose the Future." *Manufacturing Engineering*, June, p. 136

SIX

Ford on Economics, Government, and Health Care

This chapter applies Henry Ford's principles to prominent issues that include the economy, government, and health care. Readers can use the information to educate the public and help shape policy. Stock market analysts, trade journal editors, and even business managers talk about business cycles and economic cycles. *Semiconductor International*, for example, often has editorial commentary on the cyclical semiconductor market (Baliga, 1999). Circular diagrams show the history and future prospects for rising and falling demand for transistors, integrated circuits, equipment for making these products, and factory cleanroom space.

Suppose we could "just say no" to business and economic cycles, as Henry Ford did:[1]

> Through all the years that I have been in business I have never yet found our business bad as a result of any outside force. It has always been due to some defect in our own company, and whenever we located and repaired that defect our business became good again—regardless of what anyone else might be doing (Ford, 1930, 2).

BUSINESS CYCLES

> The fault, dear Brutus, is not in our stars,
> But in ourselves, that we are underlings.
> —*Julius Caesar*, Act I, Scene 2

Henry Ford discussed the business cycle issue in the "Why Not Always Have Good Business?" chapter of *My Life and Work*. His contention is that a well-managed business does not depend on whether times are good or bad. If times are bad and people do not have much money to spend,

> Then why flounder around waiting for good business? Get the costs down by better management. Get the prices down to the buying power.
>
> Cutting wages is the easiest and most slovenly way to handle the situation... It is, in effect, throwing upon labour the incompetency of the managers of the business. If we only knew it, every depression is a challenge to every manufacturer to put more brains into his business—to overcome by management what other people try to overcome by wage reduction. To tamper with wages before all else is changed, is to evade the real issue. And if the real issue is tackled first, no reduction of wages may be necessary. That has been my experience (Ford, 1922, 136).

The Ford Motor Company sold 1.25 million cars during the 1920–1921 depression that followed the First World War and the 1918 influenza epidemic. This was about five times more cars than the company sold during 1913–1914. That year was supposed to have been a "dull" year but Ford's company sold 33 percent more cars than it did in 1912–1913. Ford continues,

> There is no use in waiting around for business to improve. If a manufacturer wants to perform his function, he must get his price down to what people will pay. There is always, no matter what the condition, a price that people can and will pay for a necessity, and always, if the will is there, the price can be met.
>
> It cannot be met by lowering quality or by shortsighted economy, which results only in a dissatisfied working force. It cannot be met by fussing or buzzing around. It can be met only by increasing the efficiency of production and, viewed in this fashion, each business depression, so-called, ought to be regarded as a challenge to the brains of the business community. Concentrating on prices instead of on

service is a sure indication of the kind of business man who can give no justification for his existence as a proprietor (Ford, 1922, 138).

Lean manufacturing, a system for "increasing the efficiency of production," is the way to get the price down while maintaining wages and profits. It provides the means of saying no to economic cycles. The next sections discuss the roles, both real and perceived, of the stock market, monetary systems, and unemployment on national prosperity.

THE STOCK MARKET SHOULD BE IRRELEVANT TO NATIONAL PROSPERITY

The stock market's reactions to Federal Reserve Chairman Allen Greenspan during the late 1990s were something like a movie vampire's reaction to a cross. A comment about the weather from Greenspan was almost enough to drop the market by one or two percent. A remark about "irrational exuberance" had even greater effects. Low unemployment, a sign of good business, makes stocks fall because everyone is afraid that the Federal Reserve will raise interest rates to curb inflation. The stock market rises and falls on rumors and sentiment. Dot-com stocks commanded price-earnings ratios of 100 or more, if they had any earnings against which to divide their prices. There is indeed very little rationality in the stock market. Per Ford,

> The most common error of confusing money and business comes about through the operations of the stock market. And especially through regarding the prices on the exchange as the "barometer of business." People are led to conclude that business is good if there is lively gambling upwards in stocks, and bad if the gamblers happen to be forcing stock prices down.
>
> The stock market as such has nothing to do with business. It has nothing to do with the quality of the article which is manufactured, nothing to do with the output, nothing to do with the marketing, it does not even increase

or decrease the amount of capital used in the business. [That is, market capitalization is a meaningless term!] It is just a little show on the side. . . .

When the chief function of any industry is to produce dividends rather than goods for use, the emphasis is fundamentally wrong. The face of the business is bowed toward the stockholder and not toward the consumer, and this means the denial of the primary purpose of industry.

The absentee stockholder is one of the principal, though concealed, items in the unnecessary and preventable costs of living. . . .

Wealth is not increased by stock activity; at best, it only changes hands. Wealth is not created; it is but a score in a game. I was once quoted as saying that the stock market was a good thing for business. The reporter omitted my reason—"because it drives so many men back to legitimate business by breaking them" (Ford, 1926, 234–235).

In Tom Clancy's novel *Debt of Honor*, Japan precedes an attack on the United States with a computer virus that shuts down the stock market.[2] An assassin, meanwhile, takes out the Chairman of the Federal Reserve. The plan almost succeeds in creating economic chaos until one of the heroes, Jack Ryan, reminds the nation that the events have done *nothing* to the nation's productive capacity. The September 11, 2001 attack on the Pentagon and the World Trade Centers tested Clancy's theories, and the stock market fell precipitously during the following week.[3] The human casualties were, however, the only irreplaceable losses. The attack touched neither our manufacturing nor our military capability. Stockholders who gave in to the attack's psychological effects provided some excellent bargains to foresighted investors.

We have already seen that Japan learned a lot from Henry Ford about manufacturing. Could this also be where Japanese stockholders learned to be patient and look for long-term results instead of focusing on the annual report or quarterly income statement?

Monetary Systems Can Help or Hurt Wealth Creation

Ford identified the inherent dangers in monetary systems, and even the roots of economic depressions. "To make business wait on gold is like making the passenger traffic of a main line dependent on the facilities of a local branch with one train a day. If gold did the work it might be as acceptable as anything else; but it doesn't" (Ford, 1922a, 268).

During the reign of Louis XIV, French commerce was, to use Ford's words, "waiting on gold." Crossen (2000) describes how John Law (1671–1729) introduced his ideas for paper money into France:

> In 18th-century France, the scarcity of gold impaired the country's ability to trade its surpluses with other nations.
>
> ... "My secret is to make gold out of paper," he [John Law] once said.... Law's demonstration of the flexibility afforded by paper currency and by the creation of money by bank or government fiat has been the basis of finance ever since.
>
> ... He had proved that the value of money is an agreement among people, not an objective standard measurable in nuggets or ingots, a distinction that fostered future stages of wealth creation.

Money is not wealth but only a medium of exchange. It is a necessary tool (unless we wish to return to a primitive barter economy), but one must look past it to perceive genuine wealth.

Unemployment and Inflation

It is widely accepted that higher unemployment means lower inflation. As unemployment falls, people expect the Federal Reserve Bank (Fed) to tighten the money supply to fight the expected inflation. This, in turn, drives stock prices down.

Look at this again: when *more* people are working and businesses are creating *more* value, stock prices go down! Ford recognized this paradigm:

> There are those who claim that a certain proportion of unemployed men is desirable from the industrial standpoint.

A crowd of men clamoring around the factory gates for jobs helps keep the men inside steady and helps keep wages down, they say.

... This is a detestable philosophy. It is cold speculation in flesh and blood and anxiety and hunger. We don't want any condition that is dependent on unemployment for steadiness (Ford, 1922a, 76).

He adds that there are enough jobs to go around because there is more than enough work to go around. That is, there are enough unmet demands in any society to create more work for everybody.

The stock market also reacts negatively to rising wages. Rising wages are supposedly a harbinger of inflation that will prompt the Fed to raise the interest rates. Higher wages are inflationary only if they do not come with higher productivity. If they accompany higher prices—remember that Ford wanted to reduce prices—this is indeed a warning sign. A business should not have to increase prices so it can pay better wages. Higher wages that come from higher productivity are, on the other hand, necessary to drive economic growth. They allow the economy to absorb higher levels of production.

In addition to these cyclical elements, inexpensive energy plays an important role in national prosperity. Readers can use the material in the following section to educate the public about dysfunctional energy policies (such as the Kyoto Global Warming Treaty or Kyoto Protocol) that can harm the economy and cost manufacturing jobs.

THE ROLE OF INEXPENSIVE ENERGY

The location of a new plant is largely determined by the cost of its power and the price at which it may make and ship goods to a given territory...

Our civilization—such as it is—rests on cheap and convenient power.... The source of material civilization is developed power.

—Henry Ford, *Today and Tomorrow*

This principle has major implications for American energy policies. The nation's economic prosperity depends on the continued availability of reliable and inexpensive power. Energy shortages in California drove this point home during 2000 and 2001, as did the United States' withdrawal from the Kyoto Global Warming Treaty (or Kyoto Protocol) in 2001.

Henry Ford pointed out (1926, 165) that "developed power" made the poorest Americans, even tramps who were "poor by profession," more prosperous than Old World peasants. Even Americans who could not or would not work—and this was before the days of welfare relief—could not begin to imagine the poverty of peasants or coolies in what we now call developing nations. The following statement answers complaints that the United States' 4 percent of the world's population uses 25 or 30 percent of its energy.

> And this is because we use so much developed power in this country that even the most ingeniously indolent cannot escape its effects. And at that we are using only a small fraction of the power we ought to use, and much of what we are using is being used wastefully. Of that, more later.
>
> One point stands out above all others. This country uses many times more developed power per head than does any other country. We use far more in our factories—which is significant and easily comprehended (Ford, 1926, 165).

There is no problem at all, therefore, with the United States' *using* 25 to 30 percent of the world's energy—noting especially that the United States also produces at least this proportion of the world's goods and services. *Wasting* energy is another matter, but market and economic forces already drive the development of ways to use power more efficiently. Who wouldn't buy a car that goes twice as far per unit of fuel *without a corresponding tradeoff in performance and safety*? Dysfunctional energy policies such as "carbon taxes" however, undermine the economic welfare of the United States by making power more expensive. The next sections describe recent events that prove this.

The Roles of Power and the Machine

> What we are entering is a power age, and the importance of the power age lies in its ability, rightly used with the wage motive behind it, to increase and cheapen production so that all of us may have more of this world's goods. The way to liberty, the way to equality of opportunity, the way from empty phrases to actualities, lies through power; the machine is only an incident.
>
> . . . the only slave left on earth is man minus the machine.
>
> —*Today and Tomorrow* (1926, 168–169)

Economic prosperity comes from power, and machines are instruments for guiding and directing power. Ford described how human society progressed and wealth grew as people learned to harness power. Animal power came first. As people came to recognize that time itself had value, the horse played a valuable role in reducing travel (non-value-added) time. The sail freed mariners from "the slavery of the oar."

Draft animals once turned grindstones to mill grain, thus freeing humans (who could not do it as well) from this task. Then came windmills and water wheels, which performed similar work and did not need food or veterinary care. The steam engine expanded the Industrial Revolution by freeing workers and factories (as well as sailors) from dependence on wind and water power.

The reference to slavery in the previous quote has a literal connotation. The machine is the death of slavery, and the Romans of the first century apparently recognized this. Roman Gaul developed the donkey-propelled *vallus*, a reaping machine with teeth that cut grain. The grain then fell into a box or hopper behind the teeth. An ox powered a larger version, the *carpentum*. The Romans discarded these inventions because they were afraid of the social upheaval that would result from putting slaves out of work. Medieval Chinese bureaucrats eschewed a push-scythe that would have idled peasant laborers; the Luddite mentality preceded the Luddites by centuries. James and Thorpe (1994, 388–389) describe these Roman and Chinese reaping machines.

England was among the first nations to industrialize, and this made slave ownership uneconomical and undesirable. As raw unskilled labor became less marketable, free workers would have doubtlessly opposed the unpaid labor of slaves. Britons who thought it quite natural to own slaves in the eighteenth century could moralize about slavery's evils in the nineteenth after machinery relegated it to anachronism. The same phenomenon took place in the Northern United States prior to the Civil War.

Consequences of Rising Energy Costs

Energy shortages in California during 2000 and 2001 show exactly what happens when power costs rise. "California Energy Problems Still Continue As More Companies Do 'Less With Less'" (2001) shows that the problems developed from shortsighted and irrational attitudes toward electrical power. This article cites opinion columnist William Safire:

> ... in San Jose, epicenter of the computer industry's drain on electric power, voters rejected a new power facility because it offended their 'aesthetic sensibilities.' ... Environmentalists recoil in horror at suggestions of nuclear power, now a safe and clean source of electricity, or the use of cleaned-up coal to lower the price of natural gas that generates it.
> ... Reducing pollution sensibly is laudable, but clean-air extremists become local heroes without telling constituents the danger of the loss of Intel jobs and cheap electricity's household convenience.

The article lists the following consequences of rolling blackouts and energy shortages.

- "Rolling blackouts in the San Francisco Bay area last June 14 cost an estimated $100 million in Silicon Valley."
- "[California Steel] had to shut down seven times last December alone, causing havoc on production schedules and worker productivity."

- "Temporarily ceasing production is straining California businesses, making them vulnerable to permanently shutting down."

The West Coast's shortsighted energy policies also helped turn value-adding manufacturers into non-value-adding middlemen. It recently (2000–2001) became more profitable for West Coast aluminum plants to resell power than to make aluminum. "Locked into long-term contracts at $22 per megawatt-hour (while the going rate shot up to $300), many closed their mills and resold their electricity—realizing hefty profits even after paying idled workers" (Lavelle, 2001). Cheap electricity, not convenient access to bauxite, is in fact the principal consideration in deciding where to put an aluminum plant. Womack and Jones (1996, 39) describe how bauxite is mined in Australia but shipped halfway across the world to Scandinavia for processing. The reason is cheap hydroelectric power in Scandinavia.

These are perfect examples of dysfunctional economic driving forces that promote wasteful performance. The same goes for proposals to allow companies to trade carbon emission credits under Kyoto. National wealth and prosperity do not come from reselling electricity or trading emission credits. They come only from getting raw materials or adding value to those materials through manufacturing.

Lavelle continues, "Indeed, high fuel costs have been cited repeatedly as a factor in a string of bankruptcies in the energy-hungry steel industry since November [2000]." Higher energy costs also hurt the paper and chemical industries, which employ 660,000 and 1,000,000 Americans respectively. The effect of OPEC price increases on the economy also is well known. The very thought of carbon taxes, and similar measures that raise energy costs, should therefore concern anyone who cares about our nation's energy policy.

Chapter 7, however, supports efficiency improvements that have the incidental effect of reducing carbon dioxide emissions.

Modern fuel cells did not exist in Henry Ford's day, but he would have liked them. The high-temperature reaction of coal and steam generates hydrogen gas that fuel cells can convert into electricity with high efficiency. This process requires less coal, and therefore generates less carbon dioxide, per kilowatt-hour than conventional steam power cycles. The bottom line is that power costs less, not more. This helps both to address global warming (if it is in fact a real problem) and promote economic growth instead.

The United States withdrew from the Kyoto Protocol or Kyoto Global Warming Treaty in 2001. This treaty would have required the United States, but not developing nations, to curtail its carbon dioxide emissions. Lower carbon dioxide emissions would be achieved, for example, by carbon taxes on fossil fuels like coal and oil. About half the United States' electrical power comes from coal.

Carbon taxes, along with the Kyoto alternatives of sequestering carbon dioxide or scrubbing it out of stack gases,[4] raise the cost of electrical power. This raises the cost of American-manufactured goods and makes them less competitive with those from developing nations:

> Gasoline would rise by 50 cents or more a gallon [about 33 percent versus 2000 prices]; the cost of running industrial plants and energy-hungry computers would soar. According to a consensus of projections, the growth of gross domestic product in the U.S. would be cut by more than half as businesses moved offshore to escape the high [carbon] tax (Glassman, 2000).

The Kyoto Protocol would therefore encourage investors to move the smokestacks, all their carbon dioxide, and the jobs underneath the smokestacks to other countries. It would accelerate the loss of American manufacturing jobs and thereby undermine the nation's prosperity and military security. If the reader wants to explain this to the public, there is nothing about the phrase, "ship jobs offshore," that the American worker does not understand.

The California of 2001 is, in fact, a microcosm of what would have happened to the entire country under Kyoto. Streisand (2001) describes how other states are converging on California like sharks on wounded prey. Minnesota put up billboards in Silicon Valley to tell high-tech employers, "White Outs—Occasional. Black Outs—Never." Michigan sent 4,500 glow-in-the-dark computer mousepads to California businesses with the words, "Michigan. We never leave you in the dark." Tennessee, the home of the Tennessee Valley Authority's hydroelectric power, gave automotive, high-technology, and steel executives flashlights with the message, "the lights are always on in Tennessee." Pennsylvania, Arizona, New Mexico, Texas, and South Dakota are also telling California employers that there's inexpensive and reliable power elsewhere. That is the message that developing nations would have sent to American manufacturing firms under Kyoto.

The argument that the United States is now the only nation out of a hundred-something (the number changes as countries ratify, or withdraw from, the treaty) that isn't going along with the Kyoto agreement is meaningless. Teenagers, say "everyone else is doing it" when they want to get their noses pierced or, even worse, try recreational drugs. Furthermore, as with the teenage community, "everyone else" is *not* doing it. As of mid-2001, while every Western European nation had *signed* the treaty, *none* had ratified it.[5] Japan also dropped restrictions on greenhouse gas emissions ("Sayonara, Kyoto Treaty," 2002). The government realized that regulations were too expensive and they would prolong the country's economic problems. Furthermore, only some Kyoto signatories have any obligations under the treaty. It's very easy to sign a treaty for whose provisions someone else must pay. South American signatories are, in fact, chopping or burning down rain forests to clear land for agriculture. This shows that they do not take global warming very seriously.

The next section describes how government can undermine national prosperity.

THE ROLE OF GOVERNMENT

Government can easily become a source of economic and social rot, a force that undermines personal and national vitality by offering the illusion of a free lunch.

> But most harmful of all is the thought that the economic machine can ever be repaired by the government. Interference by the Government usually boils down to having the Government levy taxes and give the proceeds to those who clamour loudest for them. What are called "progressive programmes" simmer down to: "We can force the country to do things for us." The whole list of programmes which assume that the "Government" is an inexhaustible source of privilege and favour, the whole list of proposals that the country do this for this class and that for that class, is the expression of the mendicant type of mind. Mass weakness looks like strength, but it is not. It does not propose itself to do the thing it suggests, it proposes that the "doers" do for it. This type of mind never proposes to serve the country, but to make the country serve it.
>
> It is true that the strong ought to serve the weak, but not to confirm them in their weakness. Service to the weak is a disservice, unless it has the effect of bringing the weak to strength and independence. Fostering the hand-out attitude of mind is extreme unkindness. That is why our customary charity is such a contemptible thing. It weakens those who are willing to give, and it weakens those who are willing to receive. Charity is an evasion of effort. . . .
>
> Legislators have in large measure begun to think that their function, as members of government, is to serve as nursemaids to the people, instead of clearing the field of action that the people may do things for themselves. . . .
>
> Few seem to have studied the relation between high taxes and poverty—that high taxes breed poverty by making production less efficient (Ford, 1926, 242–244).

This could easily apply to Lyndon B. Johnson's extravagant social programs of the mid-1960s. Johnson fought the so-called War on Poverty the same way he fought the Vietnam War: without trying to win by going after the root causes. Trillions of dollars later, poverty and successive welfare generations are still endemic in twenty-first century America.

Government creates nothing of value, and the early twenty-first century's high tax rates would have appalled Ford. A worker cannot get good food, clothing, housing, and pleasure:

> ... by any political device or through any bargaining organization, such as a labour union, for goods are created neither by law nor by bargaining—which, strangely enough, does not seem generally to be recognized.
>   ... people have fallen into the habit of asking politics to do what only industry can do. The professional reformers do not understand this. They think that politics can do what only industry can do, and they propose regulations of prices and of this, that, and the other thing, on the ground that they can thus bring prosperity" (Ford, 1926, 14–15).

Government cannot legislate prosperity and a high standard of living. Industry must create them.

Why Government Is Rarely Efficient or Responsible

The only government operations that work reasonably well are the U. S. Postal Service and the Armed Forces. Ford pointed out that government monopolies do not face competition or penalties for poor service. The Post Office must, however, run like any other business and it has competitors in the parcel delivery sector. Even the Post Office's efficiency is questionable in 2002, in light of very hefty rate increases and proposals to end Saturday deliveries. Inefficiency, waste, or incompetence in an army can result in death or serious injury. This was doubtlessly an incentive for military organizations to develop techniques centuries ago that are now recognizable as leading-edge quality, productivity, and leadership methods. Frank B. Gilbreth said this of motion study:

> The United States government has already spent millions and used many of the best of minds on the subject of

motion study as applied to war; the motions of the sword, gun, and bayonet drill are wonderfully perfect from the standpoint of the requirements of their use. This same study should be applied to the arts of peace (Gilbreth, 1911).

When such incentives do not exist, however,

There is no profit and loss account staring a government in the face. There is no check on high prices or poor service, such as customers can exercise upon private concerns. A government can monopolize a service and thus compel one to use it, it can under-serve and over-charge and make one pay a deficit in the form of taxes. All these conditions are utterly destructive of all the elements of business (Ford, 1930, 117).

Some people want national health care or socialized medicine. "Be careful what you wish, you might get it," and several European nations have. The Netherlands got this:

An estimated 5,981 people—an average of 16 a day—were killed by their doctors without their consent . . . And these numbers do not measure several other groups that are put to death involuntarily: disabled infants, terminally ill children, and mental patients.
    . . . As the cost of socialized medicine in the Netherlands grew, doctors were lectured about the climbing cost of care. In many hospitals, signs were posted indicating how much old-age treatments cost taxpayers (Miniter, 2001).

"Putting someone to death *involuntarily*" is of course murder unless the subject of this action was convicted of a capital crime—in a jurisdiction that has capital punishment, which Holland does not. The same article points out that Holland was the only Nazi-occupied country in which doctors universally disobeyed or ignored orders to euthanize patients or withhold treatment. The economics of socialized medicine apparently succeeded where Nazi coercion failed.

Most professional politicians have never worked in an enterprise that had to deliver a product or service for a competitive price while meeting a payroll and balancing its budget. According to Ford, people with engineering experience are better qualified to run a government:

> Substituting the engineer for the politician is a very natural step forward. The engineer can do that which the politician can never do under any circumstances. The engineer creates and harmonizes while the politician can at best only rearrange what he has in hand (1930, 249–250).

Engineers also recognize the conservation principle that says a system's output plus accumulation must equal its input. The professional politicians, however, try to convince the people and perhaps themselves that there is a free lunch and that a system can disburse more wealth then it creates.

There is certainly no pressure on the government for the kind of continuous improvement that Ford practiced. The truth is that the national debt never gets any smaller and the government always finds a way to squander surpluses. The idea of trusting such an organization with even more responsibility, like national health care or educational programs, is appalling. On the local level, the monopoly of public schools on tax-funded education allows the delivery of substandard education.

Ford on the Inheritance Tax

As of mid-2000, there was a controversial bill in Congress to abolish the inheritance tax. Here is what Henry Ford said about this tax's effect on family-owned businesses.

> Think of the inheritance tax as collectable in actual possessions rather than in money. Suppose the collector says:
> "We must take one of the furnaces, four of the ovens, two of the elevators, ten of the machines, 25 percent of your coal pile, as an inheritance tax."
> ... Inheritance is always expressed in dollars, yet the dollars are seldom there. What most heirs inherit in these

days is a job, a business to be maintained, a responsibility to be shouldered (Ford, 1926, 244–245).

This provides a new perspective on the arguments that tax cuts are too costly to the government. Taxes cost businesses and taxpayers wealth that the government had no hand in earning or creating. The government is not entitled to a single penny that does not serve that wealth's creators.

Another argument against income and estate tax reductions is that they favor the rich, as if the rich were a class of evil pariahs or parasites. There is nothing wrong with the rich getting richer because they must share their wealth to gain its benefits. Ford points out (1930, 54–55, and elsewhere) that selfishness and greed are fundamentally impossible. The rich cannot enjoy their wealth without sharing it through spending or investment. The only way the rich (or anyone else) can avoid sharing, in fact, is to put their money under a mattress, in which case they might as well not have it at all.

Government as the Problem

Social degradation comes from excessive reliance on government. "When you get a whole country—as did ours—thinking that Washington is a sort of heaven and behind its clouds dwell omniscience and omnipotence, you are educating that country into a dependent state of mind which augers ill for the future (Ford, 1922, 7)."

Charles Sorensen added a similar remark about the New Deal. Where the government had once been the people's responsibility, the government became responsible for the welfare of the people. "Large segments of our people were willing to exchange personal freedom for a sense of social security" (Sorensen, 1956, 253).

The dependency against which Ford and Sorensen warn is responsible for many of today's social and economic troubles. Here are some examples:

- Successive generations of families go on welfare because they have learned to rely on the government to care for them. Ford said that charity in the form of a handout destroys the self-respect of the person who receives it. Someone who lives his or her entire life on government handouts can have little self-respect, and this carries over into lack of respect for others. Lyndon Johnson's Great Society was one of the worst disservices that anyone ever did the United States, for it created a class of perpetually-dependent welfare recipients. Ford did not want to let poor people starve in the streets or freeze, he wanted industry to create economic opportunities for them.

- The Social Security system does not invest its receipts the way a legitimate retirement plan does. It is a criminally fraudulent pyramid scheme because it relies on future receipts to pay future obligations. Even its advocates describe it as a pay-as-you-go system. Because it relies on several workers to support one retiree, it is actually like the retirement plan that is popular in Third World countries. Parents in many developing nations have as many children as they can so the children can divide the task of caring for the parents when they get old. The problem with this system is that it requires exponential population growth, and people in developed nations are now having fewer children instead of more.

- Although the Constitution authorizes Congress only to regulate interstate commerce, federal influence has spread into totally unrelated activities. Pork barrel legislation, in which representatives and senators negotiate for federal grants to their own districts or states, bloats government even further.

The remedy to the United States' deteriorating social structure and the expected inability of Social Security to pay its future obligations does not lie in more government. These dysfunctional conditions are, in fact, largely the result of bigger government. Giving government more authority and more money to solve these problems is a lot like seeking relief from a hangover in another bottle of hard liquor.

Taxes Cause Poverty

An argument against tax reductions is that they hurt poor people by reducing funds for social programs. This is like saying that cutting off an alcoholic's whiskey harms him by preventing him from drinking to forget that he is ashamed of his drinking problem.[6] Alcohol is the heavy drinker's problem and taxes are the poor person's problem—even if he or she does not pay them. "Few seem to have studied the relation between high taxes and poverty—that high taxes breed poverty by making production less efficient" (Ford, 1926, 243).

This is not merely a rising-tide-lifts-all-boats argument, nor was it originally Reagan Republicanism; Ford once ran for Senate as a Democrat (and lost). Nor is it an unproven argument; Ford's industries did abolish poverty wherever they appeared. Taxes can provide handouts in the form of welfare, but they cannot turn welfare recipients into producers. The government cannot afford to give welfare recipients enough money to make them into consumers who will create more jobs. Sorensen (1956, 146) actually blamed the New Deal for perpetuating the Depression by putting the unemployed on subsistence-level handouts. The beneficiaries could not consume enough goods to stimulate the economy, and the taxes for their support stifled consumption by workers.

Ford (1930, 14) said the same thing before there was a New Deal: it is better to hire fifty workers at eight dollars a day than two hundred at two dollars a day. The people who are earning eight dollars a day have surplus spending power that will create work for others. Those on subsistence wages (or government handouts) cannot spend enough to create more jobs. It is the task of intelligent management to make each of the fifty jobs worth eight dollars (or its modern equivalent) a day.

European nations have not learned much from the lessons of 75 years, for Ford described their problem in 1926.

> The largest single cause of poverty in Europe since the [First World] war has been the abject dependence upon government to do what government cannot do. The irony of this system is that the government which adopts it must continue to do more and more; and as the demand for more increases, the ability to do anything decreases. For there is nothing in government that does not come from the people; and a people in whom the spirit of self-help is killed contribute less and less to that which they desire until in the end both people and government fall into a common helplessness (Ford, 1926, 259).

More taxes and more government are the disease, not the cure. Lyndon Johnson's Great Society has, trillions of dollars later, fixed nothing. The Model T and all the industries that grew to support it created a prosperous American middle class, gave us a forty-hour work week, and made the United States the most prosperous and affluent nation in history. The results speak for themselves and they cannot speak more loudly or clearly:

> We have never put in a plant anywhere without raising the purchasing power and standard of living in the community, nor without increasing our own [sales][7] in that community (Ford, 1926, 150).
> "Henry Ford, by means of his health clinic, his schools, and employment, has changed the population from a sickly, suspicious, illiterate and undernourished group into one of the healthiest communities in Georgia" (Dr. Holton, Richmond Hill community physician in 1940, quoted in Bryan, 1997, 194).

This section has shown that we must look to industry, not government, to abolish poverty and remedy social problems. We can also look to industry, not government, to address the issue of health care, an issue upon which politicians and pundits have shed far more heat than light. The following section provides a fresh perspective on this topic and shows how Ford's lean enterprise principles apply to health care.

HEALTH CARE

The same kind of management which permits a factory to give the fullest service will permit a hospital to give the fullest service, and at a price so low as to be within the reach of everyone (Ford, 1922, 218–219)

It is simply a matter of transferring those precision methods, so well established in the Ford shops, into hospital work (Norwood, 1931, 82).

The United States' health care system is still among the best in the world. Wealthy patients even come here from countries that have socialized medicine. The United States' health care system, however, faces rising medical costs and questionable quality of care.

Godfrey (2000) shows that there is an opportunity to cut health care costs by at least 30 percent while improving quality: "Health care providers' cost of poor quality is estimated to be as high as 30 to 50 percent of the total paid for health care. For some companies the cost of employee health insurance is now higher than profits." Industrial quality control methods can reduce health care costs while improving patient care. Levinson (2000) recommends use of the ISO 9000 quality system to prevent health care mistakes, and some hospitals have adopted this standard.

HMOs (health management organizations) keep prices low by cutting corners. Henry Ford reduced prices by cutting costs and not corners, while he improved the quality of the product or service. This section focuses on the application of industrial management methods to the health care industry.

The Henry and Clara Ford Hospital

When Ford set up his hospital on West Grand Boulevard in Detroit in 1919, he instituted quality assurance and cost reduction systems. The problem of so-called professional etiquette meant that one doctor was unlikely to question another's diagnosis. The hospital's admission process routed the patient through several doctors, each of whom made an independent diagnosis. "This routing takes place regardless of what the patient came to the hospital for, because, as we are gradually learning, it is the complete health rather than a single ailment which is important. Each of the doctors makes a complete examination, and each sends in his written findings to the head physician without any opportunity whatsoever to consult with any of the other examining physicians" (Ford, 1922, 217).

Doctors and nurses worked for the hospital full-time; they were not allowed to have private practices. The salaries were good enough, however, to attract and keep Johns Hopkins graduates and members of the Royal College of Surgeons. This avoided the problem that confronts many of today's HMOs and physician practice organizations (PPOs): doctors go into private practice as soon as they have enough experience.

No nurse had to care for more than seven patients, and the hospital layout made the job easy:

> In the ordinary hospital the nurses must make many useless steps. More of their time is spent in walking than in caring for the patient. This hospital is designed to save steps. Each floor is complete in itself, and just as in the factories we have tried to eliminate the necessity for waste motion, so have we also tried to eliminate waste motion in the hospital (Ford, 1922, 218).

Ford recognized the need for preventive medicine and preventive diets. "Men who are careful of their diet do not often fall ill, while those who are not careful always seem to have something or the other the matter with them" (1926, 193). The key idea is that, as with manufacturing, Ford looked to prevention instead of correction.

Error-proofing (Poka-Yoke) in Health Care

The Institute of Medicine reported in November 1999 that 44,000 to 98,000 hospital patients die every year from avoidable mistakes

(Shapiro, 2000, 50). Crago (2000) cites the same estimate and adds Harvard School of Public Health adjunct professor Lucian Leape's estimate of 120,000 deaths a year from all medical mistakes. This is more than the United States' combined death rate for motor vehicle accidents, firearm misuse, falls, drowning, and fire.

Crago cites Leape's observation that "health care's three-sigma to four-sigma quality is 'roughly equivalent to a jumbo jet crashing every day.'" This does not exaggerate the total loss of life. A daily plane crash with 329 fatalities would add up to about 120,000 deaths a year. Even one such crash gets plenty of investigation into root causes and preventive measures to preclude recurrences. This is exactly what happens in many manufacturing establishments, where a big assignable or special cause loss gets plenty of attention. The same organizations may tolerate low-level scrap losses from random or common causes whose cumulative impact may be far greater, while doctors bury their mistakes. Nonfatal mistakes can lengthen hospital stays and cause problems that require additional treatment. From what we know of industrial quality management, the system in which the doctors work may well be the root cause of most of these losses. A better system can reduce such errors and drive down malpractice insurance premiums, a form of overhead. The cost of care goes down while its quality improves.

The ISO 9000 requirement for product traceability prevents parts from receiving the wrong process recipes and operations, and the same methods can apply to hospital patients. Patients' wrist identification bands can, like parts in a factory, have bar codes or other machine-readable labels. This can preclude the administration of someone else's medicine or even surgical procedure. A "patient control" database can also cross-reference each prescription for interactions with the patient's other medications. It can even check for unusual dosages (e.g. "100 milligrams" instead of the usual "10 milligrams")."

Citizens General Hospital in New Kensington, Pennsylvania, is actually using at least part of this approach. A robot reads bar-coded prescriptions and retrieves the right medications for each patient. Each dose goes into a bar-coded bag. The nurse scans the bar codes on the patient's wristband and the medication bag. This even avoids medication errors that result when confused elderly patients enter the wrong rooms and fall asleep there (Shapiro, 2000, 56).

The same article reveals problems the hospital has recognized and evaluates some of the practices they have instituted to address them:

- An intravenous solution with prophylactic antibiotics was known as "bug juice," and the pharmacist knew what went into it. The hospital finally realized that a new pharmacist might not know the ingredients of "bug juice," and it began to require precise names for this order. This one is a no-brainer under ISO 9000, which requires precise specifications for every operation that affects quality.
- Intravenous and spinal chemotherapy agents came in lookalike vials. It is easy to imagine injection of the former into a patient's spine resulting in paralysis or worse. The nurses suggested that the spinal drug be wrapped in red plastic. Bar codes on the vials would be even better because the system should not rely on having someone remember to wrap the vials in red plastic.
- An anesthesiologist announces the name and dose of each drug she administers, along with the patient's weight. This "invites" (to use the article's word) other doctors and nurses in the operating room to double-check what she is doing. It's better than the old procedure but "inviting" bystanders to verify what one is doing is not error-proof. The military communication practice of having a specific person repeat back any verbal instruction or information is even better.
- Semi-legible prescriptions are legendary and unfortunately true. The hospital tried to educate the doctors about this by posting blowups of illegible prescriptions that the phar-

macy had received. It would be more to the point to have the doctors type the prescriptions into a computer, which could not only relay the instructions to the pharmacy but also generate a bar-coded label for the dose.

An editorial says that doctors' bad handwriting causes as many as 25,000 deaths every year ("Message to physicians: Better read than dead," 2000). The solutions it cites focus on improving physicians' handwriting, but there is little difference between a handwritten prescription and a sticky-backed note in a factory work area—and the latter is anathema in any ISO 9000-conscious workplace. "Little sticky notes with work instructions stuck to documents or machinery won't cut it" (Bakker, 1996).

Shapiro (2000, 64) adds, "And some managers said that their colleagues still believe that many errors do come down to incompetent employees, not bad systems." A key premise of poka-yoke is that any system that relies on human intervention to prevent errors is a set of mistakes waiting to happen. If parts can be assembled backward they will be, and if the wrong medication can be administered, it will be. It's only a question of when and how often.

Scientific Management versus Rationing and Cutting Corners

HMOs claim to reduce costs, but they do so by rationing care and cutting corners. Some HMO administrators come dangerously close to the unlicensed practice of medicine by telling doctors what procedures to use. Whatever doesn't add value is waste. An HMO's or insurance company's profit and entire administrative system are waste as far as the patient and doctor are concerned. A combination of high-deductible medical insurance (with lower premiums) and personal medical savings accounts (MSAs) would cut the HMO out of the loop completely. Patients would pay for routine or minor care out of their tax-deductible MSAs and the insurance would cover major care.

Genuine managed care—scientifically managed care—is another matter entirely. While patients are justifiably outraged over cost-cutting through denial of treatment, they are very happy if the HMO saves money by not providing the wrong medicine or, even worse, the wrong operation. The treatment that causes the patient the least discomfort and inconvenience while curing the disease is also likely to be the least expensive treatment. As an example, laparoscopic surgery is often preferable to conventional surgery. It causes less discomfort and scarring, the patient is out of the hospital much more quickly, and it is therefore far less expensive. Other scientific management practices include best practice deployment and knowledge retention. Medicine, unlike manufacturing, is unlikely to offer a single "one best way" for a given case, but scientific management would keep physicians updated on the prevailing best options.

Scientific management also suggests preventive maintenance by calling patients in for vaccinations and screenings. Vaccinations against flu, for example, save money for the health care system by avoiding the need to treat the disease and its complications. They also guard the patients from the discomfort, danger, and lost work time that come with this ailment. Screening for cancer and other diseases save money as well because it is far less costly to treat cancer that is discovered early. The treatment is usually far less invasive and uncomfortable, and the patient is more likely to survive. HMOs that try to save money by denying patients "experimental" cancer treatments while not performing regular screenings for the disease are guilty of gross stupidity and managerial incompetence, if not an actual crime (i.e., the unlicensed practice of medicine).

Not an Argument for Socialized Medicine

This section is absolutely not an endorsement for a national health care system that would try to implement Ford's methods on a nationwide basis. Ford's hospital excelled because it hired the best medical personnel from the private sector and provided an environment in which they could do their best. The so-called cost controls of socialized medicine and HMOs require them to pay health care professionals as little as possible.

This section should instead serve as a model for health care organizations that want to emulate Ford by paying their doctors and nurses more, charging their patients less, and improving their quality of care. It would be refreshing to see such organizations grow at the expense of both HMOs and government-controlled programs that try to deliver as little service as possible at the highest price they can command.

This chapter has dissolved the illusion that something can come of nothing. Taxing, borrowing, and cutting wages are short-sighted and often ineffective solutions to problems. Wealth comes only from work and from brains that make the work more efficient. The next chapters, "Eliminate Waste" and "Ford's Factory," provide specific examples that show how, to use Ford's words, to "put brains into the method."

Notes

1. Taylor (1911a, 24) says scientific management equips a company to maintain high wages and low (per piece) labor costs and, even in dull times, find enough work to keep its employees busy.
2. Modern military experts consider information warfare a serious threat. There is a story that a virus was introduced into the Iraqi air defense system via printers—which everyone knows as output devices but which also send information to the computer—as a prelude to Desert Storm.
3. On the day of the attack, retired General Norman Schwarzkopf recalled that *Debt of Honor* ended with a suicidal pilot crashing an otherwise-unoccupied airliner into the Capitol.
4. Proposals have been made to sequester carbon dioxide by injecting it deep into the ground or under the sea instead of discharging it into the atmosphere. Carbon dioxide can be scrubbed from smokestack gases by caustic solutions, in which it dissolves. Both methods cost money and neither adds value to the business activity.

5. http://www.greenyearbook.org/agree/atmosphe/m-kyoto.htm, "Yearbook of International Cooperation on Environment and Development," as of May 6, 2002.

6. Antoine de Saint-Exupery's *The Little Prince* describes this scene: the drunkard drinks to forget that he is ashamed of his drinking problem.

7. The text says "scales," probably a misprint.

SEVEN

Eliminate Waste

He perfected new processes—the very smoke which had once poured from his chimneys was now made into automobile parts.

—Upton Sinclair, *The Flivver King* (1937, 61)

Black smoke is unconsumed carbon—nascent heat—lost energy—wasted coal. A smoking chimney registers money lost (*The System Company*, 1911a, 28).

This chapter is about making money—a lot of money. Henry Ford achieved unprecedented profitability by eliminating waste that most people would have overlooked, and this chapter's mission is to equip the reader to identify such waste. Taiichi Ohno (1988, 4) cites "absolute elimination of waste" as the basis of the Toyota production system. We cannot, however, eliminate waste until we recognize it.

Ford grew up on a farm and he was appalled by the inefficiency of farm work.

I believe that the average farmer puts to a really useful purpose only about 5 per cent of the energy he expends. . . . Not only is everything done by hand, but seldom is a thought given to a logical arrangement. A farmer doing his chores will walk up and down a rickety ladder a dozen times. He will carry water for years instead of putting in a few lengths of pipe.[1] His whole idea, when there is extra work to do, is to hire extra men. He thinks of putting money into improvements as an expense. . . . It is waste motion—waste effort—that makes farm prices high and profits low (Ford, 1922, 15).

This single paragraph offers the reader enormous treasure in the form of these principles:

- *Friction*, or chronic problems and inefficiencies that become accepted aspects of a job, limits productivity (Levinson, 2000, 2).
- People and organizations are unwilling to make capital expenditures that will improve their business's long-term health. They economize by keeping antiquated and unreliable equipment.
- Profitability can be improved by getting rid of wasted motion and effort.

The concept of friction is so important and pervasive that sources as diverse as Carl von Clausewitz's famous book *On War* and prominent Japanese and American management experts describe it:

- Friction is General von Clausewitz's (1976) term for "... the force that makes the apparently easy so difficult. ... countless minor incidents—the kind you can never really foresee—combine to lower the general level of performance, so that one always falls short of the intended goal."
- Ford (1930, 187) almost quotes Clausewitz on friction: "It is the little things that are hard to see—the awkward little methods of doing things that have grown up and which no one notices. And since manufacturing is solely a matter of detail, these little things develop, when added together, into very big things."
- Dr. Shigeo Shingo echoes this idea (Robinson, 1990, 14): "Unfortunately, real waste lurks in forms that do not look like waste. Only through careful observation and goal orientation can waste be identified. We must always keep in mind that the greatest waste is the waste we don't see."

- Tom Peters writes (1987), "The accumulation of little items, each too trivial to trouble the boss with, is a prime cause of miss-the-market delays."
- Masaaki Imai (1997) defines waste or *muda*, of which strain or *muri* is an example.
- Taiichi Ohno (1988, 59) says, "In reality, however, such waste [waiting, needless motions] is usually hidden, making it difficult to eliminate. . . . To implement the Toyota production system in your own business, there must be a total understanding of waste. Unless all sources of waste are detected and crushed, success will always be just a dream."
- Halpin (1966, 60–61) writes of chronic inefficiencies such as poorly placed equipment, "They turned out to be the little things that get under a worker's skin but are never quite important enough to make him come to management for a change."

The next section explains the Ford thought process for identifying waste. Remember that if the waste was obvious someone would probably have done something about it. Success comes from seeing the waste that isn't obvious.

"EVERYTHING BUT THE SQUEAL"

It's said that good meat packers use every part of a hog except the squeal—a practice that may have prompted Otto von Bismarck's comment that people who respect laws and like sausages should not watch the making of either. The adage, however, exemplifies Ford's thoughts about getting every possible bit of utility out of a resource.

"Nothing will come from nothing," said King Lear, but Ford wrote (1926, 124), "It is not possible long to continue to get something for nothing, but it is possible to get something from what was once considered nothing."

He continues (1926, 124), "We treat each tree as wood until nothing remains which is serviceable as wood, and then we treat what remains as a chemical compound to be broken down into other chemical compounds which we can use in our business." The daily output of waste wood distillation was worth $12,000 in 1926, or enough to pay 2,000 workers who were earning Ford's minimum wage. Only after Ford extracted all the structural wood and useful chemicals did he burn what was left for heat and power.[2]

A half-million dollar question on "Who Wants to Be a Millionaire" was, "Who invented the charcoal briquette?" Per Bryan (1997, 119–120), Ford's Iron Mountain (Michigan) sawing operations produced enough hardwood chips to make about a hundred tons (91 metric tons) per day of charcoal briquettes. As of 1997, Kingsford Products Company of Oakland, California, was still making and selling them under the Kingsford name.

The Smorgen Steel Group Ltd.'s North Laverton plant in Melbourne, Australia, recently decided to use electric arc furnace slag for, among other things, a replacement for natural aggregates in asphalt roads and low-strength concrete. The slag is also useful as an antiskid surfacing material for roads ("Australian Steel Mill Takes Recycling to Commercial Level," 2002). The article quotes Smorgen executive Joe Italiano, "But until now, there has been little interest in the use of leftover slag that has been either stockpiled, land-filled, or used to stabilize boggy private roads in the rural areas near our plant." Such an interest, however, existed more than 75 years ago.

Ford's blast furnaces produced 500 tons (455 metric tons) of slag per day, or about 180,000 tons per year (three times the 60,000 tons cited for Smorgen). The company found similar uses for it: 225 tons (205 metric tons) per day became cement and the rest was crushed to pave roads (Ford, 1926, 98–99). The 1 percent iron that remained in the slag did not, however, escape. The slag had to pass under powerful magnets that picked up iron particles, and they were sent back to the blast furnace. The story behind this is an outstanding example of identifying waste that everyone else has overlooked:

One day when Mr. Ford and I were together he spotted some rust in the slag that ballasted the right of way of the D. T. & I [railroad]. This slag had been dumped there from our own furnaces.

"You know," Mr. Ford said to me, "there's iron in that slag. You make the crane crews who put it out there sort it over, and take it back to the plant" (Bennett, 1951, 32–33).

Bennett admits that neither he nor Charles Sorensen (who objected when he saw a large work crew and a crane collecting the slag) thought it cost-effective to recover the iron in question. Recovery of the iron from the slag was only containment, the third step of the modern Ford Company's TOPS8D problem-solving process. Subsequent installation of the electromagnet was a permanent corrective action.

Blast furnace dust also was recycled:

Formerly, this dust, which is nearly 50 percent pure iron, was regarded as waste, and was either dumped or sold as scrap, for it was too fine to be melted in the furnaces or cupolas. This dust is caught up in collectors, unloaded in cars by gravity, and carried directly to the sintering plant, where it is mixed with steel or iron borings and agglomerated into heavy lumps, which will melt easily. This process not only reclaims a great amount of iron, but also avoids the former labour of hauling it away. At the time the sintering plant was first put into operation, we had accumulated enough blast furnace dust to furnish material for more than six hundred thousand cylinder block castings (Ford, 1926, 106–107).

Material traceability, which ISO 9000 now requires, played an important role in material reclamation. "Since all our cast iron is classified under heads according to analysis, it is a simple matter to sort scrap iron and return it to the proper [blast furnace] cupola for remelting" (Ford, 1926, 97). Ford may be referring to classification by alloy composition.

Here are some other examples of "using everything but the squeal" or "making lemonade from lemons."

- Reuse packaging. Ford (1926, 125) asks, "Why should a crate or a packing box once used be considered only as so much waste to be smashed and burned?" Ford told his workers to open boxes carefully, without using crowbars. Some companies use returnable boxes today. If a box can be folded flat for convenient disposal, it can also be shipped back to the supplier for reuse. Per Norwood (1931, Chapter XI), the River Rouge plant knocked down wooden containers and returned them to their suppliers for another load. If the container is the right size, the plant can use it to package its own products. There is a legend that some wooden boxes became Model T parts themselves. Ford supposedly asked a supplier to package shipments in boxes made of boards with dimensions suitable for Model T floorboards.
- Don't drill holes, cut them. Robinson (1990, 103) cites the wasteful practice of drilling large-diameter holes. The tool must remove the hole's entire cross-section (a solid cylinder) of metal as cuttings. A cylindrical cutter turns only a thin and hollow cylindrical section into scrap. It is often faster than a drill, and it removes the rest of the hole's volume as a solid metal cylinder that can be made into a small part.
- Recovery of silver salts from developing solutions saved Ford's Photographic Department about $10,000 (in 1920s money) per year (Ford, 1926, 98). To put this in perspective, six workers who worked 250 days a year at the company's relatively high $6/day wage (as of 1926) received $9,000. This waste reduction activity was therefore like having six workers for free.
- The paper plant could convert 20 tons (18 metric tons) of scrap paper a day into 14 tons (12.7 metric tons) of binder

board and 8 tons (7.3 metric tons) of waterproof board. The board's tensile strength was great enough for a 10-inch (25.4 cm) strip to support a Ford car (Ford, 1926, 98).

Keep Your Eye on the Doughnut Hole

There is an adage that says, "Keep your eye on the doughnut, not on the hole." It means to spend time and energy only on things of value. Modern production managers and quality managers would be happy if a stamping process that made 6-inch (152 mm) holes in sheet metal produced no defects or rework. They would be delighted if the hole diameter's specification width was at least twelve standard deviations wide, since this would be a six sigma manufacturing process.[3] That is keeping one's eye on the dough-nut: the metal sheet. The product is the doughnut; whatever is thrown away (turnings or chips from machining, cutting fluids, chemicals) is the hole. A business can achieve ordinary or even good results by keeping its eye on the doughnut. Ford achieved outstanding results by teaching his workers to watch the hole.

The principle, "Watch the hole as well as the doughnut," was part of the company culture. This is a very important consideration for modern lean practitioners. Norwood's (1931) observation about waste, "It worried the men," suggests that everyone on the factory floor was conscious of the importance of suppressing waste. Ford's workers asked, "What happened to the metal that was in those holes?" Then they realized, "Those metal discs are the right size for pressing into radiator caps." (Figure 7-1.)

Ford also introduced the principle of cutting or stamping materials to use as much of the material as possible. His woodworking departments cut logs into parallel planks without accounting for the log's shape or size. That is, logs were not cut into uniform sizes as one might expect at a lumberyard. Each plank, no matter what its dimensions, then received individual attention at a layout table. The layout workers marked part patterns on each plank until they covered it completely. They did not trim the boards to get rid of knots, they simply left the knots out of the layout. A high-speed

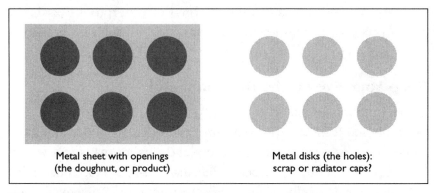

Metal sheet with openings   Metal disks (the holes):
(the doughnut, or product)   scrap or radiator caps?

Figure 7-1. The Doughnut and the Hole

band saw then cut out the parts. "From 25 to 35 percent more body parts may be obtained from logs than under the old method where the log was 'squared' and the boards edged and trimmed" (Ford, 1926, 131). The woodworking departments used not only the trunk but also branches that were more than four inches (10.2 cm) in diameter. The new layout method used even irregular branches that were formerly good only for wood distillation.

The same idea applies to cutting or stamping parts out of metal sheets. Figure 7-2 shows, however, that material waste is sometimes unavoidable; the empty squares in the metal sheet are the doughnut's hole. Ford, however, managed to eliminate this waste by changing the process: "The oil-can holder is in the shape of a cross, and we formerly stamped it out of steel with great waste at a cost of $0.0635 each. Now we cut the two parts of the cross separately with almost no scrap and weld them together, and they now cost $0.0478 each" (1926, 95).

Ford also cites windshield brackets that were cut from 18" by 32.5" (45.7 by 82.6 cm) steel sheets. Each sheet provided six brackets plus a lot of scrap. Cutting the brackets at a seven-degree angle yielded six brackets from a 15.5" by 32.5" (39.4 by 82.6 cm) sheet. This was an immediate 13.9 percent reduction in material use, and the same operation also yielded ten blanks for small parts. This saved 1.5 million pounds (682 metric tons) of steel per year (Ford, 1926, 95).

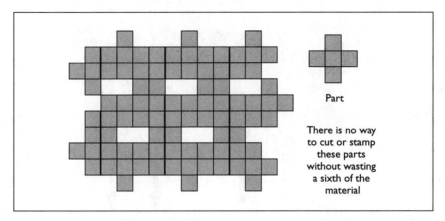

Part

There is no way to cut or stamp these parts without wasting a sixth of the material

Figure 7-2. Even the best layout wastes at lease a sixth of the material

Chipless Machining

Ford mentions another aspect of process simplification that saves money (1926, 69): "Our objective is always to minimize the subsequent machining." Compare this to an article about high agility machines (HAMs) (Mege, 2000):

> The aerospace industry produces parts in quantities from a few units to thousands of pieces. They cut a huge amount of swarf [filings or shavings] from these parts—often, the weight of the finished part is only 15–20 percent of the original rough billet, so, on average, 80–85 percent of the aluminum is reduced to a heap of chips.
>
> The first U. S. manufacturer to buy one of our HAMs four years ago posted a sign on his new "monster" reading: 'I eat 400 tons [364 metric tons] of aluminum per month!' The customer was forced to install a second swarf compactor, and now sells bricks of aluminum chips to recyclers.

This really says that the machine tool grinds about five out of six billets into shavings, which are then recycled into billets! I do not know if the process can be redesigned to reduce the waste, but the conversion of 80 to 85 percent of the raw material into scrap is hardly something about which to brag (Figure 7-3).

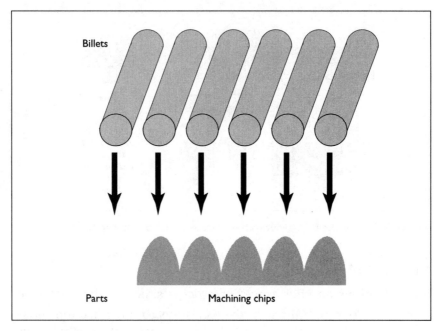

Figure 7-3. Is the idea to make parts or machining swarf?

Arnold and Faurote (1915, 211–212) noticed the same problem with the manufacture of piston rings at the Ford Highland Park plant. Piston ring "pots" were hollow cylinders of gray iron, each of which weighed 6.5 pounds (2.95 kg) when it came from the foundry. Each yielded 1.06 pounds (0.48 kg) of piston rings, so five-sixths of each pot was waste. The reference continues,

> . . . Each pot as it comes from the foundry weighs about 6½ pounds, or 104 ounces, from which 17 ounces of finished piston rings is expected to be produced—that is to say 5/6 of the pot stock is wasted.
>
> The foundry supplies the machine shop with 13,000 pounds [5909 kg] of ring pots per day, worth, at 2.5 cents per pound, $325 per day.
>
> The machine shop produces about 14,000 rings per day, 1 5/12 ounces [40.2 grams] each, say 1,240 pounds [564 kg] of finished rings from 13,000 pounds of ring stock, [leaving] 11,760 pounds [5345 kg] of stock, worth $294

wasted for the pleasure of cutting it into chips and using snap-ring piston packing.

That is to say, $325 worth of ring-stock is supplied to the machine shop, $294 of this value is wasted, and $31 of stock value utilized in the finished work.

These figures are not favorable to low-cost piston-ring production.

Although the respective weights of chips and finished rings appear inconsistent with the original five-to-one ratio, the underlying lesson reinforces what Ford said in 1926:

> The degradation of materials by conventional machining methods is of the order of 30 to 70 percent, and the more complex shapes are at the higher end. Most of the chips are recycled as scrap, but there is a severe economic penalty. As a result, there has been increasing emphasis on "chipless machining" processes by which a part is made to final, or near-net, shape. Precision forging, precision investment casting, and powder-processing techniques are good examples of such processes (Dieter, 1983, 210–211).

Consider the following example (Dieter, 1983, 210). A 6-inch (15.2 cm) long shaft with a 1 square inch (6.45 square cm) circular cross-section is to have a 1-inch (2.54 cm) long, 3 square inch (19.4 cm²) circular cross-section central hub that might later have gear teeth machined onto it (Figure 7-4).

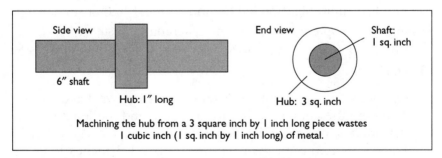

Side view End view Shaft: 1 sq. inch

6" shaft

Hub: 1" long Hub: 3 sq. inch

Machining the hub from a 3 square inch by 1 inch long piece wastes 1 cubic inch (1 sq. inch by 1 inch long) of metal.

Figure 7-4. Conventional machining wastes more than half the bar stock

Conventional machining of this piece begins with a 6-inch by 3 square inch piece of bar stock, or 18 cubic inches (295 cubic centimeters) of material. Of this, 10 cubic inches, or 55.6 percent, becomes waste. Making the hub as a separate piece and pressing it over the shaft loses only one cubic inch out of nine, or 11.1 percent. Finally, hot-upset forging or cold extruding of the hub onto the shaft loses almost no material.

Ford (1922, 101–102) cites the example of a process that required four operations to make a gear while wasting 12 percent of the steel. "One of the workmen devised a very simple new method for making this gear in which the scrap was only one per cent." He does not provide details but it does show another application of the basic principle.

Ford also points out (1930, 192–193) the benefits of forging or casting small parts and then welding them into complex ones. It was traditional to cast entire intricate metal parts, but castings could contain blowholes or other defects that the existing technology could not detect. (Nondestructive testing methods might find them today, but the piece would still have to be reworked or scrapped.) Furthermore, "A casting must be machined—sometimes by taking away thirty percent of the metal; that is a waste." The production and welding of the small forged and stamped pieces into the complex pieces added more operations to the process, but this had advantages. The smaller forgings, castings, and stampings were stronger than a large cast piece and, after assembly by welding, the final unit might be lighter and stronger than a single large casting. This approach avoided the machining waste.

Changing or customizing the size of the stock may also help eliminate waste:

> On nineteen items cut from bars or tubing we have, by changing the cutting tools and multiples and the length of the stock, saved more than a million pounds of steel a year. For instance, on one part we used a bar 143 inches long and got eighteen pieces per bar; we found that we could get the same number of pieces out of a bar 140 9/32 inches

long—thus saving more than two inches [1.4 percent of the material] per bar (Ford, 1926, 95).

Chase (1998) cites a contemporary example, a job that requires 5'8" (173 cm) boards. If the boards come in 6' (183) cm lengths, the 4" (10.2 cm) piece that remains is waste. It's the same principle.

Transportation as Waste

Imai (1997) identifies transportation as a form of *muda*. Ford points out that a company that ships green wood is shipping water. "... we save transport by the carriage of wood instead of wood mixed with water—green wood. More than that, we carry only finished wood—parts all ready to go into assembly." Here's how this principle applies to other activities.

- Bottling drinks. Drinks are usually bottled at the bottle-making plant. Trucks should not deliver empty bottles to the drink manufacturer because the shipment of air— and that's what empty bottles contain—is waste. Transportation of the drink to the bottling plant in a tank car wastes no space.
- Using packing material. A plant that receives packing material like foam "peanut" packing at its loading dock is paying for the truck to carry mostly air. It's more efficient to make the packing material where it is to be used. If the capital investment is too high for a small factory, a group of factories in an industrial park could consider a joint investment. The same principle applies to bubble wrap. (I have seen inflatable packing material in office supply stores.)
- Shipping car bodies. Ford (1926, 117) provides an example of shipping a product instead of air. "Only a few years ago, seven touring car bodies made a full load for a standard thirty-six-foot freight car. Now the bodies are shipped knocked-down to be assembled and finished in the branches, and we ship 130 touring car bodies in the same

sized car—that is, we use one freight car where we should formerly have used eighteen."

- Transporting raw materials. Process the raw material or commodity where it is mined, raised, or grown. "On meat and grain and perhaps on cotton, too, the transportation burden could be reduced by more than half, by the preparation of the product for use before it is shipped" Ford (1922, 231). Ford points out:
  - It is wasteful to transport live Texan cattle to Chicago ("hog butcher to the world") stockyards for slaughter and then ship the beef back to Texas. Hog farming areas should sell pork and ham, not hogs.
  - Site flourmills near grain farms.
  - Cotton mills should be near cotton fields.
  - Ford (1930, 273) raised the idea of extracting iron from its ore at the mine, to avoid transporting what would become slag at the blast furnace.

    Although Ford sited his woodworking operations at lumber camps, he recognized that this approach is not possible when more than one raw material is necessary. For example, coal and iron ore are rarely found in the same place.

Figure 7-5 applies to spools of tape, thread, ribbon, paper, cloth, and anything else that is relatively light. Make the core as small as possible (keeping in mind the ease of winding and unwinding the product) to reduce packaging and transportation costs. The manufacturer can lower the price (thus possibly increasing the sales volume) while making more from each sale.

Beyond Recycling

Recycling is standard practice today. Ford went past recycling: ". . . we will not so lightly waste material simply because we can reclaim it—for salvage involves labour. *The ideal is to have nothing to salvage*" (Ford, 1926, 94, emphasis is mine). Consider the

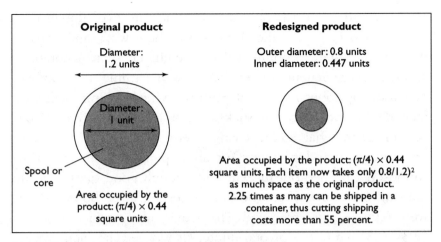

Original product

Diameter:
1.2 units

Diameter:
1 unit

Spool or
core

Area occupied by the
product: (π/4) × 0.44
square units

Redesigned product

Outer diameter: 0.8 units
Inner diameter: 0.447 units

Area occupied by the product: (π/4) × 0.44
square units. Each item now takes only 0.8/1.2)^2
as much space as the original product.
2.25 times as many can be shipped in a
container, thus cutting shipping
costs more than 55 percent.

Figure 7-5. Make spool diameters as small as possible

example of the six-inch (15.2-cm) circles from the metal stamping operation. Ordinary economy would suggest melting them for reuse. Ford's workers figured out how to turn them into radiator caps. This exemplifies the idea, Go beyond recycling; leave nothing to recycle. Ford stresses this point even further:

> It is not possible to repeat too often that waste is not something which comes after the fact. Restoring an ill body to health is an achievement, but preventing illness is a much higher achievement. Picking up and reclaiming the scrap left over after production is a public service, but planning so that there will be no scrap is a higher public service (Ford, 1926, 113).

Some recycling examples now follow. There is no way to prove or disprove Ford's belief in reincarnation for people, but his worn-out tools kept coming back:

> If a drill, a broach, or a reamer is worn out, it is cut down to a smaller size, always in accordance with the original blueprint. Cold-heading dies are all reworked to the next size, and so on down through the entire list of tools.... Tool handles of all kinds are salvaged; a broken shovel handle may make several screw driver or chisel handles (Ford, 1926, 97).

Norwood (1931, Chapter X) adds that the River Rouge plant resharpened rasps and files by blasting them with sand. Most of these tools lasted through twelve to eighteen such restorations, and they were actually better than new each time: they outlived new tools by about 10 percent. Stubs of wheel-buffing sticks were melted and made into new sticks. The stubs accounted for 15 percent of the material, so the savings were considerable. Scrap lumber became wooden rollers for shop pails. Routine testing of supposedly burned-out fuses found enough good ones to justify the wages of the worker who did the testing. Even bolts and nuts were rethreaded or retapped. The activity about which Norwood (1931, 135) wrote the pivotal quote, "It worried the men" wasted 25 percent of aluminum chips. They reduced this loss to less than 2 percent.

Per Norwood (1931, Chapter XI), the River Rouge plant also reused broken bricks. Half-bricks and larger were reusable as they were. Pulverization of smaller pieces from furnace walls made liners for steel furnace basins. Steaming removed tar from worn-out creosote blocks (tar-impregnated wood), and the wood was then re-impregnated. A special machine with claws on a revolving shaft tore nails from scrap lumber. Seventy-five kegs of these nails went into the foundry cupolas every day.

The lumber itself became foundry kindling only if it was not reusable. Even small pieces of wood could serve as wedges for casting flasks in the foundry. Scrap wood yielded 30,000 such wedges every day.

Lead-tin babbitt bearings[4] from scrap cars yielded a ton and a half (1.36 metric tons) of metal pig (ingots) every sixteen hours. These varied in composition, but they were mostly tin, which was valuable. Ford specifications called for no more than 0.2 percent lead and no less than 90 percent tin in bearings. Combining these pigs, according to their analysis, with virgin tin yielded acceptable bearings.

Norwood (1931, Chapter XII) continues by showing how boiling water separated oil from metal turnings and chips, for recovery of 2,500 gallons (9463 liters) of oil per day. The oil returned to the machine tools for reuse. This exemplifies a thought process that is typical of a chemical plant, in which materials recirculate and recycle until they are of no further use.

Machining often wastes considerable cutting fluid and lubricant. Shigeo Shingo (1987, 42–43) asks, "Why grease scrap metal?" This waste is avoidable by greasing only the surfaces that come in contact with the press dies; there is no need to grease what will become scrap metal. Furthermore (pp. 49–50), many machining processes waste up to 90 percent of the oil. An oil mist is often sufficient to provide the necessary cooling and lubrication, and spraying it removes cuttings from the tool blades as well. Water is very efficient at cooling because of its high latent heat of vaporization. Lower oil usage not only saves money on oil, the shop produces less waste oil. This is an improvement under the ISO 14000 environmental standard as well as an example of "the higher achievement" of not just recycling scrap but planning for there to be no scrap.

Waste Reduction at Ford Today

Ford Motor Company's Internet site[5] shows the application of Henry Ford's waste reduction principles today.

> Ford is a leader in the use of recycled materials. Many products that once would have been thrown away now are recycled as new and replacement parts for our cars and trucks.
>
> Recycled soft drink bottles are used in our luggage compartment carpeting, grille reinforcements and door padding. Plastic computer and phone housings are made into grilles. Used tires become step-in plates. Plastic water bottles become headlamps, old bumpers become tail lamps, and battery housings turn into splash shields.

The next section shows that there are two ways to handle the ISO 14000 standard for environmental management systems: throw money at it or, as Henry Ford would have done, make money from it.

ISO 14000 IS FREE

The Ford Motor Company was safe and environmentally clean long before either OSHA or the Environmental Protection Agency existed. Compliance with today's ISO 14000 environmental standard should be not only free but profitable. Ford's ultimate goal, *the ideal is to have nothing to salvage*, means that materials have been used productively or not at all. Even recycling, as shown by Ford's distillation of wood for its chemicals, gets rid of so-called waste at a profit.

Modern experience supports the concept of making money through environmentally friendly manufacturing.

"In general, environmentally sound companies are financially healthier companies," says University of Oregon professor Michael Russo . . . Similarly, another recent study at Vanderbilt University found that eight times out of ten environmentally sound companies outperform their higher-polluting counterparts. One reason: "If you're less wasteful, you're probably running a lean operation," says Russo (Miller and Laurenti, 2001).

Example: Fumes from a Coating Operation

Consider an ISO 14000 environmental aspect: fumes from a coating operation. Ford had a coating material for cloth that contained ethyl acetate, alcohol, and benzol (benzene, which would not be used today because it is now a suspected carcinogen). An adsorption-desorption process not only kept the solvents out of the environment, it recovered and reused them.

The fumes are drawn through charcoal made from cocoanut [sic] shells until the charcoal becomes saturated. Steam is then turned on, which drives the fumes into a condenser, from which they are separated into the original compounds. As much as 90 percent of the fumes have thus been recovered when the work of the condenser has been concentrated on one smokestack (Ford, 1926, 67).

. . . Old paint is reclaimed to the extent of 500 gallons [1890 liters] a day and is used for rough work. The salvage of oil and cutting compounds from steel shavings amounts to 2,100 gallons [7950 liters] a day (Ford, 1926, 97).

Figure 7-6 (see McCabe, Smith, and Harriott, 1985, 687–688) shows how adsorption, a common method for solvent recovery, works. In the first step, the solvent-rich gas flows through a bed of adsorbent, a role fulfilled by the charcoal in Ford's example. When the adsorbent is full of solvent, the second step, regeneration, takes place. Steam or hot inert gas flows through the adsorbent bed as shown to expel the adsorbed solvent. A condenser cools the steam (or inert gas) and solvent to turn them back into liquid.

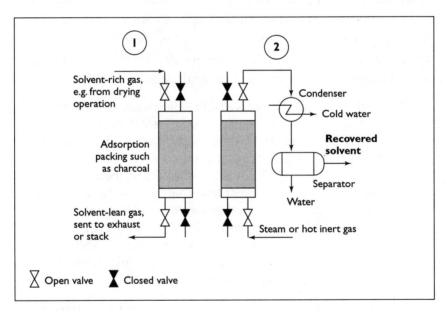

Figure 7-6. Adsorption-desorption cycle

If the solvent is water-insoluble it floats on the condensed water, and separation takes place in the vessel that appears in the figure. If it is water-soluble (like the solvents in Ford's application; alcohol is water-soluble and even benzene is slightly soluble) inert gas is used instead of steam. Ford says he used steam; it's possible that the steam passed through coils to heat the adsorbent instead of actually contacting it. In practice, two adsorbers work together. One treats the gas while the other undergoes regeneration.

Lubricating oil is an environmental issue for factories and automobile repair shops. There is often a disposal fee for used motor oil. "Scrap oil is salvaged, and what is unfit for either lubrication or rustproofing is burned for fuel" (Ford, 1926, 97).

Keeping an Eye on the Smokestack: Coking of Coal for Profitable Byproducts

Ordinary coal, especially bituminous coal, is a dirty fuel. It contains sulfur that, upon combustion, becomes sulfur dioxide. This pollutant irritates mucous membranes and contributes to acid rain. Many people see the chemicals in coal as problems that require expensive pollution control equipment like scrubbers and electrostatic precipitators.[6] Ford saw opportunities:

> With all the great factories coking their coal, thus providing a double use for it, other economies will come. A great waste will be prevented. When one thinks of the precious elements which have been consumed for decades on the furnace grates, all going up in smoke and being lost to human use, it becomes clear that the new method has not come too soon. [This is another example of keeping an eye on the doughnut's hole, which includes the smokestack.] . . . In the modern use of coal, gas is produced, and gas is a public utility. . . . The fertilizing elements extracted from coal can be utilized on the farms (Ford, 1926, 175–176).

Ford used high temperature ovens to convert bituminous coal from Kentucky into coke for his blast furnaces.

> We have one hundred and twenty "high temperature" ovens with a capacity of 2,500 tons [2270 metric tons] a day. These are all by-product ovens and beside them is the by-product plant in which we recover such of the products as may be used within the organization, excepting the ammonium sulphate which we sell outside, and we also sell our surplus of benzol [benzene]—as was said before. The coal delivered at the plant costs us about five dollars

a ton, but when converted into coke and by-products, it is worth about twelve dollars a ton. We have created an experimental paint and varnish plant further to utilize the by-products. Part of the gas produced in distillation is used to heat the ovens so as to make the process continuous, another part is piped into Highland Park while what remains is sold to the local gas companies ... The tar and oil we use in our own industries (Ford, 1926, 105–106).

Ammonium sulfate is a nitrogen carrier in fertilizers, and its production shows what becomes of at least some of the sulfur in the coal. Instead of becoming environmental waste that the company must pay to handle, it becomes a product that the company can sell.

Ford attests further to the economical and environmentally clean use of coal:

In the use of coal at the Fordson power house we have the advantage of big business in being able to treat coal as a chemical, use the derivatives in our business, and burn what remains. We use both the high temperature and the low temperature distillation of coal, although, on the low temperature, we are just making a beginning. The processes are well known—most of our processes are well known. It is the combination of processes that counts. And the result is that out of coal which costs us about five dollars a ton delivered at the plant, we get a good return per ton out of byproducts which gives us fuel for the boilers at a very low cost (Ford, 1926, 172).

Although Ford provides only a couple of pages of detail, more can be inferred from a high temperature coking process (Shreve and Brink, 1977, 68–72). Coking converts a ton of bituminous coal into 1,400 pounds (0.7 ton) of coke, 10 gallons of tar, 25 pounds of ammonium sulfate, two to four gallons of light oil, plus gas.[7] Co-product coking takes place at high temperatures in batteries of 10 to 100 ovens; Ford mentioned 120.

The principal product is the highest quality of coke for blast furnaces, where it reduces the iron ore to iron. Coke is also a fuel, and it contains less sulfur than bituminous coal.

The Fuel Cell: An Innovative Way to "Burn" Coke or Coal

Although coke may burn more cleanly than coal, this is not the final word on reducing coal-related pollution. The reaction of steam with coke at 1,832°F (1000°C) produces *water gas*, which is also known as *blue gas*; the latter name comes from the color of its flame when it burns (Shreve and Brink, 1977, 86–87). Table 7-1 shows what happens.

1. Carbon, in the form of coal or coke, reacts with steam to produce carbon monoxide (CO) and hydrogen (H2).
2. The carbon monoxide can then react with more steam to make carbon dioxide and more hydrogen.
3. Fuel cells can convert hydrogen into electricity with very high efficiencies.

Figure 7-7 (on page 184) shows why fuel cells appeal to engineers. Non-engineers can skip the technical details without loss of continuity. The bottom line is that the laws of thermodynamics have written WASTE all over traditional coal, oil, natural gas, and nuclear power generation systems. Engineers will appreciate the application of the Ford thought process in recognizing the waste. Thermo-dynamics teaches that Murphy was indeed an optimist:

- The first law of thermodynamics says we can't win. We can't get more energy out of a system (as mechanical work, which can be converted into electricity) than we put in, usually in the form of heat. TANSTAAFL.
- The second law of thermodynamics says we can't break even. No cyclic process can convert heat (e.g. from combustion of a fossil fuel or from nuclear fission) entirely into mechanical work. The maximum efficiency (η) of a Carnot power cycle—a theoretical one that real-world power generation cycles cannot achieve—is where the
$$\eta_{Carnot} = \frac{T_{hot} - T_{cold}}{T_{hot}}$$ temperatures of the hot and cold reservoirs are in degrees Rankine or Kelvin (temperature scales whose zeroes are absolute zero).

Table 7-1. Conventional combustion versus the fuel cell

Not this:	This:
$C + O_2 \rightarrow CO_2 + heat$ The Carnot cycle yields the *theoretical* maximum efficiency of a process in which heat flows from a hot to a cold reservoir. Real-world power generation cycles, such as the Rankine steam cycle, are even less efficient	$C + HO_2 \rightarrow CO + H_2$ and also $CO + H_2O \rightarrow CO_2 + H_2$ _{Fuel cell} $2H_2 + O_2 \rightarrow 2H_2O + electricity$ *Fuel cells are not subject to the efficiency limitations of thermal power cycles.*

- The third law of thermodynamics says we can't even get out of the game, because, in layman's terms, absolute zero can never be achieved. This is a problem because the Carnot cycle shows that 100 percent efficiency is achievable if the system can discharge heat to a cold reservoir at absolute zero. Now things get a lot worse. The real-world coolant must come from the environment and, even in winter, this is well above absolute zero. Next, Figure 7-7 shows that Tcold must be *warmer* than the available condenser water and Thot must be similarly *cooler* than the furnace temperature.

The turbine that recovers mechanical energy (the value-adding product) from the steam is not 100 percent efficient either. Figure 7-7 shows that there is waste in:

- The transfer of heat from the furnace to the boiler water
- The transfer of heat from the expanded steam to the condenser water
- The turbine
- The gases that go up the smokestack. These include not only the combustion products but the nitrogen (about 79 percent) in the atmosphere. Nitrogen plays no role in burning the fuel but it carries plenty of heat into the atmosphere. This is a theoretical argument for using pure oxygen to burn fuels but pure oxygen costs money. The equipment (furnace and boiler tubes) might not,

furthermore, be able to tolerate the higher temperatures that would result.

- The boiler feed water pump, although this is a minor consideration.

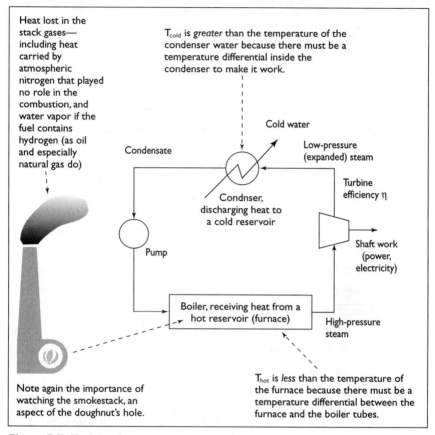

Figure 7-7. Traditional power generation cycle

The Henry Ford thought process should almost prompt revulsion at Figure 7-7. The practitioner then thinks, "Is there a way to get out of this game?" The fuel cell breaks free of the thermal power cycle; it breaks the paradigm that electricity must come from fuel-generated heat. (So does hydroelectric power, which is why hydroelectric dams are so desirable in the power industry. Furthermore, the flowing water is free.)

Fuel cells oxidize (burn) their fuels through electrochemistry, not fire; they are like electric batteries. They can use hydrogen almost twice as efficiently as a traditional combustion power plant. "In a fuel cell a fuel such as hydrogen, natural gas, or propane can be converted into twice the amount of electricity that would result from the burning of a corresponding amount of fuel indirectly through boilers, turbines, and generators to produce electricity" (Shreve and Brink, 1977, 58). "Such fuel cells are already in use to supply modest power requirements for special purposes. The efficiency of these cells ranges from 65 to 80 percent, about twice the value obtained by the conventional process of first converting the chemical energy into heat" (Smith and Van Ness, 1975, 489). Energypubs.com, 2000:

> ATLANTA, Feb. 16 /PRNewswire/ — Southern Company (NYSE: SO), the nation's largest producer of electricity, announced today that it is the first U.S. utility to join the Zero Emission Coal Alliance (ZECA) [which] is researching a new technology that, if successful, would generate electricity with coal in a process that produces no emissions or greenhouse gases. . . .
> The technology would create hydrogen from a coal-water mixture and produce pure CO_2. A fuel cell would convert the hydrogen to electricity . . . Because the coal is not burned, the process does not produce sulfur dioxide or nitrogen oxides.

We have already seen that carbon sequestration and carbon taxes (as required by the Kyoto Protocol) would raise energy costs, destroy jobs, and damage the economy. The fuel cell approach can reduce energy costs, create jobs, and promote economic growth. It also reduces carbon dioxide emissions for the same reason that it reduces costs; it requires less coal per kilowatt-hour. This is intelligent environmentalism.

Fuel cells also will find applications in vehicles like cars, trucks, and buses. There is no future in the rechargeable electric vehicle (although places like California are trying to mandate it) because recharging simply means moving the exhaust pipe from the car to the power plant. Electric vehicles that use fuel cells, on the other hand, are the future because they offer the potential for getting twice as many miles or kilometers per unit of fuel, with no sacrifice of vehicle performance (horsepower, kilowattage), size, or safety. Whoever figures out how to use fuels like gasoline (petrol), or diesel in fuel cells—and research is in progress—is going to make a lot of money. Some methods crack the hydrogen from the fuel as it is needed, thus avoiding the need to store dangerous pressurized hydrogen. Another approach might store hydrogen safely through adsorption in solids like carbon nanotubes.

General Motors has, in fact, deployed a gasoline-to-hydrogen system on the Chevrolet S10 pickup truck.

> The system works by mixing low-sulfur gasoline with air and water, then passing the mixture over a series of catalysts that extract the hydrogen. The hydrogen then is routed to the fuel cell stack, where it is combined with oxygen from the air to produce electricity.
> ...And the system achieves up to 40 percent overall energy efficiency—50 percent better than a combustion engine and the equivalent of 40 miles per gallon (Jones, 2002).

Performance is a problem, as the vehicle takes 15 seconds to go from 0 to 60 miles an hour (97 km/hour). This working vehicle shows, however, the promise of this power source. GM believes that performance similar to that of an internal combustion engine is achievable by 2010.

Reducing Greenhouse Gases from Livestock—At a Profit

Sheep and cattle, or rather bacteria that inhabit them, produce methane. Methane is 21 times as potent a greenhouse gas as carbon dioxide. Livestock generate 14 percent of Australia's greenhouse gas emissions as measured in equivalent carbon dioxide. Australian farmers are trying a drug or vaccine that suppresses methanogenic (methane-producing) archae, organisms that break down food in ruminating animals. This also is intelligent environ-mentalism because the animals, not the bacteria, would now assimilate the nutrients. The cattle make beef instead of methane while the sheep make wool instead of methane ("Australia fights methane," 2001).

Paint the Parts, Not the Air

A Japanese company spray painted fountain pen caps in a paint-ing booth, and the waste required treatment before discharge. Heavy rainfall caused polluted water from the waste treatment plant to overflow and contaminate nearby rice paddies. The com-pany had to compensate the rice farmers for damages. Dr. Shigeo Shingo asked the plant manager whether the operation's purpose was to paint the pen caps or the air. The phrase "painting the air" points straight to the waste's root cause. Until Shingo pointed it out, however, the plant took this aspect of the painting operation for granted; no one was watching the doughnut's hole.

The manager realized that the paint that missed the pen caps was waste. An equipment redesign introduced a sprayer that dis-pensed very small quantities of pigment; it moved up and down as the pen cap rotated in front of it. Very little paint missed the pen caps and no contaminated water ever left the plant. Not only had the company dealt with its environmental aspect, it paid less for paint (Robinson, 1990, 101–102). This story shows how, for a com-pany that learns and applies Henry Ford's waste reduction princi-ples, ISO 14000 is not only free but profitable.

ISO 14000 Today

Fielding (2000) cites several companies that have improved their profitability through environmental management systems (EMSs). 3M Corporation introduced its "Pollution Prevention Pays" pro-gram in 1975. Since then, it has saved more than eight hundred million dollars.

CVI's Chemical Manufacturing Division learned the same prin-ciple through its first environmental aspect identification exercise.

". . . The division identified manufacturing waste as having a significant effect on business, due not only to the excessive depletion
of natural resources but also to the added cost of lost production
time and defective parts" (Fielding, 2000). The company improved
its preventive maintenance program to suppress waste, which not
only reduced environmental emissions but also cut defects by
more than 60 percent.

The reference also shows that Ford Motor Company itself is
rediscovering its founder's principles through ISO 14000. Ford's
Michigan truck facility reduced water consumption by a million
gallons (3785 cubic meters) a day. It also cut electrical costs by
$66,000 a year by replacing fluorescent bulbs (already more
energy-efficient than incandescent ones) by metal halide bulbs.
Ten Ford plants recycle paint sludge, and the company has
replaced single-use cardboard and plywood boxes with reusable
metal and plastic containers. (Ford cars no longer have wooden
floorboards so Ford's own innovative method of dealing with
wooden containers no longer applies.)

SUMMARY

This chapter has done its job if the reader takes away two vital
concepts:

- The idea of eliminating waste is obvious, but it is very
  easy to look straight at waste (e.g. rust in slag, paint that
  misses fountain pen caps) without seeing it. One of Henry
  Ford's success secrets was his ability to see waste that
  most people would overlook. Watch the hole (everything
  that the process consumes or discards) as well as the
  doughnut (product).
- Do not take any aspect of a job or activity for granted.
  Never assume that, just because people have done a job a
  certain way for months, years, or decades, that there isn't a
  far better way to do it.

Notes

1. Recall Taylor's story about Gilbreth's discovery that bricklayers bent over to pick up each brick, thus raising and lowering their upper body's weight perhaps a thousand times a day. Pictures from Gilbreth's *Motion Study* (in Chapter 10, on Taylor) show how bricklayers performed their work before and after Gilbreth's introduction of the non-stooping scaffold. Ford's personal experience with agriculture shows that the idea of bricklayers bending over for each brick is very plausible.

2. A ton (909 kg) of waste wood yielded 135 pounds (61.4 kg) of acetate of lime, 61 gallons (231 liters) of 82% methyl alcohol, 610 pounds (277 kg) of charcoal, 15 gallons (57 liters) of tar, 600 cubic feet (17 cubic meters) of fuel gas, plus oils and creosote (Ford, 1926, 136).

3. A six sigma process is one in which the specification limits are six standard deviations (standard deviation measures the process' random variation) from the average measurement. If the measurements follow a normal distribution (bell curve), random variation will produce no more than two defects per billion. Even a process shift of 1.5 standard deviations, which a statistical process control chart should detect quickly, will result in no more than 4.5 defects per million opportunities.

4. Babbitt metal is a soft, antifriction alloy of (primarily) tin with copper and antimony. That at Ford apparently used lead.

5. http://www.ford.com/finaninvest/stockholder/stock95/leader.html, 6/9/2000

6. Scrubbers remove gases like sulfur dioxide from stack gas, while electrostatic precipitators remove particles.

7. 908 kg of bituminous coal yields 635 kg of coke, 37.9 liters of tar, 11.3 kg of ammonium sulphate, 7.6 to 15.1 liters of light oil, plus gas.

EIGHT

Ford's Factory

Then I went over to the great arms factory and learned my
real trade; learned all there was to it; learned to make
everything; guns, revolvers, cannon, boilers, engines, all
sorts of labor-saving machinery. Why, I could make anything a body wanted—anything in the world, it didn't make
any difference what; and if there wasn't any quick new-fan-
gled way to make a thing, I could invent one—and do it
as easy as rolling off a log.
                    —Mark Twain, *A Connecticut Yankee in King Arthur's Court*

This chapter covers Henry Ford's productivity and quality
improvement methods, which are as applicable today as they
were when he implemented them. This is not surprising because
they include everything we now recognize as lean manufacturing
techniques.

It is important to begin, however, by addressing some mis-
conceptions about the Ford system's effect on the worker. Many
industrial myths say that Ford, like Frederick Winslow Taylor,
wanted to turn workers into mindless automata: flesh-and-blood
robots in an era when mechanical robots existed only in science
fiction stories.[1] Allowing these myths to stand might discourage
modern practitioners from applying Ford's methods. These myths
might also breed apprehension or resistance among front-line
workers, so the chapter's first section will deal with them.

The second section covers Ford's deployment of lean manufacturing techniques such as:

- 5S-CANDO (Clearing up, Arranging, Neatness, Discipline, Ongoing improvement)
- Small-lot and single-unit processing
- Single-minute exchange of die (SMED)
- Parallel processing and assembly
- Innovative techniques for improving tool efficiencies and reducing the proportion of non-value-adding tool motion
- Cellular manufacturing (specifically, the idea that each department should make a finished part instead of performing a single operation like milling, drilling, stamping, or brazing), and the elimination of non-value-adding transportation of work-in-process (WIP)
- Unitary machines that perform several value-adding operations between loading and unloading of the part

The chapter's third major section treats Ford's extensive contributions to just-in-time (JIT) production. The Ford production control system did not use kanban; it sought to synchronize operations like clockwork. Suppression of variation in processing and work delivery times allowed Ford to do the seemingly impossible: run a balanced production line (one in which the workstations have identical capacities) at close to 100 percent utilization. *This has major implications for modern practitioners.* Ford also developed a freight management system (FMS) to support his JIT production system.

The next major section treats product design, including design for manufacture (DFM), design for assembly (DFA), and quality function deployment (QFD). The latter is also known as the "house of quality." Ford did not develop QFD as we know it today, but he applied the basic underlying principle of tying the customer's requirements to the product's features and design.

The next two sections address process simplification and improvement, self-check systems, error-proofing (poka-yoke), and variation and accuracy. The sections are related in that Ford's deliberate selection of high-precision tooling, in combination with self-check systems and error-proofing, may have been why his factories worked so well despite their apparent lack of statistical process control (SPC) charts. Neither *Moving Forward* (1930) nor Sorensen's *My Forty Years with Ford* (1956) mention SPC, which Walter Shewhart developed during the 1920s.

The next two major sections are fairly small; they deal with packaging and delivery (an important aspect of ISO 9000), and point-of-use assembly.

The next section covers industrial safety, an area in which Ford developed or deployed extremely modern techniques such as lockout-tagout. It also treats the important issue of lighting, and suggests that fluorescent lights may be a false economy in today's workplaces.

Ford also introduced techniques that we now associate with total quality management (TQM), and he even defined TQM's basis:

> There is no service in simply setting up a machine or a plant and letting it turn out goods. The service extends into every detail of the design, the making, the wages paid, and the selling price. None of these can ever be taken as right—they can only represent the best efforts of the moment (Ford, 1930, 7).

Every element of the entire business system—production, design, wages, and price—influences the enterprise's ability to serve customers. Also, every aspect of the system is subject to continuous improvement. Whereas TQM topics appear throughout the chapter, the final section treats quality control and quality auditing in particular.

This chapter will cite sections of the ISO 9000 standard for quality systems whenever they are relevant to the associated material. Lean manufacturing and ISO 9000 are synergistic and mutually supporting, not separate activities that divide the factory's attention and focus.

THE FACTORY AND THE WORKER

Some references criticize Ford for creating a "dehumanizing" workplace, but he recognized the merits of intrinsic motivation: "The man who does not get a certain satisfaction out of his day's work is losing the best part of his pay" (Ford, 1922, 120).[2] He also offered job rotation:

> We shift men whenever they ask to be shifted and we should like regularly to change them—that would be entirely feasible if only the men would have it that way. They do not like changes which they do not themselves suggest. Some of the operations are undoubtedly monotonous—so monotonous that it seems scarcely possible that any man would care to continue long at the same job. Probably the most monotonous task in the whole factory is one in which a man picks up a gear with a steel hook, shakes it in a vat of oil, then turns it into a basket. . . . Yet the man on that job has been doing it for eight years. He has saved and invested his money until now he has about forty thousand dollars—and he stubbornly resists every effort to force him into a better job! (Ford, 1922, 105–106).

Ford put automated machinery into dull and repetitive tasks whenever possible. This made good business sense because such tasks are rarely profitable for either the company or the worker. He also saw a new craftsmanship role in the development and construction of machines to perform such tasks:

> The man who helps make the machine which in turn makes the machine which actually produces goods is in a position to be paid more highly than the most skilled man in the production of goods—for he furnishes the means for high production (Ford, 1930, 40–41).

This is yet another answer to the displacement of American manufacturing jobs by inexpensive foreign labor. Dollar-an-hour labor can compete easily with $15-an-hour labor. It cannot compete with sophisticated and clever machinery even if $25-an-hour workers operate it.

Ford (1930, 123) compares his factory to the old craft system with its apprentices and journeymen. The truth was that such shops required many semiskilled and unskilled laborers but very few first-class machinists. Ford's factory had no totally unskilled positions. The proportion of highly skilled workers to those in the lowest skill class exceeded that in the traditional shops. He predicted that manufacturing would require even more skilled workers as technology progressed, and this has indeed happened.

During the mid-to-late 1920s, no production job at Ford took more than a month to learn, and about half the jobs required a week's training or less. Ford wrote in 1930 that few of his company's jobs could be learned in a week and some took as long as eight weeks to learn. The increasing need for training hardly fits the image of Charlie Chaplin tightening nuts in the movie *Modern Times*.[3] Ford even had his workers restore antiques, products of the old-style craftsmanship, presumably for his museum in Dearborn. They had no trouble making replacement parts that were far better than the originals. Even when, as an experiment, they had to use the same tools that the original craftsmen used, they could still do the job. The company's carpenters could, for example, use old-fashioned tools to restore a historical inn or old house (Ford, 1930, 126–127). This suggests that Ford's industries did *not* turn workers into two-legged automata. The next section proves, in fact, that Ford empowered and encouraged his workers to improve their jobs.

CONTINUOUS IMPROVEMENT: KAIZEN

Continuous improvement was the backbone of Henry Ford's way of business. He mentions this idea repeatedly and almost obsessively, and with justification. "If there is any fixed theory—any fixed rule—it is that no job is being done well enough" (Ford, 1922, 100). No improvement was too small to overlook; this was perhaps a lesson from Benjamin Franklin, whose books influenced Ford's thinking. Franklin stressed, for example, that a penny saved is two pence clear. Cost savings flow directly to the bottom line.

The saving of a cent per piece may be distinctly worth while. A saving of one cent on a part at our present rate of production represents twelve thousand dollars a year. One cent saved on each part would amount to millions a year. Therefore, in comparing savings, the calculations are carried out to the thousandth part of a cent. If the new way suggested shows a saving and the cost of making the change will pay for itself within a reasonable time—say within three months—the change is made practically as of course.[4] These changes are by no means limited to improvements which will increase production or decrease cost. A great many—perhaps most of them—are in the line of making the work easier. We do not want any hard, man-killing work about the place, and there is now very little of it. And usually it so works out that adopting the way that is easier on the men also decreases the cost....

[A worker] indicated that if the tool in his machine were set at a different angle it might last longer. As it was it lasted only four or five cuts. He was right, and a lot of money was saved in grinding. Another Pole, running a drill press, rigged up a little fixture to save handling the part after drilling. That was adopted generally and a considerable saving resulted. The men often try out little attachments of their own because, concentrating on one thing, they can, if they have a mind that way, usually devise some improvement....

A proposal that castings be taken from the foundry to the machine shop on an overhead conveyor saved seventy men in the transport division. ...Changing from a solid to a welded rod in one part of the chassis effected an immediate saving of about one half million a year on a smaller than the present-day production. Making certain tubes out of flat sheets instead of drawing them in the usual way effected another enormous saving (Ford, 1922, 100–101).

This citation illustrates several kaizen principles:

• Small savings add up, and they flow directly to the bottom line. Ford talks about thousands and single-digit millions of dollars but the dollar was worth far more in his time.

A Ford worker who earned the company's relatively high $6/day minimum wage got $1,500/year.

- The method that is easier on the people is often more productive. This ties in with Masaaki Imai's concept of *muri*, or strain, and its negative effects on productivity and quality.
- The frontline worker who does the job eight hours a day knows more about it than anyone else. He or she is in an excellent position to suggest improvements, and these are often achievable with small and inexpensive fixtures. Japanese experience is that poka-yoke (error-proofing) devices are often very cheap. Note especially the example of a front-line worker's initiative in eliminating non-value-adding handling after drilling. General adoption of the new method, i.e., *best practice deployment*, followed promptly.
- Part redesigns (e.g., a welded rod versus a solid one) can make production easier.

Standardization Supports Continuous Improvement

This section is synergistic with ISO 9001:1994 section 4.5 (ISO 9000:2000 5.5.6), Document Control. Standardization requires assurance that the current version of the work instruction is available at the operation, and that all workers who perform that operation are familiar with it. Standardization means:

- Finding what Frederick Winslow Taylor would call the one best way of performing a task.
- Making this method the standard for that task throughout the organization. *Best practice deployment* is another term for this.
- Recognizing that the standard is only today's best way. It can and should be superseded by a better "best way" through continuous improvement (kaizen).

Ford provided an outstanding description of standardization:

Standardization in its true sense is the union of all the best points of commodities with all the best points of production, to the end that the best commodity may be produced in sufficient quantity and at the least cost to the consumer.

To standardize a method is to choose out of many methods the best one, and use it. Standardization means nothing unless it means standardizing upward.

What is the best way to do a thing? It is the sum of all the good ways we have discovered up to the present.... Today's best, which superseded yesterday's, will be superseded by tomorrow's best.

... If you think of "standardization" as the best that you know today, but which is to be improved tomorrow, you get somewhere. But if you think of standards as confining, then progress stops (Ford, 1926, 82).

H. L. Gantt (the inventor of the Gantt chart) defined standardization similarly, "Standardization consists in reducing to written rules the best methods, and prescribing them for general use" (*The System Company*, 1911, 15).

Standardization is emphatically dynamic, not static. Taylor (1911) believed that trade workers often improved their crafts but, because they didn't keep written records (or because they kept the improvements secret), the knowledge was lost. Standardization holds the gains of continuous improvement, a key goal of the plan-do-check-act (PDCA) improvement cycle. It is therefore not a barrier to further improvement but a prerequisite for it.

Levinson (2000) points out that primitive societies transmitted knowledge through an oral tradition, which often included poetry—the rhymes reminded the speaker of what to say next. Many workplaces followed this procedure long after the invention of writing; new workers learned their jobs from experienced ones. Juran and Gryna (1988) mention *knacks*, or specific workers' knowledge of how to do a job better. When a worker with a knack moves to another job or retires, that knowledge is lost. Even while that worker is on the job, those without the knack cannot perform it as well. This underscores the need for standardization through written and controlled work instructions as required by ISO 9000.

Standardization and Best Practice Deployment

A job's work instruction or operating instruction is, to use the expression associated with Taylorism, today's "one best way." The next step is to apply today's one best way to all tasks to which it relates:

> An operation in our plant at Barcelona has to be carried through exactly as in Detroit—the benefit of our experience cannot be thrown away. A man on the assembly line at Detroit ought to be able to step into the assembly line at Oklahoma City or São Paulo, Brazil (Ford, 1926, 85).

The phrase "the benefit of our experience" underscores the concept of best practice deployment, or assurance that the entire enterprise gains whatever it can from a localized improvement. Not only do workers in Detroit, Oklahoma City, and São Paulo do the job the same way, they do it the one best way—until a better best way comes along. The document control system, as required by ISO 9000, supports this goal.

The work instruction is not, however, an injunction against the worker's innovation or creativity. Although people call the belief that workers should leave their brains at the factory gate Taylorism, Taylor wanted workers to think. He wrote of worker-initiated improvements, "And whenever the new method is found to be markedly superior to the old, it should be adopted as the standard for the whole establishment" (Taylor, 1911, 67).

Ford's Highland Park factory combined standardization, worker empowerment, and continuous improvement:

> Improvements are constantly being introduced. Hardly a week passes when some radical change is not made in the various departments. The less efficient machine is replaced by the better one. Not only the Ford engineers, but the men in the shop, are constantly trying to do things in an easier and better way (Arnold and Faurote, 1915, 308).
>
> The Ford foundries actually reduce costs every day, all the time, continually, and no Ford foundry worker, from top to bottom, ever shows the slightest hesitation in obeying any new instructions whatever (Arnold and Faurote, 1915, 327).

These two paragraphs show that:

- Everyone in the workplace, not just the technical support staff, focuses on continuous improvement. Kaizen is part of the organizational culture.
- Standardization locks the "one best way" into place. Everybody follows this "one best way" until a better one supplants it and becomes the new standard.

There is no conceptual difference between this work environment and the continually-improving worker-empowered leading-edge modern workplace.

This section has covered continuous improvement and its synergy with standardization, worker empowerment, and best practice deployment. Continuous improvement plays a central role in lean manufacturing, which the next section covers in detail.

LEAN MANUFACTURING

Lean manufacturing is essentially scientific management as described by Frederick Winslow Taylor, practiced in many early twentieth century American workplaces, and developed to the utmost at the Ford Motor Company. Remember that Shigeo Shingo, one of Japan's foremost lean manufacturing pioneers, received his flash of enlightenment from Taylor's *Principles of Scientific Management*. Ford, meanwhile, described several lean manufacturing techniques, which this section covers, explicitly:

- **5S-CANDO.** This is a program for cleanliness and neatness in the workplace. Ford's workers cleaned and repaired (i.e., maintained) their equipment continuously.
- **Small lot and single-unit processing.** Ford realized that single-piece or small lot flow is superior to batch processing. Single-minute exchange of die (SMED) often plays an important role in reducing lot sizes.

- **Motion efficiency and task subdivision.** Ford worked to reduce transportation distances and worker motion, especially handling, positioning, and walking—take the work to the people, do not require people to walk to the work. This also includes spacing machines closely. Ford says, "we put more machinery per square foot than any other factory in the world—every foot of space not used carries an overhead expense. We want none of that waste. Yet . . . no man has too little room" (Ford, 1922, 90). Keeping everything in motion also mitigates against the accumulation of inventory.

Just-in-time (JIT) manufacturing and its relatives, Goldratt's theory of constraints (TOC) and synchronous flow manufacturing (SFM), are also aspects of lean manufacturing. They receive their own major sections in this chapter. The next sections cover 5S-CANDO, small lot and single-unit processing, single-minute exchange of die (SMED), and motion efficiency and task subdivision.

5S-CANDO

The Ford Motor Company succeeded in going from what Norwood (1931, 49) calls the traditional 3S—smoke, soot, and smudge—of factory work to what Japan calls 5S (see Table 8-1). Rudyard Kipling defined the basic idea in *The 'Eathen*:

> *The 'eathen in 'is blindness bows down to wood an' stone;*
> *'E don't obey no orders unless they is 's own;*
> *'E keeps 'is side-arms awful: 'e leaves 'em all about,*
> *An' then comes up the regiment an' pokes the 'eathen out.*

> *All along o' dirtiness, all along o' mess,*
> *All along o' doin' things rather-more-or-less,*
> *All along of abby-nay, kul, an' hazar-ho,*
> *Mind you keep your rifle an' yourself jus' so!*

> *[abby-nay = "Not now." kul = "Tomorrow."*
> *hazar-ho = "Wait a bit."]*

In this situation, tools are left all over the place. With so much abby-nay, kul, and hazarho in the system, there is obviously no scheduled cleaning or preventive maintenance. This promotes dirtiness, mess, and a state of affairs in which the organization can be displaced—poked out—by a more effective competitor.

Kipling also described the key goal of the so-called Japanese 5S program (CANDO is the English acronym), whose elements appear in Table 8-1:

Gettin' clear o' dirtiness, gettin' done with mess,
Gettin' shut o' doin' things rather-more-or-less;
Not so fond of abby-nay, kul, nor hazar-ho,
Learns to keep 'is rifle an' 'isself jus' so!

When the Ford Motor Company first ventured into iron mining, here is what happened:

The first job was to clean up—that is always the first thing to do in order to find out what you are about. . . . There is a tradition that all kinds of mining have to be dirty. We cannot afford to have dirt around—it is too expensive.

This [mining] camp looks like a suburban colony—everything is painted and kept painted a light color, so the least bit of dirt will show. We do not paint to cover up dirt—we paint white or light gray in order that cleanliness may be the order of things and not the exception (Ford, 1926, 48).

When Ford bought the Detroit, Toledo, & Ironton Railroad during the early 1920s, the workforce was demoralized and the public and the shippers disliked the railroad. The roadbed was "hardly fit for use," and the rolling stock (cars) and motive power (locomotives) "were all but junk." In 1925, after the railroad had been under Ford for a few years, it earned $2.5 million dollars: about half what he paid for it. It's hard to argue with a 50 percent return on investment.

The first step was to clean up the railroad. "Put all machinery in the best possible condition, keep it that way, and insist on absolute cleanliness everywhere in order that a man may learn to

Table 8-1. 5S-CANDO

5S	CANDO
Seiri = **Clearing up**	**Clearing up**
"When in doubt, throw it out." Your best friends include your wastebasket and online auction services like e-Bay, where all kinds of serviceable but unwanted equipment is bought and sold. (Even forklifts, office equipment, and machine tools appear on E-bay.) Ford's River Rouge plant provided enough waste receptacles that no one had to take more than six steps to reach one, and these were emptied every two hours (Norwood, 1931, 56). (Walt Disney's theme parks either adopted this idea or developed it independently; waste receptacles are very copious.) Red-tag or otherwise identify items that are apparently nonessential. If no one claims them or cites a need for them, remove them from the workplace. A three-tier classification for items is useful. Keep frequently used items at the workstation. Those that require regular but not frequent use should be near the workstation. Rarely used items should be kept outside the work area.	
Seitori = **Organizing**	**Arranging**
"A place for everything and everything in its place." Every tool should have a place. For example, draw outlines on wall racks for specific wrenches. Socket wrench boxes have specific places for each socket. Employees do not have to waste time searching for tools.	
Seiso = **Cleaning**	**Neatness**
Keep everything clean. This makes it easier to find equipment leaks and dropped parts. It also prevents dirt and debris from getting into the product or the equipment. Sweeping, mopping, cleaning, and painting took place at the River Rouge plant continuously; it used 5,000 gallons (almost 19,000 liters) of machine-blue paint every month. The long-handled window cleaning sponge with a water channel through the handle was developed at Ford (Norwood, 1931, 5253). Air suction systems furnished "scores upon scores of invisible brooms that not only keep air and lungs clean, but greatly reduce the task delegated to [brooms] of corn and fibre" (Norwood, 1931, 57).	
Shitsuke = **Discipline**	**Discipline**
"Mind you keep your rifle an' yourself jus' so." Make preventive maintenance and cleaning routine activities. Incorporate them into work instructions or operating instructions. Maintenance logs should show when preventive maintenance and similar activities took place. (Under ISO 9000, such logs must be up to date and they must conform to the operating instructions.)	
Seiketsu = **Standardization**	**Ongoing improvement**
Ongoing improvement means rooting out additional forms of friction, waste, and inefficiency. Do not let friction become part of the job by working around it. Strive for continuous improvement. Deployment of best practices across the organization is a form of standardization.	

respect his tools, his surroundings, and himself" (Ford, 1926, 199). This is, in fact, one of the three Ford principles of management. The others involve breaking down organizational barriers—

a principle commonly associated with W. Edwards Deming and Tom Peters—and paying the workers well. Ford continues (1926, 201), "Give a man a good tool—a fancy polished tool—and he will learn to take care of it. Good work is difficult excepting with good tools used in clean surroundings."

Visual controls are part of 5S-CANDO, and the D.T. & I. Railroad under Ford used standard racks for all tools and materials. Each tool had a specific place for storage, so workers didn't have to waste time looking for tools. This procedure appeared in other U.S. workplaces as well. The System Company's (1911) *How Scientific Management is Applied* shows very orderly tool rooms (Figure 8-1).

From *How Scientific Management Is Applied*. Plate VI's caption reads in part, "This corner of a tool room illustrates the axiom of order—a place for everything, everything in its place." Photos © 1911, The System Company, believed to be in the public domain due to age.

Plate VII shows a wall rack for machine tools, with the explanation, "...notice that the mnemonic symbol for each tool is on a little card above it."

Figure 8-1. "Seitori" (arranging) in American factories

Preventive maintenance was standard practice at Ford during the 1920s. "... machines do not often break down, for there is continuous cleaning and repair work on every bit of machinery in the place." The Ingersoll milling machine that processed the front-axle body at the Highland Park plant is an example:

The gangs of mills are on individual arbors, so as to be removed from the machine and replaced as unit assemblies. [The arbor is the shaft or spindle that supports and rotates a cutting tool, or the part on which a cutting tool works.] Five tool-grinders are constantly employed in keeping up these gang-mill assemblies, several complete sets of which are used, so there is no delay in changing.

The regular practice is to change these gang-mill assemblies once in four hours, removing them from the milling machine before the work shows any sign of not being within gauge limits (Arnold and Faurote, 1915, 165–166).

Taylor (1911a, 117) described explicitly a "tickler system" for scheduled preventive maintenance. Notices "... come out at proper intervals throughout the year for inspection of each element of the system and the inspection and overhauling of all standards as well as the examination and repairs at stated intervals of parts of machines, boilers, engines, belts, etc., likely to wear out or give trouble, thus preventing breakdowns and delays." Scheduled preventive maintenance supports ISO 9000:1994 section 4.9, Process Control (ISO 9000:2000 section 7.5.1).

Small Lot and Single-unit Processing

An ideal manufacturing or service system handles one piece at a time. This is conducive to continuous flow; the work flows like liquids or gases in a chemical plant. Batching promotes inventory accumulation and, even if it does not affect the factory's capacity, it increases the cycle time for individual jobs. Levinson and Rerick (2002, 136–138) show that batching also complicates statistical process control (SPC) by introducing an extra variance component: batch-to-batch as well as piece-to-piece.

Lead time is the time between an order's placement and its delivery. Cycle time is the time between a job's start and its completion. The two are related, of course, unless the company keeps an inventory of finished goods from which it can fill orders. The idea of lean manufacturing is to make to order and not keep large inventories of anything. Even one batch operation in an otherwise continuous-flow environment adds cycle time and complicates just-in-time (JIT) and synchronous flow (SFM) manufacturing.

Heat treatment appears frequently, and usually in unpleasant contexts, as an issue in traditional metalworking processes. Most relevant to this discussion is the fact that heat treatment often involves batching. Heat-treatment was "Herbie [capacity-limiting constraint] II" in Goldratt and Cox's (1992) *The Goal*. The section on process simplification and improvement describes how axles from a Ford heat-treatment operation had to be straightened after-ward—a nominally value-adding operation but actually 100 per-cent rework—because of distortion. Distortion of heat-treated parts was also the reason supposedly interchangeable parts didn't interchange at the Colt Armory during the nineteenth century (Womack and Jones, 1996, 153 and note 4 on 322). Batch-and-queue operations can increase cycle time even when they are not constraints. Parts from a preceding single-unit process must wait to form at least a partial load for, as an example, a heat-treatment oven. We should worry as soon as we see the word wait, and rightly so; this is non-value-adding cycle time. When the parts come out of the oven, all but one must wait at a subsequent sin-gle-unit process.

A large heat-treatment oven at Omark, a manufacturer of chain-saw chain, prevented the company from getting its lead times below three days. The problem was specifically batching and queuing. The company considered small-lot ovens and single-unit laser proces-sors, then it found a steel alloy that did not require heat treatment (Schonberger, 1986, 83). This reduced the lead time to one day.

Ford recognized the value of single-piece flow, and he quoted a blacksmith employee's observations on this:

If I was amazed when I started to work in the forge depart-ment, how can I hope to express my feeling at the won-derful improvement in production methods? The heating of the steel stock is perhaps the best illustration of my point. The method in use when I was hired was to put twenty-five bars in the furnace at one time; then they were heated and forged and another lot put into the furnace, so there was always some time lost between "heats." But thought was applied to this business, and now the bars travel along rails through a regulated furnace which needs only one man to load, and the rest is done by an electrically operated automatic pusher. Thus there is a constant stream of correctly heated bars being supplied to the hammerman with a minimum of labour expended in the operation (Ford, 1930, 136).

The merits of single-unit flow were apparently under consideration fifteen years earlier. The Highland Park plant annealed crank box blanks in 900-unit batches with a 10.5-hour cycle time. Six cars, each with 150 blanks, went into the oven at 20:00, came out at midnight (0:00), and then cooled until 06:30.

This first annealing practice will soon be obsolete. A furnace now under construction is served by an endless chain moving up and down, which is fitted with pendulum blank-carriers to take the blanks individually as they come through the press die, carry them upward about 60 feet [18.3 m] in the furnace uptake, giving ample heating time, and then carry the blanks downward 60 feet in the open air, giving plenty of cooling time before the blanks reach the oiling table... (Arnold and Faurote, 1915, 86–87).

Shingo (1987, 54–55) shows how to reduce an oven's batch sizes if it is possible to open the oven without interfering with work in process. An annealing oven could hold 40 pieces and the process took 30 minutes. The next operation could process one piece per minute. Shingo said to divide the oven into four sections, to deliver 10 pieces every 7.5 minutes as scheduled in Table 8-2. This is better than 40 pieces every 30 minutes.

Ford's workers also found a way around making large batches of one part and then another through the following alternative to single-minute exchange of die (SMED), which the next subsection discusses. The idea appears to be that a single pouring operation could produce the entire set of bushings (these are liners or

Table 8-2. Reducing batch sizes in a large oven

Loading and unloading times for 10-piece batches			
Section 1	Section 2	Section 3	Section 4
0–30	7.5–37.5	15–45	22.5–52.5
30–60	37.5–67.5	45–75	52.5–82.5

sleeves for guiding parts into place, or reducing friction) in a car's bill of materials (BOM).

> The patterns used for casting small bushings resemble several bushings united by gates with four or five gates united at one end to form a good-sized cluster. By using such a pattern, only one mould and one pouring operation are necessary to produce a large number of bushings (Ford, 1926, 74).

Single-minute Exchange of Die (SMED)

Single-minute exchange of die eliminates non-value-adding setup times from operations. The term *exchange of die* is misleading because the underlying idea applies to any activity that involves setup, not only to machine tools that use actual die.

SMED is an important tool for reducing lot sizes. Faster setups mean there is less need to batch parts for efficiency. In an ideal (single-unit flow) world, one could do an individual setup for each piece. The basic canon of SMED is to know when the operation adds value to the product or service. Imai (1997, 22–23) says, "There is far too much *muda* [waste, often wasted time] between the value-adding moments. We should seek to realize a series of processes in which we can concentrate on each value-adding process—Bang! Bang! Bang!—and eliminate intervening downtime."

This principle predates not only Imai but Ford and Gilbreth (in whose *Motion Efficiency* an example appears). It goes back to when the value-adding moment was a literal "Bang!"—a volley from musket-armed infantry. Military necessity often drives continuous improvement. It even led to what Dr. Shigeo Shingo would later call *external setup.* An internal setup is one that requires the tool to stop; it takes time away from the tool's operation. External setups do not take time away from the tool's value-adding operation.

The musket cartridge with its premeasured powder charge was an example of an external setup. It removed the steps of opening a powder horn, measuring out a charge, and closing the powder horn. Hunters did not have to worry about loading efficiency since, if their first shot missed, the target would be long gone by the time they reloaded for a second. Soldiers had to fire as rapidly as possible because their targets rarely ran away and they shot back. A Dutch engraving from 1606 (Held, 1957, 40–41) shows a loading drill with a matchlock musket and wooden powder cartridges.

Meanwhile, Baron von Steuben's "Regulations for the Discipline of the Troops of the United States" (1779) and its loading drill for flintlock muskets (Held, 1957, 112) even specifies the number of motions for each step. For example, "Handle—Cartridge!" specifies, "One motion." Each step of the loading drill prescribed exactly what the soldier was to do. Motion efficiency and "one best way" preceded the work of Frank and Lillian Gilbreth and Frederick Winslow Taylor, by more than a century. Von Steuben's loading drill also required the soldier to count a second between each motion. This sounds like takt time, the time a factory allots to each workpiece or job, and it synchronizes all the workstations so none get ahead or behind.

SMED involves breaking the paradigm of treating what is really a setup as part of the operation. Although Shingo is the best-known exponent of SMED, it originated in the United States no later than 1911. The reference does not, unfortunately, say who was responsible for this innovation:

> In a certain shop with which we are familiar a piece had to have several holes of different sizes drilled in it, a jig being provided to locate the holes. The drills and the sockets for them were given to the workman in a tote box. The time study of this job revealed several interesting facts.

First, after the piece was drilled the machine was stopped, and time was lost while the workman removed the piece from the jig and substituted a new one. This was remedied by providing a second jig in which the piece was placed while another piece was being drilled in the first jig, the finished one being removed after the second jig had been placed in the machine and drilling started.

—Robert Thurston Kent, introduction to Gilbreth (1911)

Gilbreth (1911, Figure 17) provides another example of setup reduction: "Two horse carts with horses changed from the empty to the full carts will require fewer and cheaper motions than any other methods of transportation." The idea is that the horses need not wait for the non-value-adding activity of loading and unloading the cart. The same concept can apply to trucking operations. When it takes a long time to unload a trailer, disconnect it and connect the tractor to a full trailer. The truck driver can depart with a full load, thus improving utilization of both the driver and the tractor. Do not accept as a given that the driver and tractor must wait while the trailer is loaded or unloaded. Railroad operations have used this practice for a long time. A rail car might be left on a siding for loading or unloading while the locomotive goes off and does something else.

The Ford Highland Park factory did make specific efforts to externalize setups. "A sufficient number of spare milling cutters are provided for each operation to ensure having a newly ground set of cutters on hand before change is needful" (Arnold and Faurote, 1915, 73–74). Grinding the cutter is, or should be, external setup and there is no reason to shut the tool down while it takes place. The reference adds, ". . . the setting of the cutters is facilitated by table marks and suitable straight edges so as to consume the least possible time, and to ensure the utmost attainable accuracy in cutter placing."

SMED improves a production line's flexibility by enabling it to produce a wide variety of products. Despite its reputation for single-purpose mass production, Ford production equipment was apparently quite capable of switching product lines:

... while the Ford factory was at present equipped for building Ford cars only, yet all of the machine-tools had been designed with such cunning foresight that "by merely changing the dies" they would produce farm tractors just as well as they had before produced Ford cars (Arnold and Faurote, 1915, 63).

Ford cites an improvement in a differential housing welding operation that could qualify as SMED or, more generally (since it didn't involve changing die), a deliberate effort to reduce non-value-adding setup time. The older system, which allowed three operators to make twenty-five to thirty units per hour, involved several activities that look like non-value-adding setup. These included aligning a channel ring in its cradle ("adjust" or "align" is a non-value-adding activity), dropping clamps into place, and actuating the clamps with compressed air. A neck was slipped over an expanding collet (which also served as the electrode) and aligned. After the welding was complete, the three clamps were removed. Clamping and unclamping the work are, of course, part of the setup.

In the new system, the operator put the stock into the welding machine, applied a clamp (apparently only one), and opened a compressed air valve to clamp all the parts simultaneously (Ford, 1930, 197–198). One operator could produce fifty to sixty pieces per hour with this machine, or six times more than with the old system. The weld was also more uniform.

Another automatic welder relieved its operator of the need to place lugs by hand. It loaded them automatically from a magazine and used a magnet and a locating fixture to position them automatically for welding. When the operator had to load the lugs by hand he could produce 200 brake shoes per hour. The automatic machinery increased production to 450 an hour. It was also safer because the operator did not have to put his hand in the machine.

Under the old system the operator inserted the lugs in position, placed [non-value-adding] one end of the brake shoe between them, and completed the weld. Then he removed [non-value-adding] the shoe, inserted two new lugs, set [non-value adding] the other end of the shoe between them, and completed the weld.

The new machine feeds lugs into proper position along miniature tracks so arranged that new lugs do not take position until the previous operation has been completed. They are held in position by magnets, and the position of the brake shoe between them is controlled by the machine. [The machine thus relieved the worker of considerable non-value-adding activity.] The shoe can be fitted readily by the operator almost without watching (Ford, 1930, 199).

Robinson (1990, 322–323) uses a plastic vacuum molding process as another example of SMED. It requires the following steps:

1. Join a moveable mold and a fixed mold.
2. Pump the air from the mold to create a vacuum.
3. Inject resin.
4. Open the mold and remove the finished part.

The process adds value when the resin enters the mold—Bang! The removal of the air is a preliminary step, a part of the setup. It seems to be internal setup because the mold must be closed before the vacuum can be created. Shigeo Shingo shows how to turn it into external setup. If the mold volume is small enough, provide a tank that is 1,000 times as big. Pump the air out of the tank while the mold is making a part. When the mold is ready for the next part, close it and open the valve that connects the mold to the tank. The vacuum tank will pull 99.9 percent of the air from the mold instantly and the pump can then pull a high vacuum on what remains. The removal of 99.9 percent of the air has thus changed from internal to external setup.

In summary, to implement SMED, you must:

• Identify where the operation truly adds value (Bang!) and aspects that are really setup. Use innovative techniques to make the setup external to the operation. Apply this thinking to service as well as manufacturing activities.

- Focus on the constraint, or operation whose capacity limits the factory's production. Application of SMED at a non-constraint will not improve the factory's capacity. It does counteract the harmful effects of batch-and-queue production and may therefore reduce cycle time.

Parallel Processing and Testing to Keep Work Moving

Ford performed bushing production and metallurgical testing in parallel. A sample of the metal went to a testing laboratory before pouring, but pouring did not wait for the test results. The castings were usually ready for finishing by the time the fracture test results came back. The rough castings and their fracture testing moved in parallel and met again before finishing. The work did not stop to wait for the test results, it kept moving while the test was in progress. This probably kept inventory from building up, and it certainly kept the pouring operation from waiting for the laboratory.

If the test results were not ready the bushings did not proceed to finishing. It's possible that the time on the finishing machines was too expensive to risk on potentially bad castings. If something was wrong, however, it probably wasn't too costly to remelt the bushings and start over. The idea of letting the work progress and letting the test results catch up to it can help reduce inventory and cycle times (see Figure 8-2). (If the work is defective, it must not create problems or costs in the operations through which it progresses. It must not, under the theory of constraints, pass through the capacity-constraining operation.)

This procedure is synergistic with ISO 9001:1994 section 4.8 (ISO 9000:2000 7.5.2), Product Identification and Traceability, because the laboratory results must be traceable to the factory lots.

Tool Efficiency

Avoidance of stop-and-start actions improves tool efficiency and may avoid wear on the equipment. Ford (1926, 75–76) describes the operation of an automatic lathe:

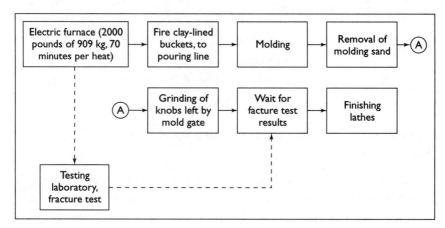

Figure 8-2. Work and inspection/testing in parallel

The automatic lathe needs but one speed and one size of arbor. Instead of being thrown out of gear every few seconds, the direction of the feed is reversed, and rather than have the machine run idle while the finished bushing is being replaced by one in the rough, two arbors are supplied, the cutting tool operating between them like a shuttle.

Here is another example of turning a non-value-adding motion into a value-adding one. The Highland Park plant made radiators by stacking the sheet metal fins in a rack. Another rack, or mold, received the tubes. This fixture then aligned the radiator tubes with the holes in the fin fixture for ramming through the fins. "The machine works in both directions so that when the ram is being withdrawn from one set of molds, it is forcing the tubes into the corresponding one on the other side" (Arnold and Faurote, 1915, 312–313). The value-adding action of ramming tubes into another mold as the machine reversed direction replaced the non-value-adding action of withdrawing the rams from the mold (see Figure 8-3).

This arrangement is also an example of SMED because a new set of tubes and fins could presumably replace the complete assembly at the left while the ram was moving to the right. A filleting machine for crankshaft bearings worked similarly:

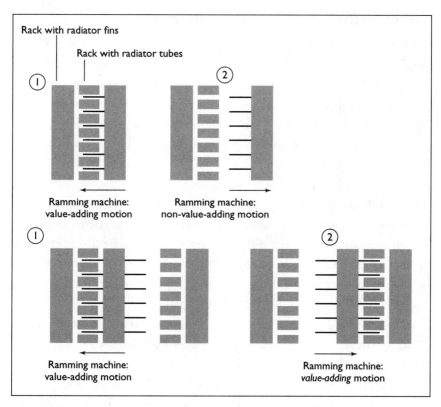

Figure 8-3. Turning a non-value-adding motion into a value-adding one

... the cutters are mounted on rapidly rotating shafts controlled by a hand lever which moves the cutters to the right or left. The cylinder casting, upside down, is deposited on a receiving table. When the lever is in neutral position, cutters are equidistant from the bearings on either side. A movement of the lever to the right fillets the left-hand side of the bearings; a movement to the left fillets the right-hand side of the bearings. The operation is performed in less time than it takes to tell about it and little care is required to perform the operation perfectly, because the movement of the lever is limited in both directions so that only the proper amount of metal can be removed (Arnold and Faurote, 1915, 320).

This machine also incorporates poka-yoke or error-proofing; the operator cannot make a mistake.

Motion Efficiency and Task Subdivision

Ford (1922, 90) cites two specific principles for lean manufacturing. "Dividing and subdividing operations, keeping the work in motion—those are the keynotes of production." Although subdivision of work goes against the concept of autonomous work, which makes a single person or team responsible for an entire assembly, it cuts out wasted motion. When one person had to build a complete product, he or she often had to pick up materials and exchange tools. "Pick up," "put down," and "exchange tools" are phrases that suggest non-value-adding work. Ford was apparently moving back, however, toward providing workers with complete tasks while retaining the efficiencies that came from subdividing them. "Now we are heading back to the old days except that where then one man did the whole of a job, now a machine as far as possible does all of a job" (Ford, 1930, 130).

Today a skilled worker is more likely to run several machines than to perform a repetitive operation. Ford advocated this. Although having each worker and each machine do only one task usually produced the most efficient results (with 1920s-vintage technology), "If a machine can be devised to perform several operations at once, then it would be a waste to have several machines. A man may sometimes as easily perform two operations as one—in which case he performs two operations" (Ford, 1926, 102).

Frank Gilbreth studied bricklayers and discovered that they lowered and raised their entire upper bodies to get each five-pound (2.3 kg) brick. Bricklaying is an ancient trade, and this is yet another example of how people can overlook waste and inefficiency for years or even centuries: "We've always done the job this way and the work gets done." (Readers who don't believe that bricklayers once worked this inefficiently will see "before Gilbreth" and "after Gilbreth" pictures in Chapter 9.) Placement of the bricks at waist level and within easy reach of the workers increased productivity immensely, and Ford adopted this principle quickly: "Stooping to the floor to pick up a tool or a part is not productive labor—therefore, all material is delivered waist-high" (Ford, 1926, 103).

Employees were not to move to the work, the work was to come to employees. Walking from one task to another was waste motion. The assembly line, and particularly the conveyor belt, brought the task to the workers. Ford (1922, 80) laid down the following rules for designing jobs. They should be very familiar to work cell designers and other lean manufacturing practitioners.

We now have two general principles in all operations— that a man shall never have to take more than one step, if possibly it can be avoided, and that no man need ever stoop over.

The principles of assembly are these:
1. Place the tools and the men in the sequence of the operation so that each component part shall travel the least possible distance while in the process of finishing.
2. Use work slides or some other form of carrier so that when a workman completes his operation, he drops the part always in the same place—which place must always be the most convenient place to his hand—and if possible have gravity carry the part to the next workman for his operation. [Arnold and Faurote (1915) mention these work slides and their contribution to efficiency frequently.]
3. Use sliding assembly lines by which the parts to be assembled are delivered at convenient distances.

Ford cited Chicago meat packing operations as an inspiration for the assembly line and for breaking jobs into small tasks:

I believe that this was the first moving line ever installed. The idea came in a general way from the overhead trolley that the Chicago packers use in dressing beef. We had previously assembled the fly-wheel magneto in the usual method. With one workman doing a complete job [autonomous assembly] he could turn out from thirty-five to forty pieces in a nine-hour day, or about twenty minutes to an assembly. What he did alone was then spread into twenty-nine operations; that cut down the assembly time to thirteen minutes, ten seconds. Then we raised the height of the line eight inches—this was in 1914—and cut the time to seven minutes. . . . The assembling of the motor, formerly done by one man, is now divided into eighty-four operations—those men do the work that three times their number formerly did (Ford, 1922, 81).

Arnold and Faurote (1915, 102–103, 105–106) cite the following improvements from assembly line operation and task subdivision:

1. Chassis assembly time by a single worker was 840 minutes. Use of a moving line reduced this to 93 minutes, a 9× productivity improvement.
2. Motor assembly required 594 minutes in October 1913. A moving line reduced this to about 238 minutes, a 2.5× or 150 percent productivity improvement.
3. Subdivision of the operation and installation of a work slide doubled the rate of piston and connecting rod assembly, with no other changes in tooling or methods. Furthermore, quality improved. There were no rejections where, under the former system of having one worker do the entire assembly of piston and rod, there were numerous returns from the motor assembly line.

Taiichi Ohno adopted Ford's and Taylor's motion efficiency principles for the Toyota production system. The physical equation for work is another way to state this principle: work equals force (or effort) times distance, not force. Effort that does not advance the process (distance) is not work even if it's exertion.

This is why I frequently emphasize that worker movement in the production area must be working, or value-adding movement. Moving is not necessarily working. Working means actually advancing the process toward completing the job. Workers must understand this (Ohno, 1988, 58).

The application of motion efficiency principles seemed to make jobs mindlessly repetitive. "The man who places a part does not fasten it—the part may not be fully in place until after several operations later. The man who puts in a bolt does not tighten it" (Ford, 1922, 83). Why shouldn't the person who places the bolt tighten it? This might require him to pick up and put down a tool for every bolt—a non-value-adding action that is no more interesting or intrinsically motivating than placing the bolt. If another person tightens the bolt, however, he can keep the tool in his hands and there is no wasted motion. Two people working this way can place and tighten far more bolts than two that each perform the entire job. They can therefore earn higher wages, and this was Ford's principal objective.

Independent work groups of the pre-Ford era actually subdivided tasks themselves for greater efficiency, per Rudyard Kipling's description of fish cleaning in *Captains Courageous* (late 19th century). The first man cut the fish open and nicked the sides of its neck (to make it easier to remove the head). The second removed the cod's liver, tore off the head, and pulled out the entrails. A third cut out the backbone and threw the cleaned fish into a tub of salt water. The autonomous complete job of cleaning a fish would have required each person to pick up and put down his knife twice per fish. Furthermore, the person who did the unpleasant task of removing the head and organs wore mittens, which might have made it harder to use a knife.

It was even better when machinery performed mindlessly repetitive tasks. The Ford Company had, by 1930, invented a machine that placed washers on screws automatically. An automatic kickback mechanism outside the hopper ejected odd-size screws and the machine was jam-proof (Ford, 1930, 190–191). A piston-rod assembly operation took three minutes, which did not seem unreasonable. A single worker performed six operations:

1. Push the pin out of the piston.
2. Oil the pin.
3. Slip the rod into place.
4. Put the pin through the rod and piston.

5. Tighten a screw.

6. Open a different screw.

An observant foreman could not understand why the task required three minutes. He watched the workers and timed their motions with a stopwatch. He discovered that the worker spent four out of nine hours walking.[5] "The assembler did not go off anywhere, but he had to shift his feet to gather in his materials and to push away his finished piece" (Ford, 1922, 88). The employee *labored* for nine hours a day but only five hours of this effort produced anything of value. The job was redesigned so that, instead of having each worker perform all six of the necessary operations, each worker performed two. They no longer had to change their positions, and production increased from 175 pieces in a nine-hour day for 28 workers to 2,600 in an eight-hour day for 7 workers: a 66fold increase.

Arnold and Faurote (1915, 108) provide some details on this job and its redesign, as shown in Table 8-3.

Arnold and Faurote (1915, 237–238) describe another job in which the worker made 7,000 pieces per day. Elimination of the following motions saved 35,000 motions per hand per day:

1. Take both hands off levers (non-value-adding).
2. Pick up (non-value-adding) a file in both hands.
3. File burrs off the part (required, but consider this as form of 100 percent rework. Can burrs be avoided? Maybe not, but think about it.)
4. Lay file down (non-value-adding).
5. Re-grasp levers, both hands (non-value-adding).

Tools were brought to workers. Ford had tried a supply room where workers lined up to get tools. However,

> We found that it often cost us twenty-five cents' worth of a man's time (not counting overhead) to get a thirty-cent tool. With that, we abolished the central tool room—a man cannot be paid high wages for standing around waiting for tools (Ford, 1926, 103).

Table 8-3. Elimination of wasted motion through job redesign

Original job design (one worker)	
Preparation, non-value-adding actions (my comments)	**Step, per reference**
Pick up the hammer.	Drive out pin with special hand hammer.
Put down the hammer.	Oil the pin by dipping its end in a box of oil. By hand.
	Slip the pin into the eye-rod. By hand.
Pick up a screwdriver.	Turn the pin to take a screw. Screwdriver.
Exchange screwdriver for hand brace.	Turn in the pinch screw. Hand brace.
Exchange hand brace for open-end wrench. Put the wrench down. Pick up the special tool.	Tighten screw with open-end wrench. Put in the cotter pin, and spread the pin end with a special tool.
185 seconds, no inspection. Average production, 175 pistons and rods per 9 worker-hours.	
Redesigned job: split into three operations	
(1) Drive out the pin, oil the pin, insert the pin-end into the piston.	
(2) Place the rod in the piston, pass the pin through the rod and the piston. Use the screwdriver to turn the pin into position to accept the screw, turn the screw in with the brace.	
(3) Tighten the screw with the open wrench, place the cotter pin by hand, and spread the cotter pin ends with the special tool.	
(4) Inspection and placement of the piston on its proper shelf. Pistons were sorted into four weight classes for pairing in the engine block.	
There were six assemblers per inspector, and the average time was 84 worker-seconds per assembly, a 120 percent improvement. (It is quite possible that subsequent improvement took place to achieve the 66-fold improvement that Ford described in 1922.)	

The undirected worker spends more of his time walking around for materials and tools than he does in working; he gets small pay because pedestrianism is not a highly paid line (Ford, 1922, 80).[6]

The River Rouge plant extended this concept even further. Assembly workers stood on conveyors—essentially moving sidewalks—so they would not have to walk while they worked on a moving chassis.

Thus a workman is not obliged to divide his attention between his legs and his work. He rides with the job. When he completes it he steps off the walk, takes a few paces to the rear, meets the next car requiring his attention, returns to the walk and again goes to work! (Norwood, 1931, 19)

The assembly line layout is not, however, the last word. Imai (1997, 80) points out that transportation of work, even by conveyor belts, is another form of waste. "Whenever we notice a conveyor in *gemba* [the real, or value-adding, workplace], our first question should be, 'can we eliminate it?'" Transportation adds no value to the parts and it can damage them. The best factory layout depends on the nature of the process and the product.

Cellular Manufacturing and Unitary Machines

A work cell consists of a closely spaced and sequential set of tools that can make a specific part, or a family of similar parts (group technology). It eliminates the need to transport work from one part of the shop to another. This reduces non-value-adding work and helps reduce inventory and cycle time. It also promotes single-piece flow because transportation encourages batching into cartloads or forklift-loads.

Although the famous assembly line seems to bear little relationship to cellular manufacturing, Ford described the concept explicitly (1922, 83–84):

We started assembling a motor car in a single factory. Then as we began to make parts, we began to departmentalize so that each department would do only one thing. As the factory is now organized each department makes only a single part or assembles a part. A department is a little factory in itself. The part comes into it as raw material or as a casting, goes through the sequence of machines and heat treatments, or whatever may be required, and leaves that department finished.

My Life and Work also says explicitly that machines are placed as close together as possible and in the sequence of operations. The concept actually goes back even further. Per H.L. Gantt, "In another shop machinery was rearranged so as to bring together allied operations and reduce the time of transportation" (*The System Company*, 1911, 21). Sorensen (1956, 116) credits Walter Flanders for showing Ford and his coworkers how to arrange machine tools at the Mack Avenue and Piquette plants, as do Standard and Davis (1999, 16–17). An excerpt from Bornholdt (1913)[7] describes the placement of machines in the sequence of operations.

Ford made another change that facilitated the work cell layout: the replacement of belt drives by electric motors. The machine tools formerly had to line up with the overhead shaft that drove their belts. Electric motors allowed their placement anywhere (Ford, 1930, 191).

Taiichi Ohno brought this approach to Toyota in 1950:

> As an experiment, I arranged the various machines in the sequence of machining processes. This was a radical change from the conventional system in which a large quantity of the same part was machined in one process and then forwarded to the next process (Ohno, 1988, 11).

Some factories use the process-oriented or job-shop layout. There are grinding departments, drilling departments, and blanking departments. A spaghetti diagram[8] is a tool for mapping the progress of jobs from one department to another (refer to Figure 8-4). It often shows that work travels enormous distances in process-oriented factories that organize departments by tool types. As with workers, pedestrianism is not a well-paid occupation for parts. The Ford Highland Park plant reduced transportation distances deliberately:

> Most of all, however, the Ford engineers have taxed the convolutions of their brain surfaces to shorten the lines of natural work-travel on the factory floors, first by crowding machine-tools together far closer than I have elsewhere seen machine-tools placed, and next by first finding the shortest possible lines of production travel of every car

component, integral or assembled, and then placing every production agent needed either directly in that shortest line, or as near that line as possible, to the extent of placing even the brazing fires where most travel-saving advantage demands.

It is of record that in the old Piquette Street days, ... the first systematizer found that the Ford en-bloc four-cylinders casting traveled no less than 4000 feet [1219 m] in course of finishing, a distance now reduced to about 334 feet [102 m]. [This paragraph shows that the company looked specifically at transportation distances, an analysis that we now associate with spaghetti diagrams.]

... Of course, after what has been here said, the visitor will not expect to find in the Ford shops any examples of orthodox machine-tool placing in generic groups, lathes together in one place, drilling machines, milling machines, and planing machines each in a group by themselves (Arnold and Faurote, 1915, 38–39).

The reference notes the novelty of placing brazing furnaces "in the natural production line of travel" instead of relegating them to separate areas.

A work cell contains all the tools necessary to convert raw materials into finished pieces. It reduces the waste of travel and it also promotes single-piece flow. Consider a three-step process of shaping, heat-treating, and forging steel bars. Figure 8-4 shows a process-oriented layout versus a cellular layout. The arrows show the movement of a hypothetical metal bar.

The arrows that show the progress of a metal bar make the layouts into very simple examples of spaghetti diagrams. In the tool-oriented system forklifts or hand trucks may have to move work from one department to another. Short conveyors may easily suffice in the cellular layout or, for smaller parts, workers can move finished work to the next station or a chute with a single arm motion.

Ford actually went beyond the work cell by taking it to its ultimate limiting case: the unitary machine that does everything. He also described its advantages explicitly. Note that the unitary

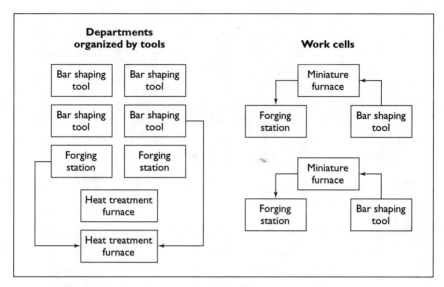

Figure 8-4. Process-oriented versus cellular layouts

arrangement reduces non-value-adding handling and the corresponding opportunity for damage.

> The best that we can do is to combine as many operations as possible, using to a very considerable extent the principle of the turret lathe—which is one of the most important principles in modern manufacturing. For example, if a part had to be drilled, bored, reamed, turned, and faced under the old system it would pass through eight or nine single-purpose machines each managed by a man and there would be a great deal of handling and of opportunity for error. Now most of these operations are performed on a single machine with a single operator who just clamps the part into a turret. At a given time, based on the number of minutes required for the job, the forging is released from the first operation and whirled along to the second station, which may be the drilling. Meanwhile, another rough forging has been loaded and revolved from the loading point to the first station. From the second station the forging goes on to a third, where remachining may be done automatically; then to a fourth, where it may be finished. . . .

Thus there is no lost time or motion; the parts are handled but twice—once in loading as a rough forging and again in removing as a finished part. The machines turn out, in a comparatively few minutes, parts which under the old system would have required hours or even days to build. The handling of parts has been cut down in many cases to two or three operations. Some parts are reduced in cost more than one half and the degree of accuracy more than doubled (Ford, 1930, 130–131).

Such a machine was apparently in use at Highland Park no later than 1915.

The top of the four-arm indexing fixture turns toward the operator. . . . The top of the fixture is the put-on-and-take-off [loading and unloading] station. As the fixture is indexed round, the piston first comes to the drilling station, and has the pin-hole drilled. At the second station a second piston is drilled while the first pin hole is being bored. At the third station a third piston is being drilled while the second piston is being bored and the first piston is being reamed. The next movement of the fixture brings the first piston to the top position, where the attendant removes it, and replaces it with another, and from thence on, so long as the attendant removes and replaces the pistons, all three operations of drilling, boring, and reaming piston pin-holes are in continuous progress, save for the time occupied by drawing the tools back and indexing the fixture from one position to the next following position (Arnold and Faurote, 1915, 208–209).

Ford also defined automatic and quasi-automatic machines (1930, 39–40). Such machines could perform several operations or even complete a part; they were therefore unitary machines. An automatic machine requires no human attention, a quasi-automatic one may require a worker to load the unfinished part and remove the finished one.

Ford also pointed out that not all parts need be made in one factory. For example, casting was moved from Highland Park to River Rouge. This was also the location of the blast furnaces and the company cast parts directly from the furnace cupolas. Decentralization created the need to transport parts from their factory to final assembly but it avoided concentrating too many workers' homes into a small area during an era when many people walked to work.

Other Techniques for Cycle Time Reduction

This chapter cites a design for manufacture principle that says to perform all assembly work from one direction if possible. The idea is to avoid reorientation of the work, a non-value-adding activity. There is nothing wrong, however, with working on a part from several directions at once. A picture of front board and steering gear assembly at the Ford Highland Park plant shows a team assembly process. "The boards travel toward us down the long line seen in the lower picture growing in completeness as they move, each 'team' working simultaneously on opposite sides of the board, adding some step to the assembly" (Arnold and Fauroute, 1915, 7).

Machines also can work on a piece from several directions. Arnold and Faurote (1915, 80) show a Foote-Burt machine that drills 45 holes at once in a cylinder casting from four directions. The reference shows another picture (p. 82) of a Foote-Burt machine that taps 24 holes from three directions. There is no reorientation of the piece during either operation. Page 79 shows an Ingersoll two-spindle milling machine that mills both ends of the engine block's cylinders at the same time.

Visual Controls and the Visual Workplace

Terms like "andon lights" are familiar to students of Japanese manufacturing techniques. The idea is that signals should be easy to understand. Ford instituted something similar for heat-treatment, in conjunction with the idea that quality should not depend on a human's judgment. The section on poka-yoke or error-proofing discusses this further. The reason is that, given enough opportunities, even the most careful and diligent workers make mistakes.

And then there is the pressing to take away the necessity for skill in any job done by any one. The old-time tool hardener was an expert. He had to judge the heating temperatures. It was a hit-or-miss operation. The wonder is that he hit so often. The heat treatment in the hardening of steel is highly important—providing one knows exactly the right heat to apply. That cannot be known by rule-of-thumb. It has to be measured. We introduced a system by which the man at the furnace has nothing at all to do with the heat. He does not see the pyrometer—the instrument which registers the temperature. Coloured electric lights give him his signals (Ford, 1922, 102).

An electrical camshaft timing tester also used lights—one for high and one for low contours—to indicate quality problems. The camshaft was placed in the tester, where it operated valve push rods exactly as it would do in an engine. The tester's push rods, however, opened and closed electrical contacts as the shaft rotated. If all the cams were within specifications no light flashed. If a light flashed the operator could check an index on the hand-wheel that identified the faulty cam. The electric gauge could detect errors of two tenths of a mil (5.1 microns) (Ford, 1926, 77). No operator judgment was necessary.

Gilbreth (1911) discusses the use of colors in the workplace, and Ford's River Rouge plant used uniform colors for certain features. Per Norwood (1931, 5354), all fire alarms and hydrants were red, as were first aid stations. "Things needed quickly can be seen quickly."

This section has covered many familiar lean manufacturing techniques, of which the early Ford Motor Company provides outstanding examples. The next section covers JIT manufacturing, synchronous flow manufacturing (SFM), and their role in inventory reduction.

JUST-IN-TIME (JIT) MANUFACTURING AND INVENTORY REDUCTION

There is no question that Henry Ford and his associates invented JIT:

We have found in buying materials that it is not worth while to buy for other than immediate needs. We buy only enough to fit into the plan of production, taking into consideration the state of transportation at the time. If transportation were perfect and an even flow of materials could be assured, it would not be necessary to carry any stock whatsoever. The carloads of raw materials would arrive on schedule and in the planned order and amounts, and go from the railway cars into production. That would save a great deal of money, for it would give a very rapid turnover and thus decrease the amount of money tied up in materials. With bad transportation one has to carry larger stocks (Ford, 1922, 143).

Sorensen (1956, 231) added that materials went into operations, stayed there, and never stopped until they had become part of a product. He called this situation "a production man's dream come true." Inventory ties up capital, inventory reduction releases capital for productive use. A major part of Goldratt's and Cox's (1992) *The Goal* was enacted at Ford seventy years earlier:

The extension of our business since 1921 has been very great, yet, in a way, all this great expansion has been paid for out of money which, under our old methods, would have lain idle in piles of iron, steel, coal, or in finished automobiles stored in warehouses. We do not own or use a single warehouse (Ford, 1926, 112).[9]

The storage of automobiles on dealer lots is as wasteful as storage in warehouses, and this excerpt supports former Ford CEO Jacques Nasser's proposal to make cars to order on a just-in-time basis.

Inventory and Production Control at Ford

The Highland Park plant held inventory down deliberately.

The factor of safety of component supply is placed by the official production head at a sufficiency for 25,000 cars, a month's assembling supply at the production rate of 1,000 cars per day. This is official, but, as will be seen from the "shortage-chaser" story, the factory practice does not follow the production-head schedule, but quite to the contrary, places a maximum component supply at a sufficiency for 5,000 cars, three-days' assembling, with a danger line at components enough for 3,000 cars (Arnold and Faurote, 1915, 63).

Shortage chasers circulated between customer and supplier departments to ensure that downstream operations never ran out of work. The reference reveals a lean operating philosophy of maintaining the lowest possibly inventory at Highland Park. In fact, the authors question whether the benefits of such a low inventory outweigh the drawbacks of encountering serious shortages:

> This story shows how the Ford shops manage to face a constant shortage probability—perhaps it might be said that the real condition is that of actual shortage of components constantly—and yet escape serious delays.
> ... On the other hand, the shortage chaser now avoids disastrous shortages only by the use of extraordinary care and exertions, together with sudden changes, which are always costly factory expedients and conditions ... The ideal factory condition is undoubtedly that of perpetual tranquility, all operations balanced and co-ordinated, so that there is no "hurry up" pressure required in any direction whatever. Yet this condition of permanent tranquility necessitates the carrying of large values of finished components, with an inevitable increase of fixed charges ...There is a point, of course, where abundant supply carried in the finished stock department becomes an extravagance, and is hence reprehensible; so that it is not easy to say with certainty that the hand-to-mouth component production, even when coupled with the anxieties and makeshifts of the shortage chaser, really costs more than it would cost to carry an ample supply of finished components of all kinds (Arnold and Faurote, 1915, 71–72).

Phrases like "shortage of components constantly" and "hand-to-mouth component production" leave little doubt as to the inventory-lean nature of the Highland Park plant.

The Theory of Constraints

Eliyahu Goldratt's theory of constraints (TOC) is a vital concept in JIT manufacturing, and it is worth explaining here. The theory of constraints says that no process can work more quickly than its slowest operation (see Figure 8-5). This operation is sometimes known as the capacity-constraining resource (CCR).

TOC applies at the factory level only when the factory can sell everything it can make. When it cannot, the market is the constraint. Levinson and Rerick (2002, 195-197) and Goldratt and Cox (1992, 311–313) treat the market-constrained situation in more detail.

The transition from market-constrained to factory-constrained throughput has some very interesting and profound effects on manufacturing economics. For example, rework that is a minor annoyance under an unconstrained system (i.e., in a factory that has excess capacity) can inflict massive opportunity costs in a constrained one.

No factory's production can exceed the capacity of its constraint, or rate-limiting operation. Consider the simple four-step process shown in Figure 8-5.

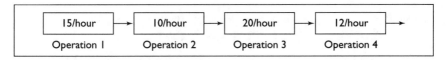

Figure 8-5. The Constraint Operation

The following should be apparent from the figure:

- The factory cannot make more than ten units an hour.
- Operations 3 and 4 cannot make more than 10 units an hour, so management should not blame those departments for "not making their numbers" or "underutilizing their equipment."
- If operation 1 runs at full capacity to maximize equipment utilization, a big pile of inventory will develop in front of operation 2.

- A buffer of inventory should be kept there so Operation 2 never lacks work, but there is a difference between a buffer and a big pile.
- JIT comes into play because Operation 2 *pulls* production starts.

Ford introduces a premise of Goldratt's and Cox's (1992) *The Goal*: time lost at the constraint operation is lost forever.

> Time waste differs from material waste in that there can be no salvage. The easiest of all wastes, and the hardest to correct, is this waste of time, because wasted time does not litter the floor like wasted material (Ford, 1926, 114).
>
> Time, energy, and material are worth more than money, because they cannot be purchased by money. Not one hour of yesterday, nor one hour of today can be bought back. Material wasted, is wasted beyond recovery. These things are in the front rank of values. They are the precious elements out of which all wealth is made (Ford, 1922a, 329).

The irrecoverability of time losses at the constraint has very important and profound economic implications:

- Rework in the constraint can easily be as bad as scrap before the constraint. Rework consumes an irreplaceable unit of the constraint's capacity, and time losses at the constraint are irrecoverable. The factory loses the opportunity to sell a unit of product. The real economic cost—one that the traditional cost accounting system will never detect—is the opportunity cost of the lost sale.
- Experiments that go through the constraint and do not produce sellable product have the same effect. This is why it is best to perform such experiments when there is idle capacity.
- The factory can make up scrap before the constraint because there is excess capacity there.
- It is imperative to keep defective pieces and materials from entering the constraint and wasting its irreplaceable capac-

ity. Error-proofing (poka-yoke) and self-check systems, as described by Shigeo Shingo and used extensively by Ford, help achieve this.

- Scrap after the constraint is irrecoverable.
- Productivity improvement activities like single-minute exchange of die (SMED) improve overall capacity only through deployment at the constraint. (SMED can reduce cycle time at any operation.) In this example, shorter setup times at operations 1, 3, or 4 yield only shorter cycle times and possibly smaller lot sizes. A 10 percent capacity increase at operation 2 increases the factory's capacity 10 percent.

Murphy and Saxena (Levinson, 1998, 159–161) discuss the managerial economic aspects of the theory of constraints (and synchronous flow manufacturing) further, as do Levinson and Rerick (2002). The traditional cost accounting system is completely blind to the economic effects of a switch from market-constrained to factory-constrained sales.

The Origin of JIT and the Assembly Line

Gourley's (1997) *Wheels of Time*, a short biography of Henry Ford, is primarily for children, but the intuitive connection between clocks and Goldratt's and Cox's (1992) drum-buffer-rope (DBR) production management system induced me to buy it. Gourley describes how, as a young boy, Ford took watches apart—and put them back together so they worked. He began to repair watches for neighbors, and he made his own watchmaking tools from his mother's knitting needles and corset stays. "Henry had learned an important lesson. Time was a machine that could be taken apart and put back together" (Gourley, 1997, 12).

Inside a watch, the mainspring slowly unwound and drove the clock wheels. The hour wheel made one revolution every hour. The minute wheel moved faster, making sixty revolutions every hour. Henry realized that his factory could operate the same way. . . .

The speed of the work was carefully timed so that the assembly line did not run too fast or too slow. Where the workers put together the chassis, the line moved 6 feet (2 meters) per minute. Where the workers bolted the front axle to the chassis, the line moved faster, 15 feet (4.5 meters) per minute.

It was like setting the mechanism of a clock.

Henry had created a giant moving timepiece (Gourley, 1997, 30).

The idea of timing, or running a factory like clockwork, recurs in Goldratt's drum-buffer-rope (DBR) production management system. The slowest operation, or constraint, beats the drum; it sets the pace at which the factory can work. A rope (production control information link) ties the release of raw material to the constraint. There is a buffer of inventory only in front of the constraint; this assures that the constraint never falls idle for lack of work in process.

Suppress Variation in Processing and Work Arrival Times

The Charlie Chaplin movie *Modern Times* (1936) satirizes assembly line work. The worker played by Chaplin struggles to keep up with the widgets on the conveyor belt. He sometimes gets ahead and sometimes falls behind, which disconcerts the workers downstream from him. This concept recurs in Goldratt's and Cox's *The Goal* (1992), where some operations cannot keep up with incoming work while others stand idle for want of work. These problems result from variation in processing times and work arrival times. This section shows how suppression of such variation supports lean manufacturing and JIT, specifically by reducing cycle time.

Study of the Ford production system offers enormous rewards when we consider its actual premise. Ford wanted to run a balanced production line (i.e., one in which all the operations have the same capacity, at almost 100 percent utilization). Readers of Goldratt and Cox's *The Goal* (1992) understand the apparent folly of trying to do this. Equation 8-1 (Standard and Davis, 1999, 234–235) reinforces the idea that one cannot run even a single operation, let alone a balanced factory, at 100 percent utilization without accumulating cycle time due to waiting in queue (inventory).

$$CT_q = \left(\frac{c_a^2 + c_e^2}{2}\right) t_e \text{ where}$$

CT_q = cycle time in queue, waiting for the workstation

$c_a = \dfrac{\sigma_a}{t_a}$ = coefficient of variation, arrivals at the workstation

$c_e = \dfrac{\sigma_e}{t_e}$ = coefficient of variation, effective processing time   **(Eq. 8-1)**

$u = \dfrac{t_a}{t_e}$ = utilization

t_a = average time between arrivals at the workstation

t_e = effective processing time

The u/(1u) factor also appeared in a semiconductor manufacturing-related paper demonstrating why it is impossible to even approach 100 percent utilization. Figure 8-6, a plot of the u/(1u) factor, shows why Henry Ford's system "could not have worked." When we consider both *The Goal* and Equation 8-1, Ford's statement that each worker should have all the time he needed but not a second more, not merely at one operation but all operations, sounds like a formula for a deranged nightmare in which inventory buries the entire factory.

This exercise provides excellent and logical reasons the Ford system couldn't have worked. The fact that it *did* work is a perfect illustration of Ford's answer to anyone who says something can't be done: "Go do it." There is enough truth in the u/(1u) factor to be dangerous to anyone who swallows it whole. This is because it is only a half-truth, and the other half is the $\left(\dfrac{c_a^2 + c_e^2}{2}\right)$ factor in Equation 8-1. I have not personally verified its accuracy through simulation and modeling but it is reasonable to expect some factor that is a function of variation in arrival and processing times. The function will have the following nature:

Cycle time in queue = $f(c_a, c_e)$ such that $\dfrac{df(c_a, c_e)}{dc_a} > 0$ and $\dfrac{df(c_a, c_e)}{dc_e} > 0$

Multiplier for cycle time

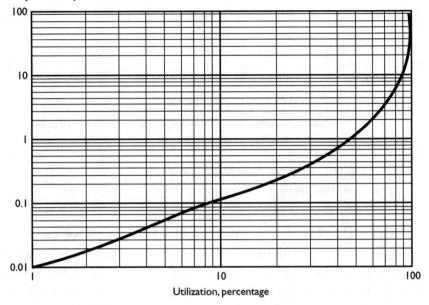

Utilization, percentage

Multiplier for cycle time

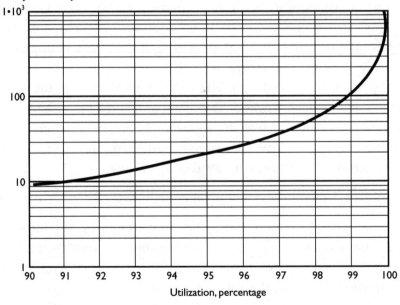

Utilization, percentage

Figure 8-6. Effect of utilization on cycle time in queue

This means cycle time in queue decreases as c_a and c_e, the coefficients of variation for work arrival and work processing times, decrease. The limiting case is $\lim\limits_{c_a \to 0,\ c_e \to 0} f(c_a, c_e) = 0$, and this is almost certainly why Ford's production system worked. If the process requires, for example, exactly ten seconds, and if work arrives at exactly ten-second intervals, there is no reason the operation cannot achieve 99.9999 percent utilization without accumulating any inventory whatsoever, despite the terrifying appearance of the rightmost sides of the graphs in Figure 8-6.

Now recall that Ford subdivided tasks. This not only eliminated non-value-adding steps like picking up and putting down tools, it suppressed variation in processing time (σ_e in Equation 8-1). Since variation in the first workstation's processing time is variation in the arrival time for the second station's work, this approach also suppressed variation in arrival times (σ_a in Equation 8-1). The concepts of clockwork (Ford's thought process) and takt time tie in very closely with suppressing both forms of variation.

Standard and Davis (1999, 83–85) show how task subdivision might reduce variation in task completion times. Consider an operation with a mean completion time of nine minutes and a standard deviation of one minute: $\bar{t} = 9m, \sigma = 1m$. The coefficient of variation is $\frac{\sigma}{\bar{t}} = \frac{1m}{9m} = \frac{1}{9}$. If the coefficient of variation remains constant, subdivision of the job into nine one-minute elements results in individual standard deviations of 1/9 minute. Then $\sigma\left(\sum_{i=1}^{n} t_i\right) = \sqrt{\sum_{i=1}^{n} \sigma_i^2} = \sqrt{9 \times \frac{1}{9^2}} = \frac{1}{3}$.[10] It still takes an average of nine minutes per piece, but the standard deviation is now one-third of what it was.

The opposite applies, however, to automated machine operations:

It should here be noted that in hand-work time is saved by dividing operations, while exactly the reverse is true in automatic-machine work, where time is saved by combining operations performed at one setting or chucking of the work (Arnold and Faurote, 1915, 189–190).

This supports the unitary machine concept, in which a single machine tool performs several tasks and thus avoids non-value-adding loading and unloading cycles.

Assuring Machine Availability

The previous discussion showed how suppression of variation in work arrival and processing times may have allowed the Ford system to run a balanced production line at almost 100 percent capacity. Unplanned machine downtime would, of course, have wreaked havoc in such a system. Avoidance of such downtime may have been another key factor in the system's success.

The River Rouge plant had provisions for machine stoppages and for the too-rapid arrival of work. Empowerment of workers to stop the production line, and the use of andon (warning) lights to draw attention to the stoppage, is a well-known characteristic of advanced Japanese production lines. Norwood (1931, 10) says that workers at the River Rouge plant were not only authorized but expected to stop the line if materials were coming too quickly, as they might during transfer from one line to another. They were also to stop the line if anything else interfered with smooth workflow.

Throwing a switch or pulling a cord at the Rouge lit a warning light in a control booth, and the light identified the stoppage's location. If the light stayed on for more than two minutes the problem required the attention of a "trouble mechanic." If the workers could fix the stoppage within two minutes they did so, and a siren warned everybody that the line was about to start up again. In either case the stoppage's cause and the lost time were recorded. If the conveyor was moving too quickly for the workers its speed was reduced. Mechanical problems were identified and corrected.

Notice that the River Rouge plant logged even those stoppages that the line workers could clear by themselves. Gardner and Nappi (2001) of National Semiconductor reinforce the importance of dealing with the root causes of so-called minor stoppages. The following characteristics help make these stoppages appear to be less important than they are:

1. They are very short: a few minutes at most.
2. The workers can clear them.
3. It is unnecessary to actually repair equipment or use spare parts.

The reference points out correctly that even minor stoppages can not only add up to major losses of production time, but also indicate more serious underlying problems. It's worthwhile to remember that a characteristic of friction is that people can often work around it or fix it. Failure to correct these problems can lead to rework, scrap, or major stoppages that require extensive repair work. The River Rouge plant apparently considered no stoppage too minor for attention.

The Effectiveness of Continuous Flow

Shigeo Shingo compares Japanese and Euro-American manufacturing (1986, 267) as follows. Euro-American manufacturing uses lots and batches. This lengthens lead times, requires anticipatory production, and causes large inventories. Japan uses one-piece flow, which reduces lead times and inventory. Many American companies do produce in inefficient batches, but the one-piece flow method is not originally Japanese:

> We start with the blast furnace and end with a completed motor stacked in a freight car. The casting leaves the foundry on a moving platform or conveyor to one of the assembly lines, it is machined, the other parts are added as it moves along, and when it reaches the end of its line, it is a completed and tested motor—and all of this without a stop (Ford, 1926, 108).

Continuous-flow operations can reduce inventory. Ford describes the progress of a load of iron ore that arrived at the Fordson plant at 8:00 A.M. Monday; it had already been on the ore boat for 48 hours. "Ten minutes after the boat is docked, its cargo will be moving toward the High Line and become part of a charge for the blast furnace. By noon Tuesday, the ore had been reduced to iron, mixed with other iron in the foundry cupolas, and cast. Thereupon follow fifty-eight operations which are performed in fifty-five minutes. . . ." The motor is complete by 3:00 P.M., whereupon it must be sent to an assembly plant. (It was less wasteful to ship subassemblies to assembly plants than it was to ship complete cars.) It could be expected there by 8:00 A.M. on Wednesday; "By noon the car will be on the road in the possession of its owner." If, however, the buyer was in Detroit, the motor did not have to go to a distant assembly plant. The car could be delivered before 5:00 P.M. Tuesday (Ford, 1926, 118–119). In other words, a load of iron ore became automobiles only 33 hours it came off the ore boat.

Arnold and Faurote (1915, 271–273) cite the paradigm, ". . . the assumption that components in progress of finishing cannot be carried in the air between factory operations, but must, of necessity, be supported on the shop floor." The reference describes the role of the work slide and the conveyor belt in promoting continuous flow. They remove the need for workers to reach for parts and then, after finishing their operations, push or carry the finished parts away. The work never pauses and never comes to rest anywhere on the shop floor. This keeps floor space clear, avoids inventory accumulation, and removes the need for movers (and hand trucks and related equipment) who would get in the way of the production workers.

Ford, Toyota, and Drum-Buffer-Rope (DBR) Production Control

SFM uses the drum-buffer-rope (DBR) production control system. The constraint "beats the drum" to set the pace for upstream operations. SFM allows protective inventory at only two places: the constraint (buffer inventory) and shipping (to assure fulfillment of delivery schedules). A rope, or information link, connects the constraint to production starts. Levinson and Rerick (2002, Chapter 7) provide more detail on SFM and DBR.

Figure 8-7 summarizes the key differences between the Ford, Toyota, and DBR production control systems. In each case, workstation A processes material X, and workstation B processes

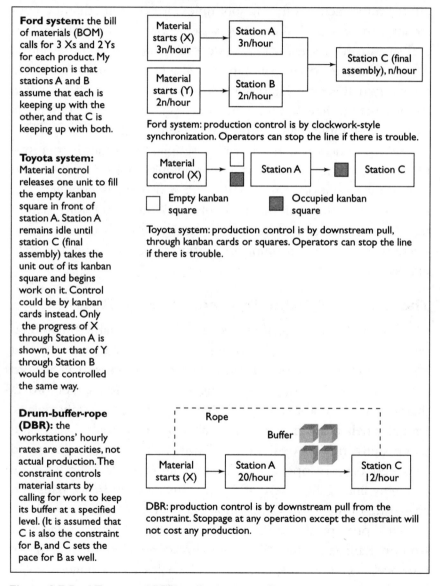

Ford system: the bill of materials (BOM) calls for 3 Xs and 2 Ys for each product. My conception is that stations A and B assume that each is keeping up with the other, and that C is keeping up with both.

Ford system: production control is by clockwork-style synchronization. Operators can stop the line if there is trouble.

Toyota system: Material control releases one unit to fill the empty kanban square in front of station A. Station A remains idle until station C (final assembly) takes the unit out of its kanban square and begins work on it. Control could be by kanban cards instead. Only the progress of X through Station A is shown, but that of Y through Station B would be controlled the same way.

Toyota system: production control is by downstream pull, through kanban cards or squares. Operators can stop the line if there is trouble.

Drum-buffer-rope (DBR): the workstations' hourly rates are capacities, not actual production. The constraint controls material starts by calling for work to keep its buffer at a specified level. (It is assumed that C is also the constraint for B, and C sets the pace for B as well.)

DBR: production control is by downstream pull from the constraint. Stoppage at any operation except the constraint will not cost any production.

Figure 8-7. Ford, Toyota, and DBR production control systems.

material Y. Final assembly at workstation C combines the sub-assemblies from A and B.

The DBR system offers an advantage over the other two. Recall that a stoppage anywhere in the Toyota system will stop the entire line. Stoppage at a non-constraint operation under DBR has no effect on the factory's throughput unless it is so long that the constraint exhausts its buffer. Otherwise, a pre-constraint operation that stops can later use its excess capacity to replenish the buffer. A post-constraint operation can increase its pace to consume the inventory that accumulated while it was stopped The system loses no production time because the constraint, whose capacity limits overall throughput, can run on the contents of its buffer.

SFM production control is also simpler than the Toyota system. In the latter, each downstream operation pulls work from the preceding operation. Under DBR, the constraint is connected to the first operation (or material releases); no other information transfer is necessary. Since the constraint sets the pace for production starts, pre-constraint operations cannot possibly generate excess inventory.

The Need for Reliable Transportation in JIT

Charles Sorensen (1956, 181) describes how unreliable transportation got Ford into the railroad business. He cited the money that was tied up as inventory and raw materials in transit (what Ford called the "float"). Longer shipping times required larger orders that swelled inventories even further and added to freight delays. Irregular deliveries to branch assembly plants increased costs and made deliveries to dealers unreliable. "This irregular demand knocked orderly operation of our Highland Park and Rouge assembly lines galley-west, and there was much biting of nails and shattering of the Third Commandment over this tangled problem."

This prompted Ford's purchase of the Detroit, Toledo, & Ironton Railroad. Once the company controlled the means of transportation, the transportation bottleneck was no longer a problem. The float decreased by 50 percent. The savings on inventory actually paid for the railroad—a harbinger of Wiremold's ability to buy suppliers by using their own inventory as described by Womack and Jones (1996, 147).

JIT manufacturing requires well-controlled and coordinated deliveries. Not only did Ford's factories operate like giant precision clocks, so did his interplant supply system.

> The average shipping time between the factory and the branches is 6.16 days, which means that there is an average of a little more than six days' supply of parts in transit. This is called the "float." If production is at the rate of 8,000 cars a day, there are parts enough in transit to make more than forty-eight thousand complete cars. Thus, the traffic and production departments must work closely together to see that all the proper parts reach the branches at the same time—the shortage of a single kind of bolt would hold up the whole assembly at a branch. The exact status of the float may be determined at any hour of the day. . . .
>
> Whenever a shipment starts, the [railroad] car number is wired to the branch. The factory traffic department traces all shipments and sees that they are kept moving until they are in the branch's territory, where the branch stock traffic man picks them up and follows them through to the unloading platform. We take no chances with the ordinary flow of traffic. Men are stationed at junctions and other points throughout the country to see that the cars are not delayed. The traffic department knows the exact time between different points, and if a car is overdue more than an hour, the fact is known at headquarters (Ford, 1926, 117).

The system achieved this level of shipment tracking without computers, bar codes, or fiber-optic communication channels.

Chapter 9 discusses transportation further, along with concepts like freight management systems (FMSs). The basic idea is that batch-and-queue deliveries, especially with long lead times, can, to use Sorensen's terms, knock the leanest production system galley-west. The same concept applies to suppliers and subcontractors that use batch operations.

Inventory as a Symptom

Inventory is often a symptom, not the cause, of an underlying problem. Standard and Davis (1999) describe inventory as the flower, not the root, of all evil. Removal of the inventory will not correct the underlying problem but correction of the problem often makes the inventory vanish.

Batching, transportation, and storage between operations are often roots of an inventory problem. Ford's Highland Park plant had workers and equipment whose purpose was to move work from one operation to another. It was probably efficient for them to wait for a full load (a consideration that also applies in freight transportation), and this led to inventory accumulation. Highland Park recognized inventory as a hiding place for problems, for example in flywheel manufacturing:

> Before the roll-way placing two truckers were kept busy in transferring the fly-wheels in process of finishing from one machine to another and piling them adjacent to the next operation machine, never in the best place for the worker's convenience. The tools were closely placed and the piles of fly-wheels at each machine and the constant journeys of the two truckers made the flywheel job a place to avoid if possible. Worst of all, the straw boss could never nail, with certainty, the man who was shirking, because of the many work-piles and general confusion due to the shop floor transportation (Arnold and Faurote, 1915, 279).

Modern practitioners recognize that the system in which people work is usually responsible for problems and inefficiencies. The problem that the reference cites might have been due primarily to the system's built-in inefficiencies instead of shirking. On the other hand, bad raw materials or subassemblies can hide in inventory (and in the transportation float, a supply chain management consideration). If parts are in continuous motion on conveyors or gravity slides, with self-check gauges between operations where appropriate, such problems cannot hide for long. The appearance of inventory where it does not belong is an automatic warning signal.

As soon as the roll-ways were placed the truckers were called off, the floor was cleared, and all the straw boss had to do to locate the shirk or operation tools in fault, was to glance along the line and see where the roll-way was filled up (Arnold and Faurote, 1915, 279–280).

Kanban systems that stop the line for trouble at any operation have the same effect. This observation reinforces the likely effectiveness of using work-in-process levels as a process diagnostic tool to help reduce cycle time. Consider, for example, synchronous flow manufacturing (SFM) and its drum-buffer-rope (DBR) production control system. The appearance of inventory anywhere but in the constraint operation's buffer points to an inefficiency that adds cycle time.

The root cause might be a batch-and-queue operation, excessive tool downtime, or unsteady production flow. The identification and subsequent eradication of the problem by conventional quality improvement methods then becomes very straightforward. The factory could, in fact, invoke the modern Ford Motor Company's team-oriented problem solving, eight disciplines (TOPS-8D) at any operation where unplanned inventory appears. The production workers are probably in the best position to discover the problem's root cause.

The following example reinforces the lesson that inventory is usually the flower, not the root, of all evil. In this case the root is long cycle times, which long transportation times promoted. Improvements in freight service at the start of the 1920s reduced Ford's manufacturing cycle time from 22 to 14 days.[11]

> We had been carrying an inventory of around $60,000,000 to insure uninterrupted production. Cutting down the time one third released $20,000,000, or $1,200,000 a year in interest. Counting the finished inventory, we saved approximately $8,000,000 more—that is, we were able to release $28,000,000 in capital and save the interest on that sum (Ford, 1922, 175).

The Value of Time in Project Management

This discussion is not related directly to JIT, but it ties in with the value of time in general.[12] Fairchild Semiconductor's plant in Mountaintop, Pennsylvania, applied this principle during the late 1990s to construct a factory to process eight-inch (200 mm) semiconductor wafers (Murphy, Lauffer, and Levinson, 1997). It took only 13 months to turn a parking lot into an operating semiconductor factory. The company achieved this by doing everything in parallel: construction, equipment purchase and installation, and worker training. It ignored traditional conventions about delaying outlays as long as possible to keep costs down. Equipment was installed as cleanroom floor space became available. The plant began to train experienced production workers who would later work in the new factory, and it hired and trained new workers to replace them in the older part of the plant.

This approach cost extra money, but cost was subordinate to speed. Murphy, Lauffer, and Levinson (1998) explain that a day's delay in opening a factory loses that day's sales revenues.[13] Fairchild followed the advice of the renowned Russian commander Aleksander V. Suvorov (1729–1800): "Money is dear; human life is still dearer; but time is dearest of all. One minute decides the outcome of a battle, one hour the success of a campaign, one day the fate of empires" (Menning, 1986). The new factory was making semiconductor devices well before the last construction worker left the site, and the project was complete in about half the usual time for such a venture. The company gained several benefits:

- An extra year or so of revenue from the new factory.
- More than an extra year of learning and process improvement. The learning curve concept says that production costs go down and yields rise as a factory gains experience.
- Entrance into the marketplace well ahead of potential competitors.

DESIGN FOR MANUFACTURE AND DESIGN FOR ASSEMBLY

Design for manufacture (DFM) and design for assembly (DFA) design quality into the product and reduce manufacturing costs. This supports lean manufacturing by suppressing at least two forms of waste: defects and reducible production costs. This section is synergistic with ISO 9001:1994 section 4.4 (ISO 9000:2000 7.3), Design Control.

Cubberly and Bakerjian (1989, 5-8 through 5-11) list the following basic principles for DFM and DFA:

The design should have as few parts as possible. "Start with an article that suits and then study to find some way of eliminating the entirely useless parts. This applies to everything—a shoe, a dress, a house, a piece of machinery, a railroad, a steamship, an airplane. As we cut out useless parts and simplify necessary ones, we also cut down the cost of making" (Ford, 1922, 14).

Modular designs should be used. Standardization means using as few different parts as possible. Off-the-shelf parts and components are preferable to new ones. "The parts of a specific model are not only interchangeable with all other cars of that model, but they are interchangeable with similar parts on all the cars that we have turned out. You can take a car of ten years ago and, buying today's parts, make it with very little expense into a car of today. Having these objectives the costs always come down under pressure" (Ford, 1922, 149). Ford (1926, 86) adds that his company standardized machine tool components like gears, keys, shafts, and levers. These could be combined to build highly specialized machinery. If a design happened to be unsatisfactory, the machine's major parts were reusable. Maintenance and repair were much easier. A series of books, *Ford Tool Standards*, provided guidance and saved thousands of dollars (1920s money) on the training of new workers. Schonberger (1986, 154) describes the same idea: ". . . standard parts are proven parts. In the past, Xerox typically put 80 percent newly designed components into a new model of copier. The results: a long design cycle followed by a long debugging cycle and tardy entry into the marketplace. Xerox's new 9900 copier used only 30 to 40 percent new components, which helped cut the design-to-market time in half".

Multifunctional parts, and parts with features that aid assembly or inspection, are useful. Keys and slots that allow only proper assembly are forms of error-proofing or poka-yoke.

Fasteners (e.g., screws, nuts, bolts, rivets) should be replaced with snap fits when possible. The cost of driving a screw may be five or ten times the screw's cost. *Today and Tomorrow* (1926, 72–73) discusses replacement of the screwdriver by a sixteen-spindle machine that could drive sixteen screws at once into a starter ring gear. While *Today and Tomorrow* (1926, 73–74) discussed the advantages of the rivet over the screw, *Moving Forward* (1930, 192–194 ff.) devotes considerable attention and enthusiasm to welding, which removed the need for fasteners. Welding interested Ford because of his interest in stamped or forged parts, which were stronger than cast parts. Cast parts also required machining, and this wasted up to 30 percent of the material. "We know that if we could build up a complicated part by joining a small number of forgings we should have something stronger than could be had by casting. But we had no method of joining except by bolts and rivets and that method of joining is not only expensive but requires such an excess of metal to hold the bolts or rivets as to make the resulting part less practical than a casting." Welding solved this problem. "Welding makes possible the uniting of forgings and stampings into integral parts of strength, lightness, and symmetry at a speed unequalled by any other known process."

Everything should be assembled from the same direction if possible. Reorientation of work or equipment does not add value. Workers should not have to walk around the job to get at its other side. Examples from the Highland Park plant showed, however, that a team can work on a part from two sides without any reorientation or walking. Machines could work on a part from four directions at once

Compliant parts should be used. These include tapers, leads, chamfers, and other features that guide parts together and prevent excessive assembly forces.

Handling, orientation, and adjustment should be avoided. They do not add value, and they create opportunities for defects and damage.

Flexible components like cables and wires should be avoided if possible, because they are difficult to handle. They also invite cable-wiring errors, although error-proofing techniques like slots and keys can suppress these. Rigid components like printed circuit boards are better; fixed-position connectors are more amendable to robotic assembly.

Ford cites weight as another design consideration. Weight does not equal strength, and Ford (1922, 15) was unhappy about the 30 pounds of water in the wood that went into a Model T. He later pointed out the strength and relative lightness of vanadium steel, which at the time was available only from France. He moved quickly to get a vanadium steel process going in the United States.

Ford apparently conceived the modern internal combustion engine himself. The Ford Model N's four-cylinder engine had four separate cylinders that were bolted together. Ford proposed casting the block as a single unit, but Charles Sorensen could not come up with a practical method for doing this. Then Ford thought of making the cylinder block and cylinder head separately (Lacey, 1986, 91). This had the following advantages:

- The block was open at both ends, thus making it easy to machine the cylinders to close tolerances. This is an example of designing for manufacture.
- The arrangement was easier to service. This is an example of designing for maintainability.

Design for manufacture and design for assembly encompass several other important design considerations, including selecting the right material of construction, designing for reliability, and designing for maintainability. Each of these is discussed in the following sections.

Select the Right Material of Construction

Ford was very enthusiastic about vanadium steel, whose merits he discovered through an accidental benchmarking event. He had entered his high-powered Model K, a six-cylinder car, in a race in Palm Beach in 1905. A French car underwent an unintentional "tear-down" when it crashed and apparently distributed several of its internal components around the track. Ford later picked up a valve strip stem and immediately noticed how light and strong it was. No one knew what it was made of, but Ford ordered his assistant to find out. This is how Ford learned about vanadium steel, which played a major role in the Model T's success.

The steels with which Ford had been working had tensile strengths on the order of 60 to 70 thousand pounds per square inch (kip/in^2) [414 to 483 megaPascals, Mpa]. That of vanadium steel was 170 kip/in^2 [1172 Mpa]. Then,

> Having vanadium in hand I pulled apart our models and tested in detail to determine what kind of steel was best for each part—whether we wanted a hard steel, a tough steel, or an elastic steel. We, for the first time in the history of any large construction, determined scientifically the exact quality of the steel. . . . The other elements vary according to whether the part is to stand hard wear or whether it needs spring— in short, according to what it needs (Ford, 1922, 66–67).

The company then performed heat-treatment experiments to increase the strength of steel even further. Ford (1926, 108) credited the Model T's success to vanadium steel, for no other steel of that era had the necessary strength-to-weight ratio. Selection of the right material can reduce the product's weight, which in turn reduces the cost of ownership. Arnold and Faurote (1915, 94) add that the use of wrought steel instead of cast metal for the Model T's crank-box made the car more reliable.

Design for Reliability

Ford recognized the need to design reliability into the product, and he recognized that a weak part could cause the entire product to fail. The idea of error-proofing or, in this case, customer-proofing, also comes into play:

> The vanadium steel disposed of much of the weight. The other requisites of a universal car I had already worked out and many of them were in practice. The design had to balance. Men die because a part gives out. Machines wreck themselves because some parts are weaker than others. Therefore, a part of the problem of designing a universal car was to have as nearly as possible all parts of equal strength considering their purpose—to put a motor in a one-horse shay.[14] Also it had to be fool-proof. This was difficult because a gasoline motor is essentially a delicate instrument and there is a wonderful opportunity for any one who has a mind that way to mess it up (Ford, 1922, 67).

Design for Maintainability

Ford wanted his cars to be reliable, but he realized that they might need repair. Design for maintainability means making it easy and inexpensive to repair or replace parts of the assembly. Ford emphasized that design for maintainability was the designer's responsibility:

> There were but four constructional units in the car—the power plant, the frame, the front axle, and the rear axle. All of these were easily accessible and they were designed so that no special skill would be required for their repair or replacement. I believed then, although I said very little about it because of the novelty of the idea, that it ought to be possible to have parts so simple and so inexpensive that the menace of expensive hand repair work would be eliminated. The parts could be made so cheaply that it would be less expensive to buy new ones than to have old ones repaired. They could be carried in hardware shops just as nails or bolts are carried. I thought that it was up to me as

the designer to make the car so completely simple that no one could fail to understand it (Ford, 1922, 69).

Quality Function Deployment (QFD)

This section supports ISO 9000:2000 5.2, Customer Focus. described the underlying foundation of quality function deployment (QFD) or the "house of quality." Ford did not use the house of quality method but the underlying idea—start with [the voice of] the customer, work back through the design, and deploy the result into manufacturing with the goal of serving the customer—is the same.

> Standardization, then, is the final stage of the process. We start with consumer, work back through the design, and finally arrive at manufacturing. The manufacturing becomes a means to the end of service.
>
> It is important to bear this order in mind (Ford, 1922, 148).

QFD is a matrix that relates customer requirements and their importance to design features as shown in Figure 8-8. It specifically converts customer requirements into design requirements, which are usually measurable product characteristics (Hradesky, 1995, 662, and Pyzdek, 1996, 89–91).

The interaction matrix "roof" shows trade-offs or synergy between characteristics. Strengthening one feature might, for example, weaken another (trade-off) or reinforce another (synergy). The importance rating is the sum of the products of the customer priorities and the numbers in the relationship matrix, which show how much the design requirement affects the customer priority.

In Figure 8-8, suppose that a strong and light alloy (e.g., titanium) can replace steel. Begin with the "roof." Titanium has a positive interaction (synergy) with weight because it's lighter than steel but it interacts negatively (trade-off) with standardized parts because the standard parts are steel. Titanium is also harder to machine (the chips can ignite) so it interacts negatively with fabrication. The zeroes for the other interactions mean there is no apparent trade-off or synergy.

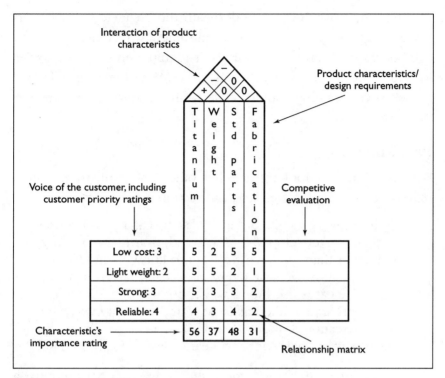

Figure 8-8. Quality function deployment/house of quality

Now compute the importance ratings. Everything is on a 1 (little or no importance, little or no relationship) to 5 (high importance or strong relationship) scale. The 5 relationship between titanium and cost does not necessarily mean that titanium helps lower the cost. It is, in fact, likely to increase it because titanium parts are expensive. The designer must keep this in mind when trying to meet the customer's needs. The 5s for light weight and strength are, on the other hand, beneficial relationships because titanium is light and strong. The importance rating is $5 \times 3 + 2 \times 5 + 3 \times 5 + 4 \times 4 = 56$.

The relationship between standard parts and cost and reliability is strong (5). Selection of standard parts usually holds the cost down, and such parts are often of proven reliability. The importance rating is $3 \times 5 + 2 \times 2 + 3 \times 3 + 4 \times 5 = 48$. In the next column, ease of fabrication has a strong relationship to cost.

There are also "floors" underneath the characteristic's importance rating for factors like technical difficulty, technical competitive benchmarks, and target values or requirements. QFD also ties in with failure mode effect analysis (FMEA) because a failure mode's severity rating should relate to the feature's importance to the customer.

Benchmarking

Benchmarking, or looking at what other companies are doing, plays a role in both design and production.

> We study every car in order to discover if it has features that might be developed and adapted. If any one has anything better than we have we want to know it, and for that reason we buy one of every new car that comes out. Usually the car is used for a while, put through a road test, taken apart, and studied as to how and of what everything is made. Scattered about Dearborn there is probably one of nearly every make of car on earth (Ford, 1922, 145–146).

Schonberger (1986, 194) describes how Nihon Chukuko, a small company that supplies metal parts for Isuzu trucks, adopted this approach. A "tear-down room" held samples of competitor's truck parts. The employees disassembled the parts, performed value analysis to deduce the parts' likely costs. They assessed the parts' tolerances, materials, and paint finishes. They also tried to figure out how the parts were made. A picture of the tear-down room shows parts from Toyota, Mitsubishi, Mazda, and Nissan. This approach is right out of *My Life and Work*.

PROCESS SIMPLIFICATION AND IMPROVEMENT

Elimination of unnecessary process steps supports lean manufacturing by reducing manufacturing costs. This section analyzes the potential benefits of process changes and discusses innovative ways to eliminate waste motion and therefore simplify processes.

It also describes self-check systems and poka-yoke, or error-proofing. Self-check systems prevent the transfer of nonconforming parts from one workstation to the next, and error-proofing suppresses otherwise-unavoidable human error.

The benefits of process simplification and improvement at Ford were unmistakable. For example, the manufacture of axles at Ford involved a heat treatment step. Failure of the axles to cool uniformly meant they had to be straightened afterward. It is easy to imagine the straightening operation becoming an accepted part of the job. An aspect of friction or muda is that people can work around it, and it becomes natural for them to work around it. Ford's workers recognized that the straightening operation was 100 percent rework.

Ford hired someone to improve the axle manufacturing operations. The man developed a centrifugal hardening machine that cooled the shafts evenly. This got rid of the straightening operation. After heat treatment, axle shafts were plunged into a caustic solution while a machine spun them. The spinning motion assured that they cooled evenly and almost instantly. The elimination of the straightening operation saved $36 million (1920s money) in four years.

Another example was a part casting operation that used molten iron directly from the blast furnace cupolas. The company ignored the so-called experts who said, "it was out of the question to pour the hot iron directly from the blast furnace into mould." "The usual method is to run the iron into pigs, let them season for a time, and then remelt them for casting. But at the River Rouge plant we are casting directly from cupolas that are filled from the blast furnaces" (Ford, 1922, 86).

Sorensen (1956, 163–164) adds that there was a problem with uncontrollable variation in the cylinder-casting metal. The solution was to develop small holding furnaces in which to analyze the iron before pouring it into molds. Sorensen uses the phrase, "control the analysis," which suggests that there was an opportunity to correct the alloy composition. This approach cut out at least a couple of operations—including making and then remelting the iron pigs—and their associated costs.

Ford (1922, 89) cites other examples, and they all reinforce the point that inexpensive offshore labor should not pose a problem for lean American manufacturers.

- The replacement of a riveting operation for crankcase arms by an automatic press allowed its operator to do five times as much work as twelve people had done with pneumatic rivet hammers.
- Radiator tubes were once fitted and soldered by hand; this arduous work required skill and patience. A machine that could make 1200 radiator cores in an eight-hour shift superseded this procedure. A conveyor then took the radiators through a furnace to solder the tubes into place.
- A rear axle assembly was dipped into a tank of enamel by hand, and this required two workers and several handlings of the assembly. A new machine allowed one worker to paint one axle every thirteen seconds.
- Camshafts came out of a heat-treatment oven with slight warpage. In 1918, the company required 37 workers to straighten them. Several employees experimented for about a year and developed a new oven in which the shafts could not warp. In 1921, this operation required only eight people and it made more parts (Ford, 1922, 102).

Process Changes Can Improve Efficiency

Waste can hide even in activities that are, under conventional definition, value-adding. For example, an operation called for making a 7/8-inch (22.2 mm) hole in a steel billet. Drilling required the capacity of thirty drill presses. Since drilling transforms the product, it qualifies as a value-adding operation. A drill, however, transforms the entire content of the prospective hole into chips. In contrast, punching expends only enough energy to shear a plug of metal out of the piece. It does not waste time or energy by converting the plug into tiny pieces (see Figure 8-9). A disc-piercing mill could make the requisite hole after Ford's workers designed a new set of tools for the mill. The new process saved significant time and labor (Ford, 1926, 86). Also remember the idea of using a circular cutter to make holes and reduce scrap, as discussed in chapter 7.

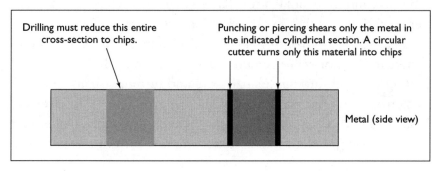

Figure 8-9. Drilling versus piercing or punching

Burrs were originally filed from crankshafts at the Highland Park plant. The job required files of different shapes. The standard was twenty-seven per hour, although the reference then says that a worker could burr no more than ten crankshafts per hour. The workmanship was often mediocre because some burrs were hard to access. A new hand-operated burring tool increased productivity to 100 per hour. The semicircular tools had spring-loaded teeth that apparently conformed to the crankshaft's case, and they scraped the burrs away in a single pass (Arnold and Faurote, 1915, 204–205).

Innovative Ways to Eliminate Waste Motion

The principle of looking for ways to get rid of wasted motion applies to everything, and is obviously a major aspect of process simplification. Consider, for example, the apparently straightforward act of tightening a bolt to set up a machine or close a pipe flange. Shigeo Shingo teaches us how to look past the obvious. Why should a worker have to turn a screw or bolt a dozen or more times to engauge all the threads? Robinson (1990, 337) shows a split thread bolt with alternating 60-degree grooves down its sides, and there are corresponding grooves in the female thread. The bolt slides all the way in and a 60-degree turn tightens it. This idea has been around for a long time, in the form of the interrupted screw artillery breech. Military operations cannot afford to waste time, so cannon manufacturers had to make breeches that the gunners could seal with a quarter turn or sixth turn.

Pear-shaped holes in flanges and clamps are another way to eliminate the non-value-added work of turning a bolt. Instead of putting the bolt through a small hole and turning it many times to tighten it, the large part of the pear-shaped opening fits over the bolt's head. Turning or pushing the flange moves the smaller part of the opening under the bolt head, and one turn or so tightens it.

Self-Check Systems

Self-check systems support lean manufacturing and JIT by keeping nonconforming parts out of downstream operations. The theory of constraints has already shown why shipment of defective pieces to the constraint operation is disastrous; it wastes irreplaceable production capacity. A defective piece can jam production equipment or, by assembly into the finished product, ruin many times its own value of work. Self-check systems also provide immediate feedback to operations that produce nonconforming units, as opposed to downstream inspections and their unavoidable time lags.

Self-check systems are synergistic with ISO 9001:1994 section 4.10 (ISO 9000:2000 7.1, 7.5.1, 8.1, 8.2.4), Inspection and Testing. ISO 9000 calls for detection of nonconforming pieces in-process, as opposed to at final test or inspection, and self-check gauges do this. They also support ISO 9001:1994 section 4.12 (ISO 9000:2000 7.5.1), Inspection and Test Status. If the only way a part can leave a manufacturing operation is through a sorting gauge, the risk of missing a required quality check is not an issue.

Shigeo Shingo points out the problems with inspections that require subjective judgment. Ford recognized this and dealt with it. "Our inspectors in only a few cases are required to use judgment—mostly they apply a gauge, but, as was shown with the bushings [see below], we are working toward mechanical inspection" (Ford, 1926, 77). Furthermore, "... some of the most ingenious machinery used anywhere is that designed to reduce the human factor in inspection" (Ford, 1930, 131).

Inspections had to be simple. Ford (1930, 131–132) describes the dynamic balancing of an engine crankshaft. That is, the crankshaft had to be in balance while it rotated. The balancing machine turned what would have been a complicated exercise into a routine task. The machine's gauge and a chart told the operator the number, depth, and angle of the holes to drill to balance the shaft. Ford does not provide the details, but whatever it was apparently solved a mechanical dynamics problem automatically, and without the aid of an electronic computer. "What would ordinarily be a complex laboratory test has to be simplified to a point where the same results as in the laboratory can be had in the shop as a matter of routine."

The best quality tests, in fact, often do not require an inspector. They allow what Shigeo Shingo calls 100 percent inspection but what is instead a 100 percent automatic sorting operation. Two-stage go/no-go gauges of the type used by Ford are examples of self-check systems. One gauge was set at the lower specification limit and the other at the upper specification limit. Good parts passed through the larger gauge but not the smaller, and anything else was a reject (Ford, 1930, 203).

Robinson (1990, 249) shows a stem tightener inspection in which pieces slide down a chute toward two successive gauges. Those that are thicker than the 10.5-mm upper specification fail to pass through the first gauge. The second gauge shunts the ones that are thicker than the 9.5-mm lower specification into the bin for acceptable units. The ones that are thinner pass through the second gauge into a reject bin.

This is exactly like the techniques that Ford used to sort bushings. One machine sorted the bushings by length, and another sorted them by outside diameter. "... the undersized ones go into one chute and the good ones into another. Those which remain on top are dropped from the end of the rollers into the over-sized chute" (Ford, 1926, 76). The self-check sorter was adjustable in 0.1 mil (2.54 micron) increments. The 3 percent scrap rate was probably quite good for 1918, and the self-check sorters prevented bad ones from getting into the product. Ford also tried to reduce scrap and defects, as shown by this operation's 1.3 percent scrap rate in 1926.

Ford describes another go-and-no-go gauge, or snap gauge, for sorting rods.

> For the rods the gauge would consist of four pieces of steel, set in a horseshoe-shaped holder, two far enough apart to allow the rods to pass between them if their diameters were not greater than the maximum tolerance specified, and the other two close enough together to keep the rods from passing between them unless the diameters of the rods were below the low limit prescribed (Ford, 1930, 212).

Pieces that were too large would not fit between the first two points, and those that were too small would drop through the second. Johansson gauge blocks set the intervals between the points.

Error-Proofing, or Poka-yoke

Error-proofing fixtures and devices make it difficult, if not impossible, to insert a part the wrong way, miss a process step, or even press the wrong button:

> While the welding operation is in progress, fan-shaped plates, operated by cams, cover in turn all operating buttons except the one needed for the next move. It is impossible for the operator to go wrong (Ford, 1930, 198).

Ford also used self-controlling tools. A sixteen-spindle screwdriver drove screws into a starter ring gear. When the torque reached a certain level a friction clutch in the spindle arm slipped; this prevented the screw slots from breaking. The tool also found the screw slot automatically. A thimble over each screwdriver aligned with the screw head and guided the driver into the slot (Ford, 1926, 73).

Even the payroll system at the River Rouge plant used a form of error-proofing, as described by Norwood (1931, Chapter VIII). Wages were in cash, with the pay envelope containing the least possible number of bills and coins. Two quarters were not an acceptable substitute for a half-dollar. Each payroll worker had responsibility for 150 pay envelopes. If an envelope was supposed to contain $90.50 and the pay clerk had a $50, two $20s, and two quarters, he or she had to empty all 150 envelopes and start over because that meant one of the pay envelopes had the wrong amount in it.

The following example (using three pay envelopes) shows how the system probably worked. Consider three payments of $80.25, $80.75, and $90.50. The least number of bills and coins for each envelope is, respectively:

$50, $20, $10, and a quarter.
$50, $20, $10, a half, and a quarter.
$50, $20, $20, and a half.

If the $90.50 pay envelope contains two quarters there is obviously a problem somewhere.

Variation and Accuracy

Ford recognized the benefits of accuracy and precision in manufacturing. Tighter tolerances for moving parts meant less vibration and better reliability. He also identified the problem of random or common-cause variation, which is a key factor in process capability. Process capability indices measure a process' ability to meet specifications consistently.

Of course, no two parts are ever absolutely alike except by accident, for it does not pay to try for accuracy beyond a certain point. But any kind of a machine which has moving parts must be accurately made or there will be an amount of vibration through play that will shorten the life of the machine and also decrease its running efficiency (Ford, 1930, 205).

This recognizes not only the issue of process variation, but also the need for design for reliability. Vibration is a cyclic stress that can lead to fatigue failure in metal parts. Design for manufacture had to account for process capability. "It cannot be too often repeated that production and design must go together. The tools have not yet been devised that will make any part exactly to a measurement" (Ford, 1930, 37). The design had to allow tolerances for this natural variation.

Walter Shewhart developed statistical methods for handling natural variation and distinguishing it from assignable or special causes (problems with the manufacturing process) during the 1920s. Neither Henry Ford nor Charles Sorensen, however, even mention statistical process control (SPC) or control charts. Ford would have had a chance to discuss them in *Moving Forward* (1930), and Sorensen wrote his book in 1956.

Remember, however, that a control chart's purpose is to detect assignable or special cause variation, which means that the process is doing something abnormal. If the quality management and process control systems prevent assignable cause events, the factory can conceivably manage quite well without SPC. The following factors may have been particularly relevant in Ford's operations:

- Continuous-flow processes that involve liquids or gases, such as those in the chemical process industries, are very amenable to automatic process controls (e.g. proportional-integral-derivative control). Such controls are far less applicable to processes that make discrete parts, but the basic idea is that processes become easier to control as they approach the continuous-flow model. Single-unit processing, as used by Ford, is the closest possible approximation to continuous-flow processing that a discrete-unit operation can achieve.

- The Ford system included diligent preventive maintenance, which doubtlessly mitigated against assignable causes like tool wearout.
- 100 percent assessment of product at all operations (by self-check systems) resulted in immediate feedback when problems did occur.

This is not a recommendation to try to do without SPC, especially in an era when computers can often update the charts automatically. SPC is, however, reactive because it warns the shop of assignable cause events. This discussion's lesson is that proactive techniques can keep these events from happening in the first place.

Process Capability and Product Improvement

Ford focused on improving process capabilities to allow tighter tolerances. When he began to make cars, tolerances of 0.01 inch (0.25 mm) were common. In 1930, 0.001 inch, (one mil, 25.4 micron) tolerances were the rule, and some were as tight as 0.0001 inch (2.54 microns). By this time, Ford had a set of Johansson gauge blocks with steps of one microinch (25.4 nanometers).

Tighter tolerances result in better product performance. By reducing vibration, tighter tolerances lengthen the lifetimes of moving parts. Ford also found (1930, 38) that precision manufacturing could double a motor's power with only a small increase in weight. Today, of course, tighter tolerances in semiconductor devices result in enormous leaps in performance.

Lacey (1986, 106–107) cites Ford's machinery as another reason for his company's success during the early 1900s. Although the theory of interchangeable parts had been around for quite a while, practice was another matter. Henry M. Leland astounded the Royal Automobile Club in 1908 by disassembling three Cadillacs and mixing their parts together. His engineers then took parts at random, assembled three Cadillacs from them, and drove the cars around the track. The idea that parts from one car would fit another without filing or adjustment was still something of a novelty. The production equipment at Ford could make parts very accurately and there was no need for hand-fitting. Process capability was a competitive weapon:

> No other plant in Detroit could match the vast Keim presses which stamped crankcases from flat sheets of steel and could produce the ninety-five tubes and sheet metal pins needed to make up a radiator at one single stroke (Lacey, 1986, 107).

The reference adds that Ford and his associates were willing to buy new machine tools and discard those they replaced to get better accuracy in milling or grinding. The same was true if the new equipment could eliminate a manufacturing operation. Although James Couzens sometimes objected to the cost, the investments usually paid for themselves. There is a lesson here for organizations whose cost accounting systems discourage replacement of fully-depreciated equipment.

Process Capability and Product Quality

Design for manufacture and design for assembly play valuable roles in assuring quality. Ford also recognized the value of building quality into the product instead of inspecting and testing it in. *Today and Tomorrow* (1926, 142) says that prior practice was to test finished cars and then take them down—partially disassemble them—for packaging and shipping. According to Womack and Jones (1996, 194–195), standard practice at Porsche was, even as late as the 1980s, to assemble the cars, test them, and fix any problems. The system delivered a very low defect level to customers although the inefficiency of inspecting, testing, and reworking quality into the product should be obvious. Ford had rendered this practice unnecessary by 1926. Porsche also retained 100 inspectors to sort out the one percent of defective parts from suppliers.

Ford used the analogy of a mint that produces silver dollars that are exactly alike, and it should be no different for cars. A manufacturing process should make parts accurately and reproducibly. Inspection should assure their quality; remember that this means automatic sorting by gauges and self-check systems, not inspections that depend on a person's subjective judgment. Then, Ford concludes, final assembly should produce identical products. If the parts are good, the final product also should be good. (This assumes that the designers have accounted for tolerance stackup, or additivity of the pieces' random deviations from their nominals.)

Gauge Calibration and Gauge Capability

This section is synergistic with ISO 9001:1994 section 4.11 (ISO 9000:2000 7.6), Control of Inspection, Measuring, and Test Equipment. Calibration assures that gauges are accurate. An accurate gauge will, on average, return the nominal measurement of a reference standard. The QS-9000 automotive quality standard requires gauge precision, as reflected by the percent tolerance (P/T) ratio. This is the ratio of the gauge's variation to the specification width.

Ford's quest for tighter tolerances, which meant better performance and better reliability due to reduced vibration, required leading-edge advances in metrology. To gain the necessary precision, ". . . we sought out the one man in the world who had made a business of absolute accuracy and brought him into the organization—Carl E. Johansson. . . . Today Johansson blocks are recognized throughout the world as the most accurate precision instruments known" (Ford, 1926, 84).

Ford boasted of owning the only set of Jo blocks in the world that had steps of a millionth of an inch (25.4 nanometers, or billionths of a meter). He also recognized the importance of temperature control in gauging and metrology: ". . . even the heat of the user's body several feet away influences the result [for the microinch-step Jo blocks]" (1926, 85). "Arguments between a mechanic on the warm side of a shop with one on the cold side often became legal battles between seller and buyer which involved broken contracts, months or even years of litigation, and often not inconsiderable damage awards by courts" (Ford, 1930, 207–208). The effects of temperature and humidity on metrology cannot be overstated (see also Levinson, 2000, 56–59).

This observation leads to an issue that falls under ISO 9001:1994 section 4.6 (ISO 9000:2000 7.4), Purchasing: the need for reproducibility of measurements between customer and supplier. In Ford's example, the supplier's machinist insisted that the parts met specification, the customer's machinist or inspector said they didn't and, according to the gauges in front of them, they were both right. The American Society for Testing and Materials (ASTM) develops standard test methods that are indeed reproducible by different labs or shops.

Ford described another problem: the tendency of heat-treated steel blocks to relieve internal stresses through gradual expansion. Nine years of experimentation led to the correct steel and proper heat treatment to produce stable gauge blocks. He also recognized the consequences of having a gauge go out of calibration. "... when one of the gauges is worn to the point that it no longer checks the limits properly, one hour's run may mean several thousand pieces of scrap, tying up of the assembly line, or the holding up of some branch in a remote part of the world" (Ford, 1930, 213). This is a very important consideration under ISO 9000.

The Johansson blocks were manufactured in a special room whose temperature and humidity controls exceeded those of most modern semiconductor fabrication plants. The temperature had to be exactly 68°F (20°C). An ozone generator replenished the room's oxygen as the workers consumed it and dehydrators removed the moisture that the workers exhaled.[15] Insulation of the room's mercury lights prevented their heat from interfering with the operation (Ford, 1930, 215–216).

Jo blocks allowed Ford's gauge inspectors to check the condition of gauges and fixtures. A calibration program was apparently in place, and Ford (1930, 216–219) describes some very sophisticated equipment for checking gauge accuracies. He said that, while one ten thousandth of an inch (2.54 microns) was workable accuracy (for the production line), assurance of the gauges' accuracies required the ability to resolve a millionth of an inch (25.4 nanometers). The Jo block provided this capability.

PACKAGING AND DELIVERY

ISO 9001:1994 section 4.15 (ISO 9000:2000 7.1 and 7.5.4), Handling, Storage, Packaging, and Delivery, requires systems for preventing expiration of perishable materials and damage during shipment. Prevention of shock, tipping, and temperature limit violations are all considerations under ISO 9000. Transportation, handling, packaging, and storage are all forms of waste, so Ford preferred not to have to package or deliver anything.

> Recently, a new type of assembly plant building has been worked out, and all new branches are being built to these specifications. This calls for a one-story structure with the conveyor lines laid out in such a way that trucking and handling are practically eliminated (Ford, 1926, 116).

In his Chicago plant, for example, no material had to be trucked for more than 20 feet (6.1 meters); this was the distance from the railroad freight car to the first conveyor.

Raw materials did, of course, have to come to the factory and finished goods had to leave. Ford recognized handling considerations that now fall under ISO 9000:

> Handling freight roughly is another source of great waste. It is absurd that an article for shipment has to be protected against other than the ordinary jarring of travel.... The labour and material involved in packing are enormous, and most of it is sheer waste—waste of human labour and of valuable lumber (Ford, 1926, 115–116).

Ford actually introduced a predecessor to modern tipping and shock indicators. Detroit, Toledo, & Ironton Railroad cars had impact recorders that showed how much vibration and jostling they had received (Bryan, 1997, 62).

Harry and Schroeder (2000) describe an example of rough handling and its effects. A Six Sigma project involved damage to boxes of plastic products in warehouses. Ninety-five percent of all the damaged boxes had two punctures at their bases. The problem proved to be … forklifts!

> The Black Belts also found that 87 percent of the damage occurred when the boxes were moved by forklift onto stacks or into trucks. It didn't take long for the Black Belt team to decide that there was a strong correlation between the number of boxes damaged in-house—as opposed to being damaged during shipping—and the number of damaged products received by customers.... The forks on the forklift protruded six to nine inches [15 to 23 cm] from under the box, so that as the fork was fully inserted under the box being retrieved, the box behind it was punctured (Harry and Schroeder, 2000, 251–252).

The Black Belt team then considered hiring very experienced forklift operators and instituting an extensive training program for existing ones. An underlying principle of poka-yoke is, of course, that an operation should not depend on human skill. The team finally decided to install shorter forks at $350 per forklift. This eliminated the problem completely. Henry Ford showed more than half a century earlier that one does not need rocket science to avoid damage from handling and transportation.

POINT-OF-USE ASSEMBLY

Ford introduced the concept of assembling an item at the point of use:

> The most economical manufacturing of the future will be that in which the whole of an article is not made under one roof—unless, of course, it be a very simple article. The modern—or better, the future—method is to have each part made where it may best be made and then assemble the parts into a complete unit at the points of

consumption. That is the method we are now following and expect to extend. It would make no difference whether one company or one individual owned all the factories fabricating the component parts of a single product, or whether such part were made in our independently owned factory, *if only all adopted the same service methods.* (Ford, 1922, 52).

We make parts, and the cars are assembled where they are to be used (Ford, 1926, 83).

The Second World War required the United States to build hundreds of destroyer escorts. These ships were smaller than destroyers, and their principal mission was to sink enemy submarines. There was not, however, enough shipyard capacity for their construction.

The problem's solution began with overcoming the paradigm that ships must be built in shipyards. A lot of the work took place in Denver, Colorado. For non-American readers, Denver is nowhere near the ocean and it is a mile (1.6 km) above sea level. A photograph (Ward, 1999, 36–37) shows prefabricated ship parts from Denver arriving at the Mare Island, California, shipyard for final assembly in 1943.

The destroyer escort project simply applied the point-of-use assembly concept on a much larger scale. The article (Ward, 1999) also cites how overcoming other paradigms increases productivity. Defoe Shipbuilding of Bay City, Michigan, realized that no rule requires ships to be built right side up. It was much easier for the welders to work down than up, and this allowed faster and better construction. When the hull was complete, a steel cradle turned it around in less than three minutes.

Ford cited the difficulty of packaging an entire machine to immunize it from damage during transportation. It was often more efficient to package the parts, ship them to the point of use, and assemble them there. This also supports ISO 9000 if it prevents handling damage.

OCCUPATIONAL SAFETY

"Don't monkey with the buzz saw," is one of New England's colloquial proverbs, to which too many four-fingered men call attention. (*The System Company*, 1911a, 114)

Charles Sorensen himself wrote off the loss of two right fingertips as an occupational hazard of his first occupation, making wooden patterns for iron casting molds. The Ford Motor Company had a very advanced and aggressive safety policy long before OSHA existed. The policy was, as described by Norwood (1931, 83-84), "'Can't' rather than 'Don't.'" That is, it is better to make accidents impossible (can't) than to post warning signs (don't) and hope the workers will be careful. The concept is similar to error-proofing.

The section on ISO 14000 in Chapter 7 showed that exposure to quarry dust was not acceptable. Mining also was to be safe. "... we wanted to make the mining as nearly safe for the miners as possible. Mining, working under the ground, is nasty work at the best, and the first effort has been to make everything safe. And it is safe; our list of accidents has been very small indeed" (Ford, 1926, 49).

Industrial Safety Principles and Practices

Ford himself (1922, 114–115) presents detailed industrial safety principles that were decades ahead of OSHA.

No reason exists why factory work should be dangerous. ... The principal causes of accidents as they are grouped by the experts are:

- Defective structures.
- Defective machines.
- Insufficient room.
- Absence of safeguards.
  - The company tried to avoid using belts whenever possible. New machines had individual electric motors, but older machines got their power from belts. Every belt had a safety guard over it.

- Automatic conveyors had bridges, so no employee had to cross at a dangerous point.
- Workers were required to wear goggles for operations that might generate flying metal. Netting around the machine reduced the hazard further.
- Railings were placed around hot furnaces.
- Starting switches of draw presses were protected by large red tags that had to be removed before the switches could be turned.
- Unclean conditions:
  - The section on 5S-CANDO shows that Ford required cleanliness and organization in every aspect of his businesses.
  - Aisles were to be kept clear of obstructions.
  - Windows were kept washed and paint was kept fresh. Normally dark corners of rooms were painted white to discourage people from spitting into them. The idea of using light colors to reveal dirt reappears in the 5S-CANDO approach.
- Bad lights.
  - The section on workplace lighting that follows discusses this issue in more detail.
- Bad air.
  - In Ford's newer buildings (1910s to early 1920s), hollow support columns provided conduits for ventilation. (See Arnold and Faurote, 1915, 389–391. The hollow columns eliminated the need for air pipes that would add cost, occupy floor space, and make the workplace unsightly). Temperature was controlled tightly.
- Unsuitable clothing.
  - Ford recognized that ties and flowing sleeves could be caught in machinery. Supervisors were to warn employees when they saw these hazards.
- Carelessness.
- Ignorance.

- Mental condition.
  - Arnold and Faurote (1915, "Safeguarding the Workmen") warn that monotonous performance of work that one can do almost without thinking can lead to dangerous conditions.
- Lack of cooperation.

Of these, Arnold and Faurote (1915, 438) write, management can eliminate all but ignorance and unsuitable clothing—and the Highland Park plant did. Accidents at Ford were rare. When one happened, a safety specialist investigated and changed the machine to make a recurrence impossible. This reinforces the point that the company did not tolerate any kind of friction in its operations; it dealt with the root causes of problems upon their discovery.

A picture of the front-axle assembly line at Highland Park (Arnold and Faurote, 1915, 191) shows that "Everything is encased with sheet metal so as to present a smooth surface, where the workmen's bodies or clothing touch it." A simple action like making sure all work surfaces are smooth and unlikely to catch on clothing can prevent injuries and property damage. The last chapter of this reference shows numerous guards around belt drives, grinding wheels, flywheels, and furnaces.

Employees had to report any injury, no matter how minor. Norwood (1931, 79–80) reports that, while he was visiting the salvaging department, a departmental boss pricked his finger on a tool. He excused himself and returned five minutes later with a surgical dressing. "'We simply must do that here,' he explained. 'It's one of our strictest rules.'" The rule had a good reason behind it because 75 to 80 percent of the infections that the plant hospital had to treat were in workers who delayed treatment for even minor cuts.

Machinery had safety interlocks that prevented startup at the wrong time. A worker made the mistake of plugging an interlock, and this resulted in the disintegration of a crankshaft grinding wheel. The fragments shattered the 3/8-inch (9.5-mm) safety hood but the guard protected nearby workers from harm. The plant decided that cast iron guards were not sufficiently strong and replaced them with boiler plate or cast steel.

The River Rouge plant foresaw the chance of disintegration of grinding wheels, whose surfaces revolved at 6,300 feet per minute (1920 meters per minute), from centrifugal force. The wheels were tested at 30 percent higher speed, behind guards, before placement in the shop machines. Blotting paper washers went between the flange and the wheel to avoid the chance of cracking (introduction of a stress concentrator) from direct pressure on the wheel.

The plant also had a policy against working alone in potentially dangerous areas, such as near coke ovens. Oxygen was available in case of carbon monoxide poisoning, and pulmotors (emergency ventilators for administering air) received weekly inspections.[16] There is no doubt that Ford would have provided defibrillators in appropriate areas had they been available.

Stairwells are excellent conduits for fires, and modern fire regulations require fire doors to remain closed when they are not in use. Arnold and Faurote (1915, 395) report that stairwells of the Highland Park plant had metallic fire curtains. A fire would melt a fusible metal and cause the curtain to seal the stairwell. (This level of heat would have presumably made the stairwell unusable as an escape route.)

Arnold and Faurote (1915, 438) describe a fire suppression system for flammable liquids that was probably well ahead of its time. Each enameling tank had a cover that hung from a cable with fusible (low-melting) metal in it. A fire would melt the metal and drop the cover over the tank to snuff the fire. A larger tank for which a cover was not usable had provisions for transferring its contents into a large underground tank within three minutes. Steam jets were available to suffocate the burning enamel that remained in the tank. A contemporary reference (*The System Company*, 1911a, 114) supports this idea: "No fire can live in live steam." Carbon dioxide might be used today.

Safety was apparently even more advanced at the River Rouge plant, where construction workers on scaffolding wore life belts. When this was not possible, netting was placed under the workers, much as circus performers use safety nets for high-wire acts. Norwood (1931, 86–87) reports that more than one worker did fall into these nets, and they avoided serious injury. Ladders had safety tubes to make falls almost impossible, and no one was to carry anything up a ladder. Hand lines were provided for raising and lowering materials and tools.

The plant once provided chemical masks for workers who had to deal with ammonia fumes or gas. Air masks with positive pressure superseded these. Modern safety engineers and industrial hygienists are familiar with confined-space entry procedures. The River Rouge plant used an innovative technique for dealing with the five-foot (1.5-meter) diameter gas mains for blast furnaces. A dutchman, or short pipe segment, was placed flush with the principal main. This allowed removal of two segments from the pipe that maintenance workers intended to enter. Natural air currents removed any remaining gases from the pipe and assured the workers' safety (Norwood, 1931, 99).

Protective Apparel

Even the past few decades have seen incidents of harmful materials remaining on workers' clothing and thus entering their homes. Safety in Ford's mining operations included countermeasures against hazardous materials following workers home. The miners wore special clothing and rubber boots (personal protective equipment, or PPE). When they finished work, they bathed in the company shower room and put on fresh clothing. Their work clothing was cleaned and dried for them before they returned to work the next day.

The River Rouge plant used extensive personal protective equipment. Anyone who handled corrosive materials had to wear goggles and rubber gloves. Those who handled these materials in bulk, however, wore rubber coats and boots as well, along with rubber hoods with glass visors. Sodium bicarbonate and vinegar eyewash bottles were available for treating acid and caustic exposures respectively.

Lockout-tagout

The River Rouge plant used a form of lockout-tagout for overhead cranes when maintenance workers had to work on the tracks. (The reference later uses the term, *lock-and-key security*.) The workers once simply told the crane pilots when they had to work on the tracks, but this relied on the crane operator's memory and violated the "'can't', not 'don't'" safety principle. The new system required the maintenance worker to obtain clamps from the crane operator, give him a receipt for the clamps, and put the clamps on the rail between the crane and the job. This made it impossible to advance the crane into the work area. If the crane pilot's shift finished he gave his replacement the receipt to inform him that part of the rail was blocked. This avoided the chance of a crane derailment. When the maintenance work was complete, the worker returned the clamps and reclaimed the check (Norwood, 1931, 87–88). Note the system's principal features:

- It required the maintenance workers to tell the crane operators what they were doing.
- The maintenance work area was locked out.
- The worker who placed the locking device (and no one else) was to remove it.

The practice of clamping crane tracks illustrates the lockout-tagout principle. Norwood (1931, 93) also describes the River Rouge plant's fully developed lockout-tagout program. A worker who had to work on a slat conveyor's running gear, which the reference compares to a sausage grinder, began by unlocking a metal box that contained the master switch. He shut off the switch, relocked the box, kept the key, and went to work. No one else had a key so he was the only one who could restart the conveyor. Modern safety practitioners will recognize this as a foundation of effective lockout-tagout.

When cranes carried loads, whistles told everyone below them to get out of the way. No suspended load was ever to pass above workers' heads. Cranes had to use steel cables for their loads because damage to a hemp rope, possibly from the load itself, could cause the load to fall. Steel cables received regular inspections, and those with even one broken wire were replaced at once.

The reference also describes a "tag and flag" system for loading docks. Someone who was loading a rail car would set up a blue flag (or lantern) and attach a tag with his badge number, the location of the work, the car number, and his foreman's badge number. No one but the worker whose badge number was on the flag could remove the flag. Modern tagout systems prohibit removal of a tag by anyone but the worker who placed it.

Ergonomics and Repetitive Motion Injuries

ISO 9000:2000 sections 6.3 and 6.4, Facilities and Work Environment, require consideration of human and physical factors, ergonomics, and avoidance of repetitive motion injuries. The danger of repetitive motion injuries became well known during the past few decades. For example, excessive repetition of the same wrist and hand motion can lead to carpal tunnel syndrome. The repetitive tasks at the Ford Motor Company sounded like prime suspects for such injuries. The company actually considered this hazard but found no incidences of repetitive motion injuries:

> After many years of experience in our factories we have failed to discover that repetitive work injures the workman. In fact, it seems to produce better physical and mental health than non-repetitive work. If the men did not like the work, they would leave (Ford, 1926, 161).

Human factors engineering and ergonomics were not as well developed then as they are now, so this statement seems surprising—until we remember Ford's injunction that no job should require a worker to apply excessive force. Job designs that conformed to this precept may well have mitigated against repetitive motion injuries in his factories. Modern meat packing factories are, in contrast, among the worst sources of repetitive motion injuries because the workers must perform the same forcible motions over and over. They must, for example, slice through muscle tissue and tendons, and this doubtlessly requires exertion even if the knives are very sharp.

The Highland Park plant recognized that stooping tires the worker and reduces his productivity, and it stressed the importance of correct posture (Arnold and Faurote, 1915, 111). Gilbreth (1911) emphasized repeatedly the need to avoid stooping.

Safety Committees

Ford recognized that the worker who is closest to the job is in the best position to recognize unsafe conditions. "A wide-awake safety committee was organized and the cooperation of the entire camp has been secured in working constantly for safe conditions" (Ford, 1926, 49). Japan later developed the safety hiyari, or scare report, which empowers workers to report unsafe conditions and even make immediate corrections if possible (Imai, 1997).

Pennsylvania's PENNSAFE initiative shows the merits of the safety committee approach:[17]

> Launched in 1996, PENNSAFE is the [former Governor Thomas] Ridge Administration's initiative aimed at increasing the level of safety in the Commonwealth's workplaces. The three prongs of the initiative are outreach and training, technical assistance, and the Governor's Award for Safety Excellence. A key component of this safety initiative is the certification of labor/management workplace safety committees, which entitles employers to insurance premium discounts.

Employers that set up qualifying safety committees receive a 5 percent discount on their worker's compensation premiums for up to five years. The state offers free training for safety committee members. Other states may enact similar initiatives.

Per Norwood (1931, 78) the River Rouge plant carried its own worker compensation risk instead of delegating it to an external agency. This saved thousands of dollars (1930s money) in worker compensation premiums even though company policy was to give injured workers the benefit of any doubt.

Workplace Comfort and Hygiene

This section also is synergistic with ISO 9000:2000 sections 6.3 and 6.4, Facilities and Work Environment. Lacey (1986, 350) describes the cleanliness of the River Rouge plant, which hired 5,000 workers for the sole purpose of keeping it clean. The plant's safety record was exemplary by contemporary standards. Grey-blue and eggshell-white paint provided the most comfortable colors for workers' eyes. Gilbreth (1911) points out the importance of proper lighting in the workplace, and the Rouge was well lit.

Ford introduced a suction machine to take up iron dust from piston ring manufacture in 1918. Per Lacey (1986), "...similar Ford systems of climate control, using blowers and exhaust fans, set the pace for industry as a whole." "Salt pellets were provided in the summer; telephones, eye goggles, and respirators were sterilized every twenty-four hours. Even the coat racks were disinfected regularly."

Per Norwood (1931, Chapter V), the River Rouge plant recognized that bacteria in cutting fluids could cause dermatitis. Addition of a low concentration of coal tar to the cutting fluid kept the bacteria down. The cutting fluid reservoirs were cleaned weekly with boiling water. Flushing the pipes to and from the reservoirs with pressurized water cleared any pockets of bacteria.

The chapter continues by noting the elimination of mercury from a certain operation, and the systematic examination of solder workers for evidence of lead poisoning. Goggles were sterilized when the workers returned them to their cribs. Respirators received similar treatment along with new filtering screens. Every twenty-four hours, 130,000 towels were laundered and sterilized. Suction systems removed dust from grinding and buffing, and fume hoods protected workers from gases and vapors. Even the air that circulated through the plant was washed with water or, when it might contain graphite that would not entrain in water, oil.

Workplace Lighting

This consideration is extremely important and, given today's reliance on inexpensive fluorescent lighting, it deserves reexamination. ISO 9000 requires appropriate lighting, especially in connection with inspection activities.

Fluorescent light is not, incidentally, white light. A prism will reveal this immediately. True white light yields a continuous rainbow spectrum, fluorescent light does not. The human eye is, of course, designed to work with true white light. Ford's newer factories (Highland Park and River Rouge) admitted copious sunlight.

The profusion of greenish factory floors with greenish machinery and even greenish workers in trade journals is further evidence of the nature of fluorescent light. The photographers who took these pictures did not understand the nature of fluorescent light so they did not use the appropriate filter (FLD) for daylight film. Fluorescent light is cheap, but its cost-effectiveness is questionable.

> The best light is the cheapest. By that is not meant that which gives the brightest light. In fact, the light itself is but a small part of the question. Go into any factory and examine every light, and you will notice that as a rule they are obviously wrong. A light to be right must pass five tests:
>
>   a. It must furnish the user sufficient light so that he can see.
>   b. It must be so placed that it does not cause the user's eyes to change the size of the diaphragm when ordinarily using the light.
>   c. It must be steady.
>   d. There shall not be any polished surfaces in its vicinity that will reflect an unnecessary bright spot anywhere that can be seen by the eyes of the worker.

e. It must be protected so that it does not shine in the eyes of some other worker.

... Go into the buildings among the workers, the students, and the scientists and see how rarely it is considered. All of this is not a question of getting the most out of the light. Light in a factory is the cheapest thing there is. It is wholly a question of fatigue of the worker. The best lighting conditions will reduce the percentage of time required for rest for overcoming fatigue. The difference between the cost of the best lighting and the poorest is nothing compared with the saving in money due to decreased time for rest period due to less fatigued eyes (Gilbreth, 1911).

Light is the first essential of low labor-cost factory production. How the last generation of factory managers (previous to those of the present hour) could have ever accepted the bat-and-mole twilights of our first large factory buildings is a question which no living person can answer, though perhaps we of today should keep our mouths shut about machine-shop lighting so long as we tolerate the present practice of overhead counter-shaft placing and belt-driving of machine tools—but that is another story (Arnold and Faurote, 1915, 404–406).

Good light to work by is an investment too infrequently made in the factory. In comparison with the cost of labor, the cost of artificial light is trifling, but there are thousands of skilled mechanics who lose efficiency because of insufficient light (The System Company, 1911a, 106).

Norwood (1931, 5253) adds that vast expanses of windows admitted sunlight to the River Rouge plant. The slightly glossy eggshell white paint on walls, girders, and ceilings helped to diffuse the light throughout the plant. The machine-blue color of machine frames, housings, safety covers, and sheathings was easiest on the workers' eyes.

This section has covered the progressive safety, ergonomics, and industrial hygiene system that existed at Ford long before anyone heard of OSHA. Many of the ideas are applicable to modern workplaces and some, like lighting, support ISO 9000. The next section treats the role of quality assurance.

QUALITY CONTROL

Ford recognized that quality reduces manufacturing costs:

> More and more quality and workmanship must be built into the product, and whenever there is a question between raising the quality and lowering the price it is better to raise the quality, for then one will shortly be able to lower the price anyway (Ford, 1930, 209).

This section covers Ford's innovative quality assurance methods, some of which also support ISO 9000's requirements.

Corrective and Preventive Action

This material is synergistic with ISO 9001:1994 section 4.14 (ISO 9000:2000 8.4, 8.5.2, 8.5.3), Corrective and Preventive Action. A question arises in modern organizations as to how much scrap or rework must occur to prompt an 8D (the modern Ford company's eight-discipline problem-solving approach) assessment, or its equivalent. The following material suggests that Ford considered even one scrap or rework one too many, and it resulted in efforts to eliminate the root cause permanently. The same policy applied to accidents and machine stoppages. Even one injury, no matter how minor, resulted in elimination of the underlying reason. The reasons for all machine stoppages went on record even if the line workers could clear them in less than two minutes.

A description of the process for the Ford *en bloc* cylinder at the Highland Park plant shows the use of inspection feedback. "A full and complete inspection record is kept so that the faulty cut in each waster [reject, scrap unit] is known and the machine fault, if such exists, is remedied at once. Should the fault be due to any workman's act, he is, of course, duly informed and his faulty practice changed" (Arnold and Faurote, 1915, 76).

The Highland Park plant used three kinds of inspectors:

- Machine inspectors moved from one machine to another to inspect work in progress. "Machine inspectors enough are placed in each department to cover all operations in that department at frequent intervals, so that no faulty operation shall proceed for any great length of time" (Arnold and Faurote, 1915, 99).
- Operation inspectors checked the work at certain points in the process.
- Floor or final inspectors checked completed components.

Rejects went to wasters (scrap) inspectors who determined whether they could be reworked. Again, any incidence of scrap resulted in feedback and corrective action on the shop floor:

> The wasters inspectors may call on the head inspector, and the head inspector may summon the foreman of the production department where the waster was originated, and the machine-shop superintendent may be notified, so that the waster makes plenty of trouble for those whose faults assisted in its production. The same procedure may be followed in the scrap-inspection quarters, so that all in fault are very likely to be made fully aware of vigorous disapproval of scrap production even as a rare performance (Arnold and Faurote, 1915, 99).

Quality Auditing

This section is synergistic with ISO 9001:1994 section 4.17 (ISO 9000:2000 8.2.2), Internal Quality Audits. Ford describes product auditing as follows:

> Of course we have other checks. We have a squad at the Dearborn laboratory whose sole duty is to go out through the shops, take anything they see, and fetch it to Dearborn for testing.... although at every stage of production every conceivable test and inspection is made, we maintain this flying squadron as an additional and independent check.

And the flying squadron itself every once in a while has to be checked (Ford, 1930, 149).

The auditors were apparently independent of the area or operation they were auditing. The audit was a check on the adequacy of the quality assurance system; it made sure the inline inspections and tests were effective. Finally, the audit system itself was subject to periodic evaluations. This sounds a lot like the foundation of the modern auditing systems, including those covered by ISO 9000.

Notes

1. "Robot" comes from the Czech *robata*, or compulsory labor. In many pre-monetary societies, people often paid taxes by laboring for the government for a certain number of days. There is even a theory that Egyptian pharaohs built their "monuments of success," the Pyramids, with the equivalent of *robata*.
2. H. L. Gantt also recognized the merits of intrinsic motivation: "It is a psychological truth that a task in which we are interested is performed with less fatigue than one we must force ourselves to do" (*The System Company*, 1911, 26).
3. *Modern Times* begins with the theme of dehumanization by machinery; sheep running through a chute turn into workers entering a factory. An Orwellian television screen in the employee restroom allows the factory owner to watch his employees even there, and he tells the worker played by Chaplin, "Get back to work!" The factory owner also orders the line speedup that Sinclair describes in *The Flivver King* (1937). A supplier even offers an automatic feeding machine that can supposedly feed employees as they work, thus cutting out the lunch break.
4. This is the payback method of product selection, and three months is an extremely conservative standard. Net present worth is more scientific. Modern experience shows, however, that workers often find ways to make improvements at very little cost.
5. This example is presumably from before Ford's introduction of the eight-hour work day.
6. Basset (1919, 71) cites an example in which poor tool arrangement resulted in an estimated 60 percent of labor costs going for "pedestrian endurance."

7. This could well be Oscar Bornholdt, who worked for Ford. See Hounshell, 1984, 271.
8. e.g., Womack and Jones, 1996, 104
9. Ford (1926, 105) admits to maintaining enormous storage bins for coal, iron ore, limestone, and lumber at the River Rouge plant because ice closed the waterways during winter and the materials could not arrive by boat. Iron ore and lumber came from Ford's mines and forests in Upper Michigan, so they had to travel by ship. Coal, however, also came by rail from mines in Kentucky.
10. The variance (square of the standard deviation) of a sum of random numbers equals the sum of their variances. Take the square root of the sum of the variances to get the standard deviation.
11. Per Ford (1926), the cycle time was reduced even further during the next several years.
12. There is, in fact, a relationship between project management and the theory of constraints (TOC). In production control, the capacity-constraining resource (CCR) limits the speed at which the factory can work. In project management, the critical path limits the speed at which the project can finish. Linear programming, simplex method can identify the CCR and also slack (excess) capacity at other operations. The critical path method (CPM) identifies slack times in project activity paths. Levinson and Rerick (2002) provide additional detail.
13. Murphy and Saxena (in Levinson, 1998, 183–185) also show the benefits of getting the factory into operation as quickly as possible despite the extra costs.
14. The reliability of n components in series is $\prod_{i=1}^{n} R_i$, where $0 \leq R_i \leq 1$ is the reliability of the ith component. Given a fixed average reliability such that $\frac{1}{n}\sum_{i=1}^{n} R_i$ = constant, series reliability is indeed maximized when $R_1 = R_2 = \ldots = R_n$.
15. This might not be acceptable today, as ozone is recognized as a health hazard. Although Ford did not willingly expose workers to hazardous conditions, some dangers were simply unknown at the time.
16. http://www.klinikum-hannover.de/nordstadt/anaesthesiologie/images/pulmotor.htm, as of this printing shows a Dräger pulmotor of 1907. See also http://www.draeger.com/us/MT/Library/CriticalCare/CriticalCare.jsp. Dräger, or Draeger, makes medical and industrial safety equipment today.
17. http://www.dli.state.pa.us/pennsafe/index.html, http://www.li.state.pa.us/bwc/health&safety/ as of 4/28/01.

NINE

Customer and
Supplier Relationships

An outstanding engineer or mechanic can design an excellent machine. Ford's genius, however, went beyond the walls of his own organization to identifying customer needs and filling them. He introduced the innovative idea of lowering prices to make a product into a mass-market commodity. This would in turn, increase sales and profits.

He also identified the need for what lean manufacturing practitioners now call *supply chain management*, or making every manufacturer, supplier, and subcontractor that is associated with making a product cooperative trading partners. *Supplier development* is the practice of helping suppliers improve their operations. This chapter's excerpts from *My Life and Work* reveal a way of thinking about identifying markets and creating demand, pricing strategies, and supply chain management. His concepts were well ahead of their time and perhaps for that reason can easily be applied to any present-day product or service.

IDENTIFYING MARKETS AND
CREATING DEMAND

Henry Ford was not the first person to make automobiles. His unprecedented success resulted instead from his industrial methods and an intelligent marketing plan.

Other carmakers built cars to order for wealthy buyers. Ford recognized that 95 percent of the potential market did not care about customization. The other five percent, who might be willing to pay for specialized work, constituted a limited market. The foundation of his plan was:

> Ask a hundred people how they want a particular article made. About eighty will not know; they will leave it to you. Fifteen will think they must say something, while five will really have preferences and reasons. The ninety-five, made up of those who do not know and admit it and the fifteen who do not know but do not admit it, constitute the real market for any product. The five who want something special may or may not be able to pay the price for special work. If they have the price, they can get the work, but they constitute a special and limited market. Of the ninety-five perhaps ten or fifteen will pay a price for quality. Of those remaining, a number will buy solely on price and without regard to quality. Their numbers are thinning with each day. Buyers are learning how to buy. The majority will consider quality and buy the biggest dollar's worth of quality. If, therefore, you discover what will give this 95 percent of people the best all-round service and then arrange to manufacture at the very highest quality and sell at the very lowest price, you will be meeting a demand which is so large that it may be called universal (Ford, 1922, 48).

Focus on 95 percent of the potential market, which had to include middle-class customers, could meet a "universal demand." Because these customers bought on the basis of price and quality, the product had to be affordable and reliable.

The proliferation of personal computers has followed a roughly parallel model. The first ones were experiments and toys for their creators, much like the automobiles of the 19th century. The next ones were relatively expensive tools for industry and academia. By the end of the 20th century they were so inexpensive that almost everyone could afford them. Their spread, and the rise of the Internet—an electronic "interstate highway system" that crosses national as well as state borders— fueled the demand for computers even further.

Identifying Customer Needs

Ford outlined the characteristics of the "universal car" that he planned to sell. This outline accounted for quality, simplicity, reliability, and ease of use as well as price (quoted directly from Ford, 1922, 68):

1. Quality in material to give service in use. Vanadium steel is the strongest, toughest, and most lasting of steels. It forms the foundation and super-structure of the cars. It is the highest quality steel in this respect in the world, regardless of price.
2. Simplicity in operation—because the masses are not mechanics.
3. Power in sufficient quantity.
4. Absolute reliability—because of the varied uses to which the cars would be put and the variety of roads over which they would travel.
5. Lightness. With the Ford there are only 7.95 pounds [3.61 kg] to be carried by each cubic inch [16.39 cubic centimeters] of piston displacement. This is one of the reasons why Ford cars are "always going," wherever and whenever you see them—through sand and mud, through slush, snow, and water, up hills, across fields and roadless plains.
6. Control—to hold its speed always in hand, calmly and safely meeting every emergency and contingency either in the crowded streets of the city or on dangerous roads. The planetary transmission of the Ford gave this control and anybody could work it. That is the "why" of the saying: "Anybody can drive a Ford." It can turn around almost anywhere.
7. The more a motor car weighs, naturally the more fuel and lubricants are used in the driving; the lighter the weight, the lighter the expense of operation. The light weight of the Ford car in its early years was used as an argument against it. Now that is all changed.

This list, in fact, ascribes all-terrain capability to the Model T. A picture from *Today and Tomorrow* (Productivity Inc. edition) shows a 1921 Model T center door sedan mounting the steps of the Benson Polytechnical High School. A Portland Oregon dealer was demonstrating the vehicle's "mountain-goat ruggedness." Another picture shows a Model T as a snowmobile, with steel treads in back and steel sled runners in place of front wheels. This was a utility vehicle for farmers and woodsmen. This reference also points out that the same principles carried over to the Taurus: "An affordable, quality vehicle that is durable and simple to operate."

Foresight and innovation also are important in market identification. Ford wrote, "There is a difference between a need and a wish. The public may need a thing and not know it because it has not yet seen the thing that it needs. The public needed the automobile long before it wished for it" (Ford, 1930, 176).[1] The manufacturer must often create a product to fill an unstated need. In this case, it was inexpensive and reliable transportation that neither horses nor railroads could provide.

The Marketing Vision Statement

Any successful venture begins with a vision statement, a clear picture of what a person or organization wishes to achieve. Ford's first advertisement began with his vision statement.

> Our purpose is to construct and market an automobile specially designed for everyday wear and tear—business, professional, and family use; an automobile which will attain to a sufficient speed to satisfy the average person without acquiring any of those breakneck velocities which are so universally condemned; a machine which will be admired by man, woman, and child alike for its compactness, its simplicity, its safety, its all-around convenience, and—last but not least—its exceedingly reasonable price, which places it within the reach of many thousands who could not think of paying the comparatively fabulous prices asked for most machines (Ford, 1922, 54).

The lesson is to draw an easily communicated mental picture of how the product will satisfy the customers' needs. Any good vision statement has this quality.

PRICING STRATEGY

Ford warns repeatedly against business relationships in which one party—whether labor, management, customer, or supplier—tries to get as much as it can at the others' expense. The same principle applies to pricing.

> If an article has been sold at too high a price and then, because of stagnant business, the price is suddenly cut, the response is sometimes most disappointing. And for a very good reason. The public is wary. It thinks that the price-cut is a fake and it sits around waiting for a real cut. We saw much of that last year. If, on the contrary, the economies of making are transferred at once into the price and if it is well known that such is the policy of the manufacturer, the public will have confidence in him and will respond. They will trust him to give honest value. So standardization may seem bad business unless it carries with it the plan of constantly reducing the price at which the article is sold. And the price has to be reduced (this is very important) because of the manufacturing economies that have come about and not because the falling demand by the public indicates that it is not satisfied with the price. The public should always be wondering how it is possible to give so much for the money (Ford, 1922, 48–49).

This approach should also offer the advantage of promoting steady and not cyclical demand. We have already seen the problem with today's automobile retailing system. Car dealers try to pack in as much markup as they can at the beginning of the new model year. Customers who don't mind buying last year's model know, however, that they can game this system by waiting until the end of the model year. Then the dealer must mark the prices down. The manufacturer must offer incentives to move the inventory, which has already run up thousands of dollars per car in carrying costs.

Sell on Quality, Not on Price

Peters and Austin (1985, 59) tell the story of a senior regional sales manager from John Deere who displayed a tie tack with the letters SOQ NOP: Sell on quality, not on price. "It's my toughest job, in down markets, to make my own people realize that the objective is to sell the benefits, not just resort to price [as the only selling leverage]."

The Deere sales manager told the story of a buyer who was about to give a sale to Deere's competitor because the latter offered a lower price. The Deere manager complimented the buyer on his leather boots, and the buyer talked about them at length. He described the fine leather and added that the boots were practical as well; that is, he described their benefits. The Deere manager asked, "How come you buy those boots and not just a pair off the shelf in an Army-Navy surplus store?" The buyer thought for about twenty seconds and gave the sale to Deere. He had effectively sold himself on the concept of buying quality.

Ford wanted to offer as low a price as possible while never skimping on quality. His first advertisement, the one that began with his vision statement, went on to stress the benefits of his product. It encouraged the customer to sell himself or herself:

> Men who are constantly complaining of shortage of time and lamenting the fewness of days in the week—men to whom five minutes' delay sometimes means the loss of many dollars—will yet depend on the haphazard, uncomfortable, and limited means of transportation afforded by street cars, etc., when the investment of an exceedingly moderate sum in the purchase of a perfected, efficient, high-grade automobile would cut out anxiety and unpunctuality and provide a luxurious means of travel ever at your beck and call.
> Always ready, always sure.
> Built to save you time and consequent money.

Built to take you anywhere you want to go and bring you back again on time.

Built to add to your reputation for punctuality; to keep your customers good-humoured and in a buying mood (Ford, 1922, 55).

The advertisement reminds the reader that his time is worth money, especially in business. The automobile is more reliable than public transportation for meeting schedules. It's easy for the reader to convince himself that the car will pay for itself. The ad also stresses the product's reliability: "Always ready, always sure."

Ford warns against cutting corners to reduce prices. "There is no quicker or surer way of destroying confidence in a business than to make a price reduction which represents the giving of less and not of more value than before" (Ford, 1930, 9). Furthermore,

If prices are used as baits for buyers, to be raised or lowered as the buyers feel about it, it is in effect a handing over of the control of the business to the buyers to do with as they like. That is a very real control and it is exercised in very drastic fashion (Ford, 1930, 9).

We have seen the example of car purchasers who wait until the end of the model year to buy. Clothing customers who wait for the storewide sale are another. Markdowns of 20, 50, or even 75 percent tell customers that the store can really sell for less and the list price is excessive. The 2001 holiday shopping season is a perfect example:

Macy's post-Christmas sales blitz includes 50 percent discounts on furs, men's suits and sportswear, and men's sweaters. Toys R Us was offering discounts of up to 80 percent ("Shoppers Flock To Stores for Deals," 2001).

The obvious lesson to shoppers is to game the system by having Santa Claus come a couple of days after Christmas. He can deliver far more gifts (and necessities like clothing) for the same money. The article also says that retailers must clear the Christmas merchandise in time for their spring product lines. This is a glaring example of the disadvantages of retail inventory and another excellent argument for making-to-order.

This chapter has treated customer relationships, marketing, and pricing. It will now cover supplier relationships, including the lean enterprise concept of supply chain management.

SUPPLY CHAIN MANAGEMENT

Ford underscored the need for the lean enterprise concept of supply chain management very explicitly:

> The manufacturer often sees how swiftly the economies in manufacturing are swallowed up in wasteful distribution and this distribution may not be within the control of the manufacturer. There is no point in economizing in manufacturing if at the same time the suppliers and distributors charge all that the traffic will bear. This is merely to emphasize the fact that the task of putting business on better foundations depends on every department of business and not alone on the manufacturer. Nothing can be cheap when any part of a commodity is dear (Ford, 1930, 18).

This statement reveals three key points:

- It is especially pointless to shop offshore for cheap manufacturing labor when the distribution system adds bloated costs to the final price. Chinese-made American flag pins proliferated in the aftermath of the terrorist attacks of September 11, 2001. They probably cost a few pennies to make but retailed for about a dollar and a half. The final price tag doubtlessly included trans-Pacific shipment plus overhead and profits for all the middlemen.[2]
- A lean manufacturer with a JIT production system cannot realize its full potential without lean suppliers and subcontractors. Or as the adage has it: you can't soar like an eagle when you work with turkeys.
- Leading-edge manufacturers should teach lean operational principles to their business partners (Womack and Jones,

1996).This is known as supplier development, whose goal Schonberger (1986) describes as follows. "The task is complete when the supplier has taken up the crusade for simplification, waste removal, and a fast-paced campaign for rooting out causes of error."

Modern lean manufacturers stress another point: a batch-and-queue supplier or subcontractor anywhere in the supply chain has an effect similar to that of a batch-and-queue production tool. Delivery of a huge batch from a supplier or subcontractor creates inventory that must wait for processing. If a subcontractor waits to accumulate a large batch before working on it, for the sake of economies of scale or equipment utilization, the job that the lean manufacturer turned around in a day may wait another week. Everyone in the supply chain must get in step for the best results.

Daniel Gardner (2001) adds the following warning:

> . . . once merchandise enters the logistics chain, reversing the process is very difficult and expensive to handle. JIT operations cannot afford to have compromised shipments in the pipeline, particularly when the problems don't surface until they hit the port of destination.

As shown here, large batch shipments not only add cycle time as discussed earlier, they can also hide nonconforming materials or parts for considerable time. When the problem finally comes to light, it may take a long time to replace the shipment. One can easily imagine the havoc that a defective shipment from an offshore supplier could cause if the only way to replace it was by surface transportation. This is another reason supply chain management is so important.

The Value of Time in Transportation Activities

Remember that inventory, or float, can accumulate in transit. Ford showed why it is worthwhile to pay high wages to get the best available workers, especially to run large capital investments. The ore-carrying ships of his Great Lakes fleet had almost first-class hotel accommodations for their officers and crews.

> Both the officers' and the crew's quarters are finished in hardwood, with shower baths enough for everyone.
>
> ... On the whole, our wages will run considerably higher than the highest wages elsewhere paid. We make money on these wages, for really, the whole total of wages paid on a ship is not very important—the important thing is to see that you get the full use out of the big investment, which is the ship.
>
> If a ship is held a couple of weeks in port unloading and loading, the loss will probably be greater than the total wages for a year. Low-priced, irresponsible men will not care what happens to a ship or how long it stays in port. Our men are on their toes to see that our ships are kept moving. ... it is a rare thing for one of our ships to be in a port more than twenty-four hours (Ford, 1926, 119–121).

There is an obvious lesson here for employers who still think it is economical to pay workers as little as possible. There are other lessons as well:

- Consider the effect of the 55-mile-an-hour (88 km/hour) national speed limit, which was imposed because of the 1973 OPEC oil embargo, on the U.S. economy. A truck that goes 65 miles an hour (105 km/hour) is 18 percent more productive. The lower speed limit saved gasoline but wasted personal and commercial time.
- It might easily be worth a higher capital expenditure for a commercial airplane that can fly faster, a ship that can sail faster, or a train that can go faster.
- The expression "waiting for my ship to come in" takes on a whole new meaning, and a very unpleasant one, in the context of overseas transportation time. This is another argument against going offshore for cheap labor. If the product has a low price-to-weight ratio, airfreight costs are prohibitive so it must travel by ship. This encourages

accumulation of large batches (and all their disadvantages) and adds several weeks of cycle time.

Freight Management Systems

The need for small deliveries is a consideration in JIT manufacturing. The need for partial truckloads complicates JIT deliveries. The JIT warehouse—an obvious oxymoron—tries to get around this by storing full truckload deliveries and withdrawing JIT quantities for daily or sub-daily delivery to customers. Modern supply chains use truck sharing, freight management systems (FMSs), and third party logistics systems (3PLs) to deliver JIT quantities without any warehousing. The 3PLs often consolidate shipments from different suppliers to get the best rates from shipping firms. Loads travel by truck, rail, ship, air, or a combination to get the best delivery times and rates. The 3PLs also help shippers earn more money, for example by reducing the distance over which a vehicle travels empty.

Ford apparently had a good FMS that operated without the help of computers. His interplant supply system ran like clockwork, and freight consolidation played a role.

> The problem of coordination is simplified by standard carloads—of which we have twenty-five. The standard carload for front axles, for example, contains exactly 400 sets. Limited quantities of smaller parts, such as spring hangers, are always included with the shipment of larger parts, but these, too, are standardized. This is worked out in a manner that will take advantage of the lowest freight classification.
>
> This method does away with filling out shipping orders. Instead, they are printed and books are kept on one master part only. The only time it is necessary to specify quantities is when special shipments are made (Ford, 1926, 117–118).

Note the consolidation of shipments (small parts with larger ones) to reduce transportation costs and to get the best shipping rates.

The following description underscores the effectiveness and coordination of the Ford logistics system. Norwood (1931, 20–24) described the Ford logistics system as a continent-spanning conveyor that moved millions of parts and hundreds of tons of raw materials. Deliveries were coordinated, precisely scheduled, and apparently just in time. Supply was never to exceed or fall short of requirements; surpluses as well as shortages were wasteful. "Using that multitude of additional links offered by rail, highway, water, and air, it has butt-welded them with their own time-tables and picketed them with telegraphic checkings as watchful as the straw bosses who supervise progression along the conveyor lines of the shop."

This sounds a lot like a modern freight management system. The reference continues by adding that the transportation system worked a lot like the conveyor belts in the plant. Three segments were considered: part production, transit, and final assembly in an assembly plant. The entire description is characteristic of a well-managed supply chain with just-in-time delivery from suppliers to downstream customers. The system coordinated the activities of 3,500 outside suppliers and the movement of the 6,800 different parts that went into the Ford Model A. Raw materials might be delivered to a plant, which then shipped parts to several assembly plants; the schedules for all these activities had to coordinate.

Transportation was by highway, air, water, and/or rail. In the latter case rail cars had to be formed into trains. The cars were arranged for later detachment in the correct order for transfer to connecting lines. Waybills and bills of lading were prepared while freight cars were being loaded and moved; these activities took place in parallel to save time. The idea of performing independent tasks in parallel seems like common sense, but Norwood (1931, 32) cited an average 24-hour delay at other railroads while these activities happened sequentially.

The system was sufficiently robust to deal with unforeseen events like wrecks and rail line blockages. The fact that a 24-hour delay in a certain delivery would idle the Houston assembly plant attests to the JIT nature of Ford operations. If a rail car for Houston suffered a breakdown, a car with the same parts that was on its way to Dallas could be diverted to Houston if the Dallas plant could stand the delay. The car that was going to Houston would then go to Dallas after repair. The transportation department's knowledge of every car's location at all times facilitated such remedies. The system was apparently good enough to keep the company running despite a major flood that cut rail routes through the St. Louis gateway.

As for water transportation, Norwood (1931, 38) adds that a maximum variation of 48 hours was allowed for deliveries from 6,000 miles (9654 km) away that had to pass through the Panama Canal. Deliveries by sea from New York or Philadelphia to Jacksonville, Florida, were expected within 24 hours of the planned delivery time.

Demurrage (charges for delaying a railroad car for loading or unloading beyond its scheduled departure time) was insignificant in comparison with the freight system's total activity. The reference even cites "less-than-carload lots," evidence that the Ford Motor Company recognized the LTL (less than load) issue in modern logistics systems.

Supplier Development

Recall that a lean manufacturer cannot achieve its full potential if it must rely on non-lean suppliers and subcontractors. Customers also sometimes require education so they can work effectively with their supply chain partners. Consider the basic concepts of Polaroid's zero base pricing (ZBP) approach: "target pricing and cost containment for suppliers" (Schonberger, 1986, 157).

> The first step is for a Polaroid buyer to ask the supplier to fork over data on its unit costs. . . . Buyers are not to accept cost increases as justification for a price rise. Instead, at that point, Polaroid people visit the supplier's plant and offer tips on how to contain costs (Schonberger, 1986, 157).

This is a good summary of how Ford handled an automobile body supplier who complained about his low profits. Instead of giving him a higher price, Ford's company examined his operation and discovered that the bodies should cost half as much.

> The man finally consented to try to manufacture at exactly one half his former price. Then, for the first time in his life, he began to learn how to do business. He had to raise wages, for he had to have first-class men. Under the pressure of necessity, he found he could make cost reductions here, there, and everywhere, and the upshot of it was that he made more money out of the low price than he had ever made out of the high price, and his workmen have received a higher wage (Ford, 1926, 43–44).

Sorensen (1956, 81) identifies the supplier as the C. R. Wilson Body Company, of which Fred Fisher was then superintendent. Fisher and his brothers later went on to make "Bodies by Fisher." Wilson had wanted $152 per body. Sorensen built a model body and tabulated the labor and materials costs. The total came to fifty dollars, and Fisher later persuaded Wilson to accept $72 per body. These improvements came, of course, from lean manufacturing methods.

A business does not exist as an isolated entity, but rather as a member of a supply chain that begins with raw material providers and ends with the customer. This chapter began by treating Ford's approach to the customer, which included considerations such as identifying customer needs and expanding market share through continuous price reductions. It then showed the importance of supply chain management and of removing waste from the transportation system. The next chapter treats one of Henry Ford's contemporaries, Frederick Winslow Taylor. Taylor's scientific management work may have influenced the Ford Company, and it played a major role in laying the foundations of what we now call lean manufacturing.

Notes

1. The Prussian field marshal Helmuth von Moltke actually expressed a need for trucks in 1868. "[A truck] can travel by itself, consumes but a

fraction of its load, and covers greater distances. Military authorities will undoubtedly gain much from the use of trucks when they have been invented" (Hughes, 1993, 257). Moltke was referring to steam-driven vehicles, *Strassenlokomotives*.

Strassenlokomotives may have been similar to a "road engine" that Henry Ford saw in 1875, when he was twelve years old. "It was intended primarily for driving threshing machines and sawmills and was simply a portable engine and boiler mounted on wheels with a water tank and coal cart trailing behind" (Ford, 1922, 22). Ford had seen horses transport such engines to work sites but this one had a chain drive that allowed it to propel itself. The chain could be disconnected and replaced with a belt to drive machinery.

2. Mainland China was meanwhile selling, presumably to the other side, statuettes of a triumphant Osama bin Laden holding the Pentagon, and figures of the burning World Trade Center.

TEN

Frederick Winslow Taylor and Scientific Management

History is often unfair. Consider what was named for Edsel Ford, a very competent leader and manager. People remember Frederick Winslow Taylor best for his association with the bankrupt idea that workers should leave their brains at the factory gate. I must admit to including a picture of brains at a factory gate in Levinson (1998, 101) and a "Taylorsaurus Rex" dinosaur in Rose and Buckley (1999, 20), although in both cases I was referring to Taylorism taken to an extreme. Many twentieth century managers did, unfortunately, take Taylor's writings to the extreme of trying to turn their workers into robots. Purtell (1991) says Taylor's followers "divorced his philosophy and married his methods."[1] Taylor, like Ford, actually developed many management principles that became popular only in the late twentieth century, and this chapter will describe them.

Taylor even introduced the idea of the modern business school:

> Unfortunately there is no school of management. There is no single establishment where a relatively large part of the details of management can be seen, which represent the best of their kinds. The finest developments are for the most part isolated, and in many cases almost buried with the mass of rubbish which surrounds them (Taylor, 1911a, 200–201).

This statement ties in with standardizing the best available practices (the "one best way") and with knowledge retention. Standardization preserved improvements that many trades lost repeatedly because their inventors never recorded them. Taylor applied this to the shop; this excerpt shows its application to business management as well.

This chapter details the similarities between Ford's principles and Taylor's theories of scientific management. It dispels some popular myths about Taylorism, particularly his ideas on labor relations. It also illustrates how some current management practices are quite similar to Taylor's nineteenth and early twentieth century ideas. It describes the relationship between Taylor's scientific management and today's lean manufacturing techniques. Transformation to the ideal lean enterprise of today can, in fact, occur only through successful change management. This chapter later describes how Taylor addressed this topic at length.

DID TAYLOR INFLUENCE FORD?

Charles Sorensen (1956, 41) said outright that Frederick Winslow Taylor had no influence on the Ford Motor Company. Lacey (1986, 107) says, however, that James Couzens was very interested in Taylor's methods.

Ford may well have developed some of Taylor's key principles independently. His observation of waste effort in farming during his boyhood doubtlessly spurred his obsession with attacking waste in every activity. It's also possible that Ford (or people working with him, like Couzens) read Taylor's publications but did not hire Taylor or a Taylor-trained consultant. The System Company (1911, 12) recommended, "They [principles of scientific management] should be introduced, in their entirety, in no factory except under the direct supervision of Mr. Taylor or of men trained by him or trained directly under his influence." Sorensen may mean simply that the Ford Motor Company did not do this. His comments on experts are consistent with Henry Ford's view that so-called experts are often useless. Ford would probably not have hired an external consultant even of Taylor's reputation and caliber. Ford's and Taylor's ideas, however, correlate very strongly.

Correlation between Ford's Principles and Scientific Management

> Flavius: But wherefore art not in thy shop today?
>   Why dost thou lead these men about the streets?
> Cobbler: Truly, sir, to wear out their shoes to get myself
>   into more work.
>
> —*Julius Caesar*, Act I, Scene 1

Taylor wrote (1911, 5) that after the mechanization of shoemaking working-class people could buy one or two pairs of shoes per year , whereas before that they often went barefoot because they could afford new shoes only every five years or so. Ford (1922, 153) wrote, "When shoes were made by hand, only the very well-to-do could own more than a single pair of shoes, and most working people went barefooted in summer. Now, hardly any one has only one pair of shoes, and shoe making is a great industry." Both Ford and Taylor cite this example to show what happens when a trade is mechanized.

The change displaces workers on a short-term basis; the mass production of shoes forced most traditional cobblers out of business. As shoes became cheaper, however, the demand for them increased, and this created more shoemaking jobs. Shoe companies needed workers to run and maintain the shoemaking machinery. Since each worker could produce far more shoes than a traditional cobbler, he or she could earn better wages. The lesson is that while jobs are initially lost to improvements in manufacturing technology, they are eventually replaced with better jobs that raise everybody's standard of living.[2] The following excerpt illustrates this point further.

> If production costs have been high, the manager's method of attacking the problem in the past has been simply to try to lower wages or to add machinery. If selling costs have increased, he has tenaciously tried to increase selling prices.
>   . . . But a changed mental attitude suggests a new approach. If costs of production are high the business man will study the equipment that he already has.

... [Because] the reduced cost to make, the increase in wages, [and] the reduction in prices [all] come from the application of principles of efficiency—not by skimping material, but by finding how to use the least amount of the best—not by increasing the workman's pace, but by cutting his lost motions and applying his energy intelligently—not by increasing prices, but by increasing profit, by reducing costs (Frederick M. Feiker, "What Scientific Management Is," *The System Company*, 1911, 14).

This describes exactly what Ford always tried to do. The next section treats the relationship between Taylor's scientific management and what we now call lean manufacturing.

SCIENTIFIC MANAGEMENT, LEAN MANUFACTURING, AND KAIZEN BLITZ

Much of what people now call lean manufacturing is a reapplication of the scientific management principles of the early twentieth century. Layout changes (as described in Chapter 8) that make work flow more easily are an aspect of scientific management, as are task studies and task redesigns.

Modern programs improve on the original form of scientific management by recognizing that the front-line employees often know more about the job than anyone else. The old method divided responsibilities into planners (management) and doers (workers). It was the planners' responsibility to observe and time the workers, change equipment layouts, and redesign tasks. This was the origin of the "leave your brain at the factory gate" paradigm for the doers.

Modern programs like kaizen blitz ("lightning continuous improvement") use Taylor's principles but the doers apply them. Basset (1919) cites two examples that show, in fact, that empowered workers of that era performed activities that modern practitioners would call kaizen blitzes or kaizen events, and they achieved similar productivity gains. "In another factory, within six months from the time the workers were given a voice in the management, they devised more improved machinery than had been known in that particular industry within twenty years" (Basset, 1919, 133).

The next section shows the correlation between Taylor's, Ford's, and Frank Gilbreth's motion efficiency principles.

TAYLOR AND MOTION EFFICIENCY

Taylor identified wasted motion and its enormous detrimental effects on productivity. He cited Frank B. Gilbreth's discovery that the motion of bending over to pick up each brick had become a habitual part of the bricklaying trade. The worker actually lowered and raised his upper body to lift a five-pound (2.3-kg) brick, and he did this perhaps 1,000 times a day. It should be obvious that performing the equivalent of 1,000 toe touches (from a sitting position) does not add value to the job, but bricklayers had always done it that way. The phrase, "we've always done it that way" is now a widely recognized warning flag.[3]

Figure 10-1 suggests that placement of the bricks at about waist level (B) will allow the mason to work more quickly than placement on the ground (A). In addition, as you can see in the revised figure, it's also useful to know which hand the mason holds his trowel with. In the original figure the mason would have

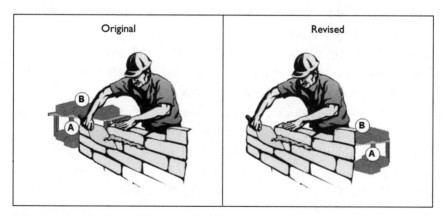

| Original | Revised |

Figure 10-1. Place the bricks to minimize wasted effort and motion[4]

to either put down his trowel or turn around completely to get a new brick, even from position B. It might also be desirable to have a table whose height can increase as the wall grows. Richard Schonberger (1986) says that he once worked for the fastest brick-layer in North Dakota, who insisted that his helper place the bricks where he could retrieve them without looking. He also says (1982, 94) that this practice made the bricklayer four or five times faster than others: "The champion did less bending, stoop-ing, turning, and reaching."

Arnold and Faurote (1915, 162–163) cite the same advantage for the work slides at Ford's Highland Park plant, and the reference says specifically that they reduced labor costs. These work slides conveyed parts from one workstation to the next, to positions that were easy for the workers to reach. The reference adds (p. 274), "In every instance of work-slide placing there was a gain of from 30 to 100 percent in the production volume, with the same meth-ods, machines, small tools, and men; seemingly nothing was done to decrease labor costs, yet large savings shown immediately." The same underlying principle applies to any job in which people must handle tools and materials.

If this seems obvious and trivial, Figure 10-2 shows just how easy it is for waste to become an accepted and ingrained part of any job. This figure is an outstanding illustration of a bedrock prin-ciple of lean enterprise: *waste often becomes an ingrained and accepted part of the job. The joke about how underachievers install a light bulb*—by turning the ladder while one worker holds the bulb—*suddenly seems a lot less funny when we identify similar built-in waste in jobs in our workplaces.*

Ford applied Taylor's concept of motion efficiency extensively. "What is the use of putting a tremendous force behind a blunt chisel if a light blow on a sharp chisel will do the work? . . . For any one to be required to use more force than is absolutely nec-essary for the job in hand is waste" (1922, 18–19).

Ford also said that no job should require a worker to take more than one step in any direction. Edward Mott Woolley (*The*

| "The usual method of providing the brick-layer with material" (Figure 9 in Gilbreth, 1911. The photo is dated 9/5/1906, believed to be in the public domain). | "Non-stooping scafold designed so that uprights are out of the bricklayer's way whenever reaching for brick and mortar at the same time" (Figure 1 in Gilbreth, 1911). Notice the bricks' orderly arrangement in packets, and the fact that the bricks and the wall are both at approximately waist level. |

Figure 10-2. Bricklaying, before and after Gilbreth

System Company, 1911, 41) wrote the following of a fabric folding operation in a bleaching and dyeing factory in Wilmington, Delaware:

> But all [employees] took two steps to the right to secure their cloth, returned to the tables, folded the stuff and deposited it on another pile two steps to the left. That had always been the practice; no one had ever thought to question it.

Redesign of the job doubled its output without adding more workers or requiring the existing ones to put forth more effort.

Break the Job into Steps

The book has already shown how Ford subdivided tasks to make their performance more efficient. Taylor (1911a, 48) wrote, ". . . divide the man's work into its elements and time each element separately." He identified the following elements of loading pig iron onto a rail car:

1. Pick up the pig.
2. Walk with it on flat ground.

3. Walk up an incline to the rail car.
4. Throw the pig down, or lay it on a pile.
5. Walk back empty to get another pig.

Modern value analysis would, of course, identify the entire job as non-value-adding (transportation). The pig iron did, however, need to go onto the rail car, and this might have been the only way to get it there with existing technology. Taylor's methods improved the operation's productivity (amount loaded per employee-day) about 270 percent and its wages 60 percent. The specifics of how Taylor brought about this improvement are discussed in the section "Involve those whom the change affects" at the end of this chapter.

Frederick M. Feiker (*The System Company*, 1911, 117–18) describes the subdivision of tasks in pillowcase manufacture. He begins by citing three principles for task design:

- Identify the operations and how they are performed.
- Eliminate any unnecessary operations and shorten the distance that each piece must travel.
- Develop the best way to perform each operation.

Pillowcase manufacturing involved eleven operations, which began with tearing the cloth into the correct lengths. The second and third operations were to sew the side and the end respectively. The first worker took the cloth, sewed the side, and passed it on a slide to the second worker. This person sewed the end. The same person did not sew the side and the end because this would have presumably required her to turn the piece ninety degrees. Reorienting the piece is waste motion. If the second worker and her machine were ninety degrees to the first (the reference does not describe the layout, but see Figure 10-3) she would not need to reorient the work. Subdivision of labor according to Feiker's principles increased output from 53 to 142 per hour, a 167 percent improvement.

In Figure 10-3, the "turn pillowcase" step is necessary if one person performs the entire job. Task subdivision allows removal of

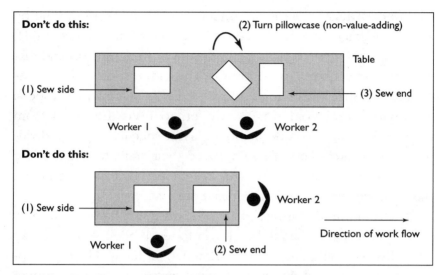

Don't do this:

(2) Turn pillowcase (non-value-adding)

(1) Sew side

Table

(3) Sew end

Worker 1   Worker 2

Don't do this:

(1) Sew side

Worker 2

Worker 1   (2) Sew end

Direction of work flow

Figure 10-3. Possible job design for pillowcase manufacturing

this non-value-adding motion, but it may easily remain part of the job unless everyone knows how to identify friction.

The principles of layout change and task study and redesign (or Taylor's view on motion efficiency and breaking jobs into steps) help underscore friction's treacherous and insidious nature and its ability to hide in plain view of the entire workforce.

The next section dispels the "leave your brain at the factory gate" myth about Taylorism. It also shows that Taylor described concepts and principles that modern practitioners consider state-of-the-art:

- The idea, which Ford also emphasized, that management and labor are partners instead of adversaries
- Avoidance of dysfunctional performance measurements
- Management by wandering around (MBWA), or gemba ("real place," value-adding workplace) management

THE TRUTH BEHIND TAYLORISM

Taylor did write, "Thus all of the planning which under the old system was done by the workman, as a result of his personal experience, must of necessity under the new system be done by the management in accordance with the laws of the science" (1911, 16). Managers were to identify the best way to do the job and that is how workers were to perform it. This is the source of the misconception that Taylor regarded workers as automata or robots.

Taylor's real goal was, however, to hold the gains from improvement in the work methods. Taylor speculated that individual trade workers had often improved their crafts throughout the centuries but, because they often never recorded or even taught the improvements, the discoveries were lost.

Gilbreth found that masons' work was much harder than necessary because they had to bend over for each brick. A mason may have discovered that he could work much more quickly if the supply of bricks was at about waist level instead of on the ground. During the era of trade guilds, he might have taught his journeymen and apprentices this helpful procedure, but he would not have taught it to his competitors. Also recall that workers often found it necessary to soldier, or deliberately limit their productivity. If the mason was paid by the day, for example, finishing in half the usual time would halve his pay. Juran and Gryna (1988) mention *knacks*, or individual workers' knowledge of how to do a job better than the standard practice.

Scientific management included provisions for recording, teaching, and institutionalizing discoveries. Taylor expected these to come from engineers, scientists, and managers, but he recognized that they could also come from workers. A surgeon operates with

> . . . standard implements and methods which represent the best knowledge of the world up to date, [but] he is able to use his own originality and ingenuity to make real additions to the world's knowledge, instead of reinventing things which are old. In a similar way the workman who is cooperating with his many teachers under scientific management has an opportunity to develop which is at least as good as and generally better than that which he had when the whole problem was 'up to him' and he did his work entirely unaided (Taylor, 1911, 66).

Furthermore,

It is true that with scientific management the workman is not allowed to use whatever implements and methods he sees fit in the daily practise [sic] of his work. Every encouragement, however, should be given him to suggest improvements, both in methods and in implements. And whenever a workman proposes an improvement, it should be the policy of the management to make a careful analysis of the new method, and if necessary conduct a series of experiments to determine accurately the relative merit of the new suggestion and of the old standard. And whenever the new method is found to be markedly superior to the old, it should be adopted as the standard for the whole establishment. The workman should be given the full credit for the improvement, and should be paid a cash premium as a reward for his ingenuity. In this way the true initiative of the workman is better attained under scientific management than under the old individual plan (Taylor, 1911, 67).

There is little difference between Hewlett-Packard's "best practices" program and the preceding statement by Taylor:

Each job at HP has standard operating procedures (SOPs) associated with it. These SOPs are called practices. If an employee can find a better way to accomplish a job, he or she is encouraged to document the new method. Management then reviews the new method and its estimated advantages and, if approved, it becomes a new "best practice." Each procedure guide is updated and the employee receives credit for the new method. Appropriately, the reward system is geared to benefit those employees who actively seek a better way to do their own jobs (Bakerjian, 1993, 1–8).

These passages show that Taylor at least described key leading edge management concepts, specifically standardization and best practice deployment, if he didn't actually invent them:

- Tom Peters emphasizes that the person who does the job knows more about it than anyone else, and is thus qualified to improve it.
- Taylor introduces the modern suggestion system by saying that workers should receive cash premiums for successful improvements.
- Taylor also describes the concept of designed experiments, including the comparison of the new method with a control (the current method), to judge the merits of a proposed change.
- This idea actually preceded the invention of statistical techniques that would make multivariable experiments practical. Taylor's efforts to run a controlled experiment with nineteenth-century analytical methods required a small fortune, 400 tons of iron and steel, and 26 years—and it couldn't account for interactions between process factors.
- The lack of worker discretion in the daily practice of his job. This is consistent with ISO 9000, which prescribes work instructions and standards for each operation.
- The institutionalization and standardization of worker-initiated improvements. Holding the gains is part of the plan-do-check-act (PDCA) cycle as described by Juran (1988, 10.26) and was described by Taylor in the excerpts shown above.
- Best practice deployment. This means adopting the best method for, to use Taylor's words, "the entire establishment."

Taylor and Labor Relations

Despite Taylor's undeserved reputation for turning workers into mindless automata, his view of employer-employee relationships matched Ford's. He assigned employers, not workers, the biggest share of the blame for soldiering. What did the employer expect when it responded to a productivity improvement by cutting the workers' piece rates?

. . . after a workman has had the price per piece of the work he is doing lowered two or three times as a result of his having worked harder and increased his output, he is likely entirely to lose sight of his employer's side of the case and become imbued with a grim determination to have no more cuts if soldiering will prevent it.

There should be instead:

. . . mutual confidence which should exist between a leader and his men, the enthusiasm, the feeling that they are all working for the same end and will share in the results . . . (Taylor, 1911, 8).

Taylor and Ford reduced their workers' piece rates, but they also made it possible for the workers to make far more pieces without working harder. It was reasonable that, if the employer's science, management, and capital made it possible for a worker to double his or her hourly output, the worker and the employer should share the fruits of the improvement. The worker was better off making, for example, 200 pieces at 15 cents per piece than 100 at 20 cents if the necessary time and effort remained constant. The wages per piece went down but the wages per hour went up. This, of course, allowed the employer to lower the price of the finished item, for which the worker was often a customer. The employer had a duty to use some of the profit to make the worker even more productive and thus able to earn an even higher wage.

Taylor on Dysfunctional Labor Relations

Taylor warned his readers against what Ford called the "spokesperson who does not work in the shop, who does not work in any shop, whose sole ambition perhaps is to never again have to work in a shop." He said that when workers paid union dues they expected the union's leaders to do things for them. The leaders obliged them by looking for grievances or creating them if none existed; they had to justify their pay and positions.[5] He also warned against limiting production for, "If their employers are in a competitive business, sooner or later those competitors whose workmen do not limit the output will take the trade away from them, and they will be thrown out of work" (Taylor, 1911a, 187–188).

Taylor added that productivity restrictions (institutionalized soldiering) were already causing poverty in England. He thus exposed part of the rot that had set into the British Empire even before the First World War. Henry Ford later offered (to paraphrase that famous Briton, Rudyard Kipling) to "take up the White Man's burden" for fixing the supposedly dominant world power's social and economic problems:

> ... with management attuned to high wages and no individual limits on production, England can be made a high wage and therefore a high consumption country (Ford, 1926, 264–265).

Taylor recognized, however, that unions could perform beneficial functions. He wrote a paper in 1895 that said trade unions, especially English trade unions, had helped not only their members but society in general. They had gained shorter work hours (during an era in which people often worked twelve hours a day, six days a week). They had also played a role in improving working conditions. He does not go into further detail, but nineteenth century workplaces were not particularly safe. Even photographs of shops in 1911 (e.g., *The System Company*, 1911) show machinery with exposed belts. The motion picture *The Molly Maguires* shows the conditions in which coal miners worked, and the mine owners found ways to cheat the miners of their meager pay. Unions doubtlessly played a constructive role in putting an end to such conditions, although progressive employers like Henry Ford also drove advances in workplace safety. Taylor summarizes,

> Union labor is sacred just so long as its acts are fair and good, and it is damnable just as soon as its acts are bad. Its rights are precisely those of nonunion labor, neither more nor less. The boycott, the use of force or intimidation, and the oppression of non-union workmen by labor unions are damnable; these acts of tyranny are thoroughly

un-American and will not be tolerated by the American people (Taylor, 1911a, 191).

Labor's Response to Taylor

Front-line workers were apparently receptive to Taylor's methods:

At least 50,000 workmen in the United States are now employed under this system; and they are receiving from 30 per cent to 100 per cent higher wages daily than are paid to men of similar caliber with whom they are surrounded, while the companies employing them are more prosperous than ever before.... During all these years there has never been a single strike among the men working under this system. In place of the suspicious watchfulness and the more or less open warfare which characterizes the ordinary types of management, there is universally friendly cooperation between the management and the men (Taylor, 1911, 11).

Management and Labor as Partners

Ford emphasized that the employee and employer were partners. Taylor wrote that the principal goals of management were "prosperity for the employee, coupled with prosperity for the employer." Workers were not to regard their bosses as slave drivers, "but as friends who were teaching them and helping them to earn much higher wages than they had ever earned before. It would have been absolutely impossible for anyone to have stirred up strife between these men and their employers" (1911, 35). Taylor later (1911, 73) identifies the public as a third stakeholder in the manufacturing enterprise. Like Ford, Taylor says the public will compel both employer and worker to deliver their best work at the lowest possible cost. Economic Darwinism culls out both managers and workers who will not uphold their ends of the work.

Dysfunctional Performance Measurements

Modern management experts recognize the truth in the adage, "Be careful what you wish, you might get it." Managers express their wishes through performance measurements, and bad measurements result in bad performance. Taylor recognized the danger of measuring workers solely on output. "One of the dangers to be guarded against, when the pay of a man or woman is made in any way to depend on the quantity of work done, is that in the effort to increase the quantity the quality is apt to deteriorate" (1911, 45). Firms that encouraged their workers to focus on "making the numbers" during the late twentieth century should have paid more attention to what Taylor actually wrote instead of the stereotyped image of brains at the factory gate.

"Management by Wandering Around" (MBWA)

Managers should go to the value-adding workplace (Masaaki Imai's gemba, or "real place") and see how workers actually do the job. A manager who stays in his or her office cannot really understand what happens in the factory, which is where the enterprise adds value to its product. The manager's presence is also conducive to morale. William Shakespeare describes how King Henry V practiced what Tom Peters calls "management by wandering around" (MBWA) on the night before the Battle of Agincourt (25 October, 1415):

> *A largess universal like the sun*
> *His liberal eye doth give to every one,*
> *Thawing cold fear, that mean and gentle all,*[6]
> *Behold, as may unworthiness define,*
> *A little touch of Harry in the night.*
> —*King Henry V*, Act IV, Prologue

The French nobles, in contrast, boasted to one another about their armor and horses, much as unenlightened modern executives might show each other color transparencies in their corner offices instead of visiting the shop floor. King Henry and the Constable of France also exhibited very different views about the role and importance of their common soldiers, i.e. the equivalent of their blue-collar workers:

CONSTABLE:	KING HENRY:
...our superfluous lackeys and our peasants, Who in unnecessary action swarm About our squares of battle, were enow To purge this field of such a hilding [worthless] foe... *Act IV, Scene 2*	And Crispin Crispian [Saint Crispin's Day, 25 October] shall ne'er go by, From this day to the ending of the world, But we in it shall be remember'd; We few, we happy few, we band of brothers; For he to-day that sheds his blood with me Shall be my brother; be he ne'er so vile, This day shall gentle his condition . . . [make him as if he was part of the gentry, even if he is a commoner] *Act IV, Scene 3*

Testimony to the relative effectiveness of the two management styles includes two movies (starring Sir Laurence Olivier and Kenneth Branagh respectively) and England's decision to name a battleship of the early twentieth century the *Agincourt.*

Arthur Wellesley, the Duke of Wellington, often went to the location of the hottest action to see what was happening and to encourage his soldiers. He called this "taking trouble"—that is, taking the trouble to find out for himself what was happening.

> It [Wellington's battle tactics] also required a particularly intense 'managerial' style—'taking trouble' with the battle, as Wellington himself would later put it. The general must make himself the eyes of his own army ... must constantly change position to deal with crises as they occur along the front of his sheltered line, must remain at the point of crisis until it is resolved and must still keep alert to anticipate the development of crises elsewhere (Keegan, 1987, 149).

... he counted on word of mouth less than other generals of his age, because of his settled practice of 'taking trouble,' that is, going to see for himself (Keegan, 1987, 157).

Taylor cited the value of MBWA in promoting good labor relations.

... the close, intimate cooperation, the constant personal contact between the two sides [labor and management], will tend to diminish friction and discontent. It is difficult for two people whose interests are the same, and who work side by side accomplishing the same object, all day long, to keep up a quarrel (1911, 75).

The employer who goes through his works with kid gloves on, and is never known to dirty his hands or clothes, and who either talks to his men in a condescending and patronizing way, or else not at all, has no chance whatsoever of ascertaining their real thoughts or feelings (Taylor, 1911a, 184).

Other scientific management practitioners also recognized the value of MBWA:

I try to go through the shops as often as I can, to shake hands with the men and talk to them of their work. I do not believe an employer can be too familiar with his men; I have never found that I endangered discipline so.

I know all my superintendents, foremen, and office men intimately and many of the workers in the shops are my old friends.

My personal contact with my employees and the establishment of friendly relations with them is the chief factor in the success of my business (Richard T. Crane, "Personal Contact Pays," in *The System Company*, 1911a, 144).

Henry Ford also practiced MBWA. Gourley (1997, 38) writes, "Henry didn't much care for sitting in his office. He preferred to walk through his factories and talk to his workers."

This section has covered Taylor's description and deployment of modern leading-edge management methods, including very progressive ideas about labor relations. The next section adds Taylor's observations on change management, a prerequisite for successful transformation to lean enterprise.

PRINCIPLES FOR CHANGE MANAGEMENT

> The worst mistake that can be made is to refer to any part of the system as being "on trial." Once a given step is decided upon, all parties must be made to understand that it will go whether any one around the place likes it or not. In making changes in system the things that are given a "fair trial" fail, while the things that "must go," go all right.
> —Frederick Winslow Taylor, *Shop Management* (1911a, 136)

> Do, or do not. There is no try.
> —Yoda (*The Empire Strikes Back*)

The father of scientific management was about three-quarters of a century ahead of George Lucas's fictional Jedi master in stating this key principle for success.[7] Yoda admittedly phrases it in a form that's easier to remember. Successful change agents recognize the need for absolute management commitment to any new program.

Lip service is among the surest ways to make a program fail. The organization's members will view every new productivity or quality improvement initiative as the program of the year (or month, depending on executive management's attention span). Taylor added the following specific warning:

> The writer would again insist that in no case should the managers of an establishment, the work of which is elaborate, undertake to change from the old to the new type unless the directors of the company fully understand and believe in the principles of scientific management and unless they appreciate all that is involved in making this change, particularly the time required, and unless they want scientific management greatly (Taylor, 1911, 71).

Taylor (1911a, 129–31) also emphasizes the need to change not only procedures but also organizational culture. Culture includes the attitudes and habits of everyone in the workforce and the way they relate to and think about their work. Taylor promises his readers, "A complete revolution in [the workers'] mental attitude toward their employers and their work." Patience and persistence are critical, and managers can expect lasting change to require from two to four years of steady effort.

Use Visible Successes to Promote Change

A key advantage of kaizen blitz is instant gratification for the participants. Workers make a change and see higher productivity, often in a few days. Taylor identified the role of successes, which could be small but had to be visible, in organizational change.

> [The workers'] real instruction, however, must come through a series of object lessons. They must be convinced that a great increase in speed is possible by seeing here and there a man among them increase his pace and double or treble his output. They must see this pace maintained until they are convinced that it is not a mere spurt; and, most important of all, they must see the men who "get there" in this way receive a proper increase in wages and become satisfied. It is only with these object lessons in plain sight that the new theories can be made to stick (Taylor, 1911a, 132-133).

The key points are equally applicable today:

- The "great increase in speed" comes not from greater effort but from deployment of productivity and quality improvement techniques. This is exactly what happens in a successful kaizen blitz.
- The results are visible to the rest of the workplace.
- Recognition need not come in the form of immediately higher wages. Teams can receive immediate recognition such as an article in the company newspaper. Wages should, however, increase as greater productivity enables the employer to pay more. Ford and Taylor both stressed the point that workers should share the rewards of higher productivity.

Involve Those Whom the Change Affects

Taylor used the carrot instead of the stick to get workers to cooperate with his motion efficiency experiments. He observed pig iron handlers at Bethlehem Steel, who loaded about 12.5 long tons (12.7 metric tons) a day into railroad cars. He believed that a worker who used the most efficient methods could load 47 tons a day without greater exertion. He also realized that the workers who handled the 92-pound (41.8-kg) iron pigs would probably not believe this.

He selected a worker and asked if he would like to earn $1.85 a day instead of his current wage of $1.15 a day. To do this, the worker had to do what Taylor's assistant told him. "When he tells you to pick up a pig and walk, you pick it up and you walk, and when he tells you to sit down and rest, you sit down" (Taylor, 1911, 21).

The worker succeeded in loading 47.5 tons of pig iron onto the railroad car without tiring himself. Taylor found that a worker who was handling 92-pound iron pigs should be under load 43 percent of the time and free from load the rest of the time. Having the worker rest 57 percent of the time sounds wasteful but, had he been told only that he could earn a 61 percent higher wage by loading 47.5 tons of iron, "...in his desire to earn his high wages he would have tired himself out by 11 or 12 o'clock in the day. He would have kept so steadily at work that his muscles would not have had the proper periods of rest absolutely needed for recuperation, and he would have been completely exhausted early in the day" (Taylor, 1911, 28).

It was almost as tiring to hold the iron pig as it was to carry it. The thought of workers standing around with 92-pound loads sounds ludicrous but remember the bricklayers who bent over to get each new brick. The worker therefore had to move whenever he was holding a pig. Some workers found it more convenient to run with the pig up the inclined plank into the rail car, and Taylor apparently allowed them to do this. The extra energy they used by running repaid itself by ridding them of the load more quickly—a concept that can easily apply, in a business sense, to other activities.

Chapter 9 showed, for example, that a truck that burns more fuel per mile by going 65 mph (105 km/hour) instead of 55 mph (88 km/hour) may still save money by delivering its load more quickly. The basic principle is, "Beware of false economies."

When other workers saw that it was indeed possible to load more than three times as much pig iron into a rail car without working harder, and to earn more pay by doing so, they were willing to accept the new methods. This method of change management was far more effective than telling them they had to do it the new way.

Frederick Winslow Taylor was therefore well ahead of many modern management scientists in identifying change management as an issue, and in implementing it.

The next section shows that Taylor recognized the value of controlled experiments. Statistical methods to support a 12-variable experiment did not, unfortunately, exist in his era. Engineers who are familiar with modern industrial statistics—specifically factorial and fractional factorial experimental designs—will find this story entertaining, if somewhat tragic. Applied statisticians can use this story to underscore the merits of modern design of experiments (DOE) techniques.

AN EXPERIMENTAL DESIGN DISASTER

In 1880, Taylor wanted to identify the best angles and tool shapes for cutting steel, and also the best cutting speed (Taylor, 1911, 54–58). "At the time that these experiments were started it was his belief that they would not last longer than six months . . ." Taylor did everything that an experimenter should do. He identified the factors that affected the results:

1. The metal's qualities that affected the cutting speed, on a 1–100 scale.
2. The chemical composition and heat treatment of the tool steel, on a 1–7 scale.

3. The thickness of the shaving that the tool was to remove from the workpiece.
4. The shape or contour of the tool's cutting edge, on a 1–6 scale.
5. Coolant, on a 1 (dry) to 1.41 (copious water stream) scale.
6. The depth of the cut.
7. The duration of the cut; time between tool regrindings.
8. Lip and angle clearances of the tool.
9. The elasticity of the work and the tool, as reflected by chatter.
10. The diameter of the casting or forging that was to be cut.
11. The pressure of the chip or shaving on the tool's cutting surface.
12. The pulling power and the speed and feed changes for the machine.

Fractional factorial experimental designs were unknown in 1880, and here is what happened:

> It may seem preposterous to many people that it should have required a period of 26 years to investigate the effect of these twelve variables on the cutting speed of metals. . . . And in fact the great length of time consumed in making each single experiment was caused by the difficulty of holding eleven variables constant and uniform throughout the experiment while the effect of the twelfth variable was being investigated. Holding the eleven variables constant was far more difficult than the investigation of the twelfth element (Taylor, 1911, 56).

The one variable at a time approach was, of course, not only inefficient but incapable of identifying interactions between factors. This sad affair required not only 26 years but $150,000 to $200,000 in the money of the late nineteenth century (a small fortune), 400 tons of steel and iron, and 30,000 to 50,000 experiments that were worth recording. (Other experiments were not recorded.)

The experiment led to the development of twelve equations that had to be solved to get the best cutting speed and feed for a given job. Hand calculations are not practical for shop operations. Bethlehem Steel invented a slide rule that allowed a mechanic to get the best conditions in half a minute. The cutting speed and feed were probably not the best because the experiment did not identify the interactions, but the key point is that Taylor and his associates gave the workers a tool they could use easily and quickly to set the conditions for each job.

For readers who are not intimately familiar with designed experiments, Taylor's application had twelve *factors* that could influence the operation's performance. Each factor could have several *levels*: as an example, a 16 scale described the shape or contour of the tool's cutting edge. The typical 2^n factorial design assesses *n* factors at only two levels: absent versus present, or low versus high. Its purpose is to determine which factors and interactions between factors (synergistic effects) affect the operation's performance significantly. There are, as the description suggests, 2^n possible low/high combinations of factors. A full 2^{12} experimental design would thus have required 4096 tests, not the 30,000 to 50,000 that Taylor performed.

In practice, a fractional factorial design that examined only some of the possible low/high combinations might have required only 128 or 256 tests. This would probably have been adequate to identify all the significant main effects (i.e. which among the 12 factors was significant) and two-way interactions. More detailed experiments could then have focused only on those factors, to quantify a model as Taylor desired.

The next chapter treats the influence of inventor Benjamin Franklin on Henry Ford. It shows that Franklin actually laid the basic foundation of the lean enterprise by pointing out specifically:

- Lost time is irrecoverable
- It is often more profitable to reduce costs than to increase sales ("A penny saved is two pence clear").
- It is often poor business to buy inventory simply to get a "great deal."

The chapter will also show a clear connection between Franklin's work and some of Ford's other principles.

Notes

1. My notes on this APICS meeting add the speaker's citation of Weisbrod, Productive Workplaces. Amazon.com shows that the author is Marvin Ross Weisbrod. An excerpt (available online) says that, in 1986, National Steel Corporation and the United Steel Workers of America agreed to restructure the organization to reduce the labor force (through attrition and voluntary termination instead of layoffs) while assuring job security for remaining workers. Recall that job security is a prerequisite for lean cultural transition, and this is consistent with Taylor's principles.
2. Basset (1919, 72) makes a similar point.
3. Robinson (1990, 18) cites an entertaining story about a British artillery drill from the mid-20th century. "Everything looked quite good, except that there was one man who spent a long time just standing still doing nothing. When we looked back over the drill to discover what he was supposed to be doing, we found out that he was in fact holding the horses! The horses had, of course, disappeared about twenty years earlier, but this task had not been eliminated when the gun drill had been rewritten."

   The persistence of the sample range (R) chart on modern statistical process control (SPC) computers is another example. The R and the sample standard deviation (s) chart both detect changes in process variation. The s chart is actually somewhat better but it was not practical for routine hand (pencil and paper, and possibly adding machine or slide rule) calculations on the shop floor. R is simply the difference between the sample's largest and smallest measurements, so workers could calculate it quickly. R charts are, however, common on modern SPC computers that can compute s in microseconds!
4. I noticed an error in the original figure but I left it in for comparison to the revised figure. In the original figure, the bricklayer would have to either put down his trowel or turn around completely to get a new brick, even from position B.
5. Machiavelli's The Prince warns against allowing anyone to make war his sole profession, for similar reasons.
6. "mean and gentle all" = commoners and gentry, i.e. Henry V gives his attention to followers of all ranks.

7. Lucas collaborated with the famous scholar Joseph Campbell, who was very knowledgeable about the roles of myths and legends in human society. Star Wars' success probably involved the incorporation of anthropological material from Campbell. Yoda's comment is therefore far more than pop culture. A principle in karate, for example, is that a person who wants to break a board must have no doubt that the blow will penetrate. The word "try" suggests that failure is possible.

ELEVEN

The Influence of
Benjamin Franklin

Most of the wisdom of the world was in the copy books. The lines we used to write over and over again, the homely old maxims on which we practiced to obtain legibility of our p's and q's were the essence of human wisdom. They were the first aid packages which the philosophers made to assist men who might need help out in the midst of the field of life. Most of the books that have been written since the copy books are only commentaries thereon; they say with more and harder words what we used to read in our first lessons (Ford, 1922a, 290).

Henry Ford said that no one would ever get to know him, but this paragraph reveals some of the principal influences on his childhood. Benjamin Franklin's books were probably standard features in the country schoolhouses of that era. This paragraph also echoes Franklin's own observation (1986, 30), ". . . not a tenth part of the wisdom was my own, which he ascribed to me, but rather the gleanings that I had made of all ages and all nations."

Franklin was, like Ford, a Freemason and an inventor. He invented bifocals and the Franklin stove, and he experimented with electricity. Ford titled a chapter in *Moving Forward* (1930) "The Way to Wealth," which is the title of the preface to *Poor Richard's Almanack*. "In this preface, Franklin summed up all of his previously published thoughts about how to succeed in business" (Franklin, 1986).[1] Ford also wrote, "Nothing has happened in our history to render out of date the business philosophy of

Benjamin Franklin. *Poor Richard's Almanack* is still the best business compendium" (Ford, 1922a, 282–283). This chapter explores Franklin's views on waste, initiative, self-reliance, persistence; and money. Each section also identifies how Franklin's beliefs mirrored Ford's. The first section shows how Franklin may have influenced the basic principle of Ford's lean enterprise system: suppression of all forms of waste.

FRANKLIN ON WASTE

This section shows that *Benjamin Franklin actually defined the fundamental theory of lean manufacturing.* Ford put it into practice on an unprecedented scale.

The chapter on "Ford's Factory" underscored the idea that time is a precious resource. Unlike wasted material, time cannot be salvaged. Under the theory of constraints, time losses at the constraint are irrecoverable. Franklin (1986, 12) wrote, "If time be of all things the most precious, wasting time must be,' as Poor Richard says, 'the greatest prodigality;' since, as he elsewhere tells us, 'Lost time is never found again; and what we call time enough always proves little enough:'..." *Poor Richard's Almanack* adds,

> He that idly loses 5s. [shillings] worth of time, loses 5s., and might as prudently throw 5s. into the river. He that loses 5s. not only loses that sum, but all the other advantages that might be made by turning it in dealing, which, by the time a young man becomes old, amounts to a comfortable bag of money.

This principle applies especially under the theory of constraints. While the cost accounting system does not recognize missed opportunities (e.g., opportunities to make and sell a unit) as costs, recognition of opportunity costs is a vital characteristic of top performers. The same principle appears in *My Life and Work*:

> If a device would save in time just 10 percent or increase results 10 percent, then its absence is always a 10 percent tax. If the time of a person is worth fifty cents an hour, a

10 percent saving is worth five cents an hour. . . . A building thirty stories high needs no more ground space than one five stories high. Getting along with the old-style architecture costs the five-story man the income of twenty-five floors. Save ten steps a day for each of twelve thousand employees and you will have saved fifty miles of wasted motion and misspent energy.

Those are the principles upon which the production of my plant was built up (Ford, 1922, 77).

On Waste Avoidance and the Cost of Quality

A penny saved is two pence clear. A pin a-day is a groat a-year. Save and have.

It may take ten or twenty dollars in sales to yield a dollar of profit. The benefits of waste reduction flow directly to the bottom line. A penny saved is a penny earned, a dollar of cost avoidance is a dollar of profit. Waste prevention, and the use of materials that were once considered waste, were key aspects of Henry Ford's manufacturing strategy. Modern businesses recognize that cost reduction is far more effective than higher sales in increasing profits. Savings flow directly to the bottom line, while sales have associated costs like materials and labor. Lower production costs are also a decisive tool for increasing sales.

"Save and have" is exactly the principle of reducing the cost of poor quality and eliminating waste of materials or effort. Furthermore, Franklin wrote, "If you'd be wealthy, think of saving, more than of getting; the Indies have not made Spain rich, because her Outgoes equal her Incomes," and, "If you know how to spend less than you get, you have the philosopher's stone." The philosopher's stone was a legendary stone that could transmute base metals like lead into gold.

The chapter on waste avoidance discussed friction, or chronic wastes of effort and material. Masaaki Imai uses the terms *muda* and *muri*, or waste and strain. Franklin describes the underlying concept: "Beware of little Expenses: a small Leak will sink a great Ship." Ford said manufacturing is a matter of detail, and little things add up to big things. The elimination of such apparently minor inefficiencies was the foundation of Henry Ford's success.

On Inventory

Modern companies often find themselves with idle raw materials and subassemblies because the purchasing department found an "excellent deal" on low-priced or even distressed goods. Franklin wrote this about an auction:

> You call them goods; but, if you do not take care, they will prove evils to some of you. You expect they will be sold cheap, and, perhaps, they may [be bought] for less than they cost; but, if you have no occasion for them, they must be dear to you. Remember what Poor Richard says, 'Buy what thou hast no need of, and ere long thou shalt sell thy necessaries.' And again, 'At a great penny worth pause a while:' He means, that perhaps the cheapest is apparent only, and not real; or the bargain, by straightening thee in thy business [reducing your available cash–that is, straightening your circumstances], may do thee more harm than good. For in another place he says, 'Many have been ruined by buying good penny worths' (Franklin, 1986, 20–21).

Ford expressed the same principle:

> We have carefully figured, over the years, that buying ahead of requirements does not pay—that the gains on one purchase will be offset by the losses on another, and in the end we have gone to a great deal of trouble without any corresponding benefit. . . . We do not buy less if the price be high and we do not buy more if the price be low. We carefully avoid bargain lots in excess of requirements. It was not easy to reach that decision. But in the end speculation will kill any manufacturer. Give him a couple of good purchases on which he makes money and before long he will be thinking more about making money out of buying and selling than out of his legitimate business, and he will smash. The only way to keep out of trouble is to buy what one needs—no more and no less. That course removes one hazard from business (Ford, 1922, 144-145).

Any reader of Goldratt's and Cox's *The Goal* (1992) will recognize this effect in UniCo's warehouses full of "good deals" that its purchasing department obtained. These "good deals" compelled the company to pay for the inventory's carrying cost and also warehouse space.

On Government Waste

"The king's cheese is half wasted in parings; but no matter, 'tis made of the people's milk," Franklin wrote. Ford pointed out that a government does not have to answer to anyone for its bottom line. The lack of fiscal accountability often makes government a very poor steward of the people's money. Private enterprise, which is accountable for its bottom line, usually does a superior job.

FRANKLIN ON INITIATIVE, SELF-RELIANCE, AND PERSISTENCE

Benjamin Franklin speaks through Henry Ford on the need for initiative in personal and business success. Ford said that the shop that says "No help wanted" needs help before it can give any, and that the proactive worker might create a job for himself there by finding a way to start a new wheel turning. He also said that "hard times" was a poor excuse for an underperforming business. Franklin wrote,

> So what signifies wishing and hoping for better times? We may make these times better, if we bestir ourselves. 'Industry need not wish, and he who lives on hope will die fasting. There are no gains without pains; then help hands, for I have no lands,' or, if I have, they are smartly taxed (Franklin, 1986, 13).

In Franklin's time, a landowner might live off the revenues of his estates. A landless person must use his or her hands (practice a trade or profession). Franklin and Ford are saying exactly the same thing. Better times do not come of themselves, proactive and self-reliant people must create them. Industry need not wish, industry can make things happen, and this is a bedrock foundation of Henry Ford's principles.

Ford emphasized the importance of persistence, or "stick-to-it-iveness," as "the uncrowned king of world endeavor." Franklin (1986, 15) wrote, ". . . but stick to it steadily, and you will see great effects; for 'Constant dropping wears away stones; and by diligence and patience the mouse ate in two the cable;[2] and little strokes fell great oaks.'" *Poor Richard's Almanack* says, "Diligence is the mother of good luck." Franklin also described proactivity: "Drive thy Business, or it will drive thee."

Success as Failure

Franklin wrote, "When Prosperity was well mounted, she let go the Bridle, and soon came tumbling out of the Saddle," and, "Success has ruin'd many a Man." When a person or business succeeds, they may think they no longer need to practice the virtues that brought them to the top. Ford said that success could bring down many people whom failure could not touch.

> There is nothing so trying to the morale of a business as a run of success. The tendency then is to let the business run on and fill its orders while the leaders pleasantly contemplate their triumph. The danger is not apparent, but it is already present. It is the same danger that assails the football squad after the training and playing season is over: the organization goes soft. The wise manager will be oftener on his rounds in so-called good times because it is in good times that all the seeds of bad times are sown. . . . fair weather is the time when all the leaks are made (Ford, 1930, 144–145).

No organization should ever think, "It can't happen to us." We saw earlier that Ford himself was a victim of the Model T's long run of unopposed success—this despite his specific awareness of the danger that comes with success.

FRANKLIN ON MONEY

Almost a quarter of "The Way to Wealth" is an injunction against the assumption of debt. ". . . think what you do when you run into debt; you give to another power over your liberty" (Franklin, 1986, 24-25).[3] Ford said he was not against bankers or borrowing money, but he warned,

> I would not say that a man in business needs to know nothing at all about finance, but he is better off knowing too little than too much, for if he becomes too expert he will get into the way of thinking that he can borrow money instead of earning it and then he will borrow more money to pay back what he has borrowed, and instead of being a business man he will be a note juggler, trying to keep in the air a regular flock of notes and bonds (Ford, 1922, 156).

He also underscored the idea that too many people considered money a substitute for management. If the problem was poor management or complacency, borrowing simply fed the disease.

Ford pointed out repeatedly that no system, whether business, individual, or government, can disburse more wealth than it creates or takes in. Franklin wrote (1986, 22), "'Always taking out of the meal tub, and never putting in, soon comes to the bottom,' as Poor Richard says; and then, 'When the well is dry, they know the worth of water.'"

Ford (and Ralph Waldo Trine) underscored the evils of both wasting and hoarding. Neither one who wastes a resource, nor one who leaves it unused, gains from it. Franklin wrote, "The use of money is all the advantage there is in having money."

On Speculators

Franklin wrote (1986, 16), "Many, without labour, would live by their wits only, but they break for lack of stock." Ford excoriated financiers who speculated in "things already made," as he called them. Speculation in the stock market, for example, produces no wealth or value. Without Ford's principal arts of manufacturing, agriculture, and transportation (defined in the Introduction), there would soon be nothing in which to speculate.

Notes

1. This is a reprint of the original eighteenth century work.
2. Rudyard Kipling's "A Pict Song" includes the lines,
   Mistletoe killing an oak—
   Rats gnawing cables in two—
   Moths making holes in a cloak—
   How they must love what they do!
   Kipling was, like Ford and Franklin (and also apparently Alexander Suvorov, who is mentioned elsewhere) a member of the Masons.
3. This was during an era when failure to pay a debt could lead to debtor's prison.

Bibliography

Alvarado, Rudolph, and Alvarado, Sonya. 2001. *Drawing Conclusions on Henry Ford: A Biographical History through Cartoons.* Ann Arbor: University of Michigan Press.

Aquarian Tarot Deck. 1975. Illustrated by David Palladini. Dobbs Ferry, NY: Morgan Press International.

Arnold, Horace Lucien, and Faurote, Fay Leone. 1915. *Ford Methods and the Ford Shops.* New York: The Engineering Magazine. Reprinted 1998, North Stratford, NH: Ayer Company Publishers, Inc.

"Australia Fights Methane," 2001. *Chemical and Engineering News,* 18 June 2001, 104.

"Australian Steel Mill Takes Recycling to Commercial Level," 2002. *Engineering Times,* January, 2002, p. 19.

Bakerjian, Ramon (editor). 1993. *Tool and Manufacturing Engineers Handbook: Volume 7, Continuous Improvement.* Dearborn, MI: Society of Manufacturing Engineers.

Bakker, Robert M. 1996. "Why Companies Fail Quality Audits," *Manufacturing Engineering,* (News Desk), May 1996.

Baliga, John. 1999. "Economic Forecast: Slowly Turning Upward." *Semiconductor International,* January 1999, 56–60.

Bennett, Harry, as told to Paul Marcus. 1951. *Ford: We Never Called Him Henry.* New York: Tom Doherty Associates, Inc.

Blumenson, Martin. 1990. *Patton: The Man Behind the Legend.* Ashland, OR: Blackstone Audio Books.

Bornholdt, O. C. 1913. "Continuous manufacturing by placing machines in accordance with sequence of operations." *Journal of the American Society of Mechanical Engineers* 35: 1671–79.

Bottorff, Dean L. 2001. "Manage Operating Culture as it Should be Managed." *The Quality Management Forum,* Vol. 27, Number 2, Spring 2001, p. 9. Milwaukee: American Society for Quality.

Bradford, Ernle. 1981. *Hannibal.* New York: Dorset Press.

Braun, Alexander E. 2000. "Even the Old Are Fair," *Semiconductor International*, August 2000, p. 21.

Briscoe, Scott. 2001. "The Tiger: Poised to Strike." *APICS—The Performance Advantage*. April 2001, 40–44.

Bryan, Ford R. 1997. *Beyond the Model T: The Other Ventures of Henry Ford* (Revised Edition). Detroit: Wayne State University Press.

Buck, William. 1973. *Mahabharata*. Berkeley: University of California Press.

"California Energy Problems Still Continue As More Companies Do 'Less With Less'," *Engineering Times*, March 2001. (Professional Engineers in Industry practice division, National Society of Professional Engineers).

Campbell, Joseph, with Moyers, Bill. 1988. *The Power of Myth*. New York: Doubleday.

Carrière, Jean-Claude. 1987. Translated by Peter Brook. *The Mahabharata*. New York: Harper & Row.

Chase, Nancy. 1998. "Accounting for Quality: Counting Costs, Reaping Returns." *Quality*, October, pp. 38–42.

Chu, Chin-Ning. 1992. *Thick Face, Black Heart*. New York: Warner Books

Clausewitz, Carl von. 1976. *On War*. Translated by M. Howard and P. Paret. Princeton, NJ: Princeton University Press.

Coleman, Calmetta Y. and Gumbel, Peter. "St. Louis Mall Declares War on E-Retailing," *Wall Street Journal*, 11/24/99, B1.

Confucius, translation by Arthur Waley. 1938. *The Analects of Confucius*. New York: George Allen & Unwin, Ltd.

Covey, Stephen R. 1991. *Principle-Centered Leadership*. New York: Summit Books.

Cox, James F. III, and Blackstone, John H. Jr. 1998. *APICS Dictionary*, 9th ed. Alexandria, VA: APICS—The Educational Society for Resource Management (APICS was formerly the American Production and Inventory Control Society).

Crago, Michael G. 2000. "Patient Safety, Six Sigma, and ISO 9000 Quality Management." *Quality Digest*, November 2000.

Crossen, Cynthia. 2000. *The Rich and How they Got That Way*. New York: Dow Jones & Co. Excerpts in *The Wall Street Journal*, 7/19/00, B1, B4.

Crow, Carl. 1943. *The Great American Customer*. New York: Editions for the Armed Services, Inc.

Cubberly, William H. and Bakerjuan, Ramon (editors). 1989. *Tool and Manufacturing Engineers Handbook*, Desk Edition. Dearborn, MI: Society of Manufacturing Engineers.

Dieter, George. 1983. *Engineering Design: A Materials and Processing Approach*. New York: McGraw-Hill.

Donnithorne, Col. Larry R. (retired). 1993. *The West Point Way of Leadership*. New York: Currency Doubleday.

Edmondson, Gail, and Johnston, Marsha. 1997. "I'll Give You A 35-Hour Week, And You Give Me..." *Business Week*, 11/10/97, Number 3552, Pg. 106E34, Section: Industries: Labor.

Energypubs.com, 2000. "Southern Company Joins Alliance to Study Emission-Free Generation" http://www.energypubs.com/news/n000457.html.

Fielding, Stanley. 2000. "ISO 14001 Brings Change and Delivers Profits." *Quality Digest*, November 2000, 32–35.

Ford, Henry, and Crowther, Samuel. 1922. *My Life and Work*. New York: Doubleday, Page & Company.

Ford, Henry. 1922a. *Ford Ideals: from "Mr. Ford's Page."* Dearborn: The Dearborn Publishing Company.

Ford, Henry, and Crowther, Samuel. 1926. *Today and Tomorrow*. New York: Doubleday, Page & Company (Reprint available from Productivity Press, 1988).

Ford, Henry. 1929. *My Philosophy of Industry* (An authorized interview by Fay Leone Faurote). New York: Coward-McCann, Inc.

Ford, Henry, and Crowther, Samuel. 1930. *Moving Forward*. New York: Doubleday, Doran, & Company.

"France Launches the 35-Hour-Week," 2000. Deutche Welle, http://www.dwelle.de/english/topstory/script/20000201.html (as of 4/24/01).

Franklin, Benjamin. 1986. *The Way to Wealth*. Bedford, MA: Applewood Books.

Franklin, Benjamin. *Poor Richard's Almanack*. Mount Vernon, NY: Peter Pauper Press.

Gardner, Daniel. 2001. "Movers and Shapers: The Impact of Logistics on Global Supply Chains." *APICS—The Performance Advantage*. May 2001, pp. 29–33.

Gardner, Les, and Nappi, Frank. 2001. "The Total Impact of Minor Stoppages." The 6th Annual Lean Management and TPM Conference, sponsored by Productivity Inc. October 25–26, 2001, Dearborn, MI.

Gates, William H. 1995. *The Road Ahead*. St. Paul, MN: Penguin HighBridge Audio.

Gates, William H. 1999. *Business @ The Speed of Thought: Using a Digital Nervous System*. New York: Warner Books.

Glassman, James K. 2000. "Forget Kyoto." *Wall Street Journal*, 11/30/2000, editorial pages.

Gilbreth, Frank B. 1911. *Motion Study*. New York: D. Van Nostrand Company.

Godfrey, Blanton. 2000. "Managing Key Suppliers." *Quality Digest*, September, 2000, p. 20.

Goldratt, Eliyahu, and Cox, Jeff. *The Goal*. Croton-on-Hudson, NY: North River Press.

Gourley, Catherine. 1997. *Wheels of Time: A Biography of Henry Ford*. Brookfield, CT: The Millbrook Press.

Green, 1991. A*lexander of Macedon*, 356–323 B.C. Berkeley, CA: University of California Press.

Gupta, Praveen, and Pongetti, Dan. 1998. "Are ISO /QS9000 Certifications Worth the Time and Money?" ASQ *Quality Progress*, October 1998, 1924.

Halpin, J. F. 1966. *Zero Defects*. New York: McGraw-Hill.

Harry, Mikel, and Schroeder, Richard. 2000. *Six Sigma: The Breakthrough Management Strategy Revolutionizing the World's Top Corporations*. New York: Currency Doubleday.

Hayes, R. H., Wheelwright, S. C., and Clark, K. B. 1988. *Dynamic Manufacturing: Creating the Learning Organization*. New York: The Free Press.

Held, Robert. 1957. *The Age of Firearms: A Pictorial History*. New York: Bonanza Books.

Hill, Napoleon. 1928. *The Law of Success in Sixteen Lessons*. North Hollywood, CA: facsimile edition by Wilshire Book Company.

Holstein, William J. 1999. "Kicking a Virtual Tire," *U.S. News and World Report*, October 25, 1999.

Hounshell, David A. 1984. *From the American System to Mass Production, 1800–1932*. Baltimore: Johns Hopkins University Press.

Hoyer, R.W. 2001. "Why Quality Gets an 'F': What happens when the bottom line overrides a focus on customer needs." *Quality Progress*, October 2001, 32–36.

Hradesky, John L. 1995. *Total Quality Management Handbook*. New York: McGraw-Hill.

Hughes, Daniel J. 1993. *Moltke on the Art of War: Selected Writings*. Novato, CA: Presidio Press.

Imai, Masaaki. 1986. *Kaizen*. New York: McGraw-Hill.

Imai, Masaaki. 1997. *Gemba Kaizen*. New York: McGraw-Hill.

James, Peter, and Thorpe, Nick. 1994. *Ancient Inventions*. New York: Ballentine Books.

Johnson, Perry L. 1993. ISO 9000: *Meeting the New International Standards*. New York: McGraw-Hill.

Juran, Joseph, and Gryna, Frank. 1988. *Juran's Quality Control Handbook*, 4th ed. New York: McGraw-Hill.

Keegan, John. 1987. *The Mask of Command*. New York: Penguin Books

Kipling, Rudyard. 1940. *Rudyard Kipling: Complete Verse*. New York: Doubleday.

Klein, Stuart M., and Ritti, R. Richard. 1984. *Understanding Organizational Behavior*, 2nd ed. Belmont, CA: Wadsworth.

Lacey, Robert. 1986. *Ford: The Men and the Machine*. Boston: Little, Brown, and Company.

Lao Tzu, translation by D. C. Lau. 1963. *The Tao Te Ching*. New York: Penguin Books.

Lavelle, Marianne. 2001. "The power hungry get powered down," *U.S. News & World Report*, April 30, 2001, 40.

Lee, Louise. 1994. "Garment Scanner Could Be a Perfect Fit." *Wall Street Journal*, 9/20/94.

Levinson, William. 1994. *The Way of Strategy*. Milwaukee: ASQ Quality Press. (1999, iUniverse.com).

Levinson, William, and Tumbelty, Frank. 1997. *SPC Essentials and Productivity Improvement: A Manufacturing Approach*. Milwaukee: ASQ Quality Press.

Levinson, William (editor). 1998. *Leading the Way to Competitive Excellence: The Harris Mountaintop Case Study*. Milwaukee, WI: ASQ Quality Press.

Longworth, Philip. 1965. *The Art of Victory: The Life and Achievements of Field Marshal Suvorov (1729–1800)*. New York: Holt, Rinehart, and Winston.

Machiavelli, Niccolò. 1965. *The Art of War*. New York: Da Capo Press.

Mahan, Alfred Thayer. 1980. *The Influence of Sea Power Upon History*, 1660–1805. London: Bison Books.

Marciano, Michael. 1999. "How did Hartford Get Into This Mess?" *The Hartford Advocate*, New Mass Media Inc. http://books.hartfordadvo cate.com/articles/hfdmess.html.

Mascaró, Juan (translator). 1962. *The Bhagavad Gita*. New York: Penguin Books.

McCabe, Warren L., Smith, Julian C., and Harriott, Peter. 1985. *Unit Operations of Chemical Engineering*, 4th ed. New York: McGraw-Hill.

Mege, Claude Jean. 2000. "Is there a HAM in Your Future?" *Manufacturing Engineering*, July 2000, 114–124.

Menning, Bruce W. 1986. "Train Hard, Fight Easy: The Legacy of A. V. Suvorov and his 'Art of Victory.'" *Air University Review*, December 1986, 79–88.

"Message to physicians: Better read than dead." 2000. Wilkes-Barre *Times Leader*, 25 October 2000.

Miller, Annette, and Laurenti, Susanna. 2001. "Companies Find It Pays To Be Green." *National Wildlife*, February/March 2001, 70.

Miller, Lawrence M. 1989. *Barbarians to Bureaucrats: Corporate Life Cycle Strategies*. New York: Fawcett Columbine.

Miniter, Richard. 2001. "The Dutch Way of Death," *The Wall Street Journal*, 4/25/2001, A20.

Murphy, Robert, Lauffer, Jeffrey, and Levinson, William. 1997. "Project Raptor," *Future Fab*, Issue 3, Volume 1.

Murphy, Robert, Lauffer, Jeffrey, and Levinson, William. 1998. "Velociraptor—Swift Predator," *Future Fab*, Issue 5.

Musashi, Miyamoto. Translation by Victor Harris, 1974. *A Book of Five Rings*. Woodstock, NY: Overlook Press.

Norwood, Edwin P. 1931. *Ford: Men and Methods*. Garden City, NY: Doubleday, Doran & Company Inc.

Ohno, Taiichi. 1988. *Toyota Production System: Beyond Large-Scale Production*. Portland OR: Productivity Press.

Paterno, Joseph V. and Asbell, Bernard. 1989. *Paterno: By the Book*. New York: Berkely Books.

Peters, T. and Waterman, R. 1982. *In Search of Excellence*. New York: Harper and Row.

Peters, Tom, and Austin, Nancy. 1985. *A Passion for Excellence*. New York: Warner Books.

Peters, Tom. 1987. *Thriving on Chaos*. New York: Harper and Row.

Purtell, John. 1991. "Employee Involvement." Local meeting (Mid-Hudson region, New York), APICS, 9 October, 1991.

Pyzdek, Thomas. 1996. *The Complete Guide to the CQE*. Tuscon, AZ: Quality Publishing Inc.

Robinson, Alan (editor), 1990. *Modern Approaches to Manufacturing Improvement: The Shingo System*. Portland: Productivity Press.

Rose, Ed, and Buckley, Steve. 1999. *Self-Directed Work Teams*. Alexandria, VA: American Society for Training and Development.

"Sayonara, Kyoto Treaty." 2002. *Wall Street Journal*, 2 January 2002, p. A18.

Schonberger, Richard J. 1982. *Japanese Manufacturing Techniques: Nine Hidden Lessons in Simplicity*. New York: The Free Press.

Schonberger, Richard J. 1986. *World Class Manufacturing*. New York: The Free Press.

Shapiro, Joseph P. "Taking the mistakes out of medicine." *U.S. News and World Report*, 7/17/2000, 50–66.

Shellenbarger, Sue. 2000. "Workplace Upheavels Seem to be Eroding Employees' Trust." *Wall Street Journal*, 6/21/2000, B1, "Work and Family."

Shingo, Shigeo. 1986. 1986. *Zero Quality Control: Source Inspection and the Poka-Yoke System*. Portland, OR: Productivity Press.

Shingo, Shigeo (Andrew Dillon, translator). 1987. *The Sayings of Shigeo Shingo: Key Strategies for Plant Improvement*. Portland, Oregon: Productivity Press.

Shirouzu, Norihiko. 2001. "Job One: Ford Has Big Problem Beyond Tire Mess: Making Quality Cars," *Wall Street Journal*, 5/25/2001, A1 and A6.

"Shoppers Flock To Stores for Deals," 2001. Associated Press, 26 December 2001.

Shreve, R. Norris, and Brink, Joseph A. 1977. *Chemical Process Industries*, 4th ed. New York: McGraw-Hill.

Sinclair, Upton. 1937. *The Flivver King*. Second printing, 1987. Chicago: Charles H. Kerr Publishing Company.

Sisodia, Rajendra S. and Sheth, Jagdish N. 1999. "Car Retailing Needs a Tune-Up," *Wall Street Journal*, 12/20/99, "Manager's Journal" feature, editorial page.

Smith, J. M. and Van Ness, H. C. 1975. *Introduction to Chemical Engineering Thermodynamics*, 3rd ed. New York: McGraw-Hill.

Sorensen, Charles E., with Samuel T. Williamson. 1956. *My Forty Years with Ford*. New York: W. W. Norton & Company Inc.

Standard, Charles, and Davis, Dale. 1999. *Running Today's Factory: A Proven Strategy for Lean Manufacturing*. Cincinnati: Hanser Gardner Publications.

Streisand, Betsy. 2001. "Like a moth to a flame: Luring California firms out of state by promising cheap power." *U.S. News & World Report*, 28 May, 2001, 36–37.

Stuelpnagel, T. R. 1993. "Déjà Vu: TQM Returns to Detroit and Elsewhere." *Quality Progress* (September), 91–95.

Sun Tzu, translated by James Clavell. 1983. *The Art of War*. New York: Delacorte Press.

Suzaki, Kiyoshi. 1987. *The New Manufacturing Challenge: Techniques for Continuous Improvement*. New York: The Free Press.

The System Company. 1911. *How Scientific Management is Applied*. London: A. W. Shaw Company Ltd.

The System Company. 1911a. *How to Get More Out of Your Factory*. London: A. W. Shaw Company, Ltd.

Taylor, Frederick Winslow. 1911. *The Principles of Scientific Management*. New York: Harper Brothers. 1998 republication by Dover Publications, Inc., Mineola, NY.

Taylor, Frederick Winslow. 1911a. *Shop Management*. New York: Harper & Brothers Publishers.

Taylor, Wendy, and Jerome, Marty. 1999. "Karma." *PC Computing*, May 1999, p. 87.

"Too Tempting? Smuggling Makes a Comeback in China." 2001. *Chemical and Engineering News*, 10/01/2001, p. 40.

"Top 10 Reasons to Shop on the Internet- Now!" *PC Computing*, December 1999, p. 206.

Trine, Ralph Waldo. 1899. (Thorsons' edition, 1995) *In Tune with the Infinite: Fullness of Peace, Power, and Plenty*. London: Thorsons.

Trine, Ralph Waldo, and Ford, Henry. 1929. *The Power that Wins: Ralph Waldo Trine and Henry Ford Talk on Life*. Indianapolis: The Bobbs-Merrill Company.

Tsouras, Peter G. 1992. *Warrior's Words: A Dictionary of Military Quotations*. London: Arms and Armour Press.

Wagner, Richard. Translation by Stewart Robb, 1972. *Siegfried*. New York: ABC Records, Inc.

Ward, John R. 1999. "The Little Ships that Could." *American Heritage of Invention and Technology*, Fall 1999, 34–40.

Williams, Tom. "On Shaky Ground." *Quality*, February 2000 (p. 6).

Williams, Tom. "Step Right Up." *Quality*, April 2000 (p. 6).

Williamson, Porter B. 1979. *Patton's Principles: A Handbook for Managers Who Mean It. New York*: Simon and Schuster.

Womack, James P. and Jones, Daniel T. 1996. *Lean Thinking*. New York: Simon & Schuster.

Yamamoto, T. 1979. *Hagakure* ("Hidden Leaves"). New York: Kodansha International.

Index

3PLs. *See* Third-party logistics systems
3S. *See* Smoke soot smudge
5S-CANDO. *See* Cleaning up Arranging
    Neatness Discipline Ongoing
    improvement

A

Accounting book values, meaning, 131
Accumulation, 69–70
Accuracy. *See* Variation/accuracy
Achilles, 95–96
Acquisitions, 135–136
Administrator, 35
Adsorption-desorption process, 183
Advertising
    value, 125
    waste, 124–128
Air quality, 277
Alcuin of York, 94
Alexander of Macedonia, 81
    greatness, 37
Alexander the Great, 36, 95
    successor, 80
Aluminum casting, 40
Alzheimer's disease, delay, 33
Amazon.com, 109
American invention. *See* Lean
    manufacturing
American Society for Quality, 8
American Society for Testing and Materials
    (ASTM), 272
American Society of Manufacturing
    Engineers, 116
American society (transformation), Ford
    (impact), 5–6
American-manufactured goods, cost, 147
Americans with Disabilities Act (ADA), 9
Ammonium sulfate, 185–186
Anchor draggers, 90
Andon lights, 232
Anti-utopia, 5

Apple Computer, 131–132
Arjuna, 31
Armed Forces, 151
Assembly. *See* Parallel
    processing/assembly; Point-of-use
    assembly
    aiding, 253
    directions, 254
    line. *See* Ford Motor Company River
    Rouge plant
        layout, 227
        operation, 222–223
        origin, 238–239
    principles, 222
Asterix, creators, 80
ASTM. *See* American Society for Testing
    and Materials
Atago Shrine, 85
Auto-By-Tel, 120
Automatic machines, Ford definition,
    231–232
Automatic sorting, 270
Axis powers, 4

B

Bacteria, recognition. *See* Ford Motor
    Company River Rouge plant
Bar codes, usage, 249
Barbarian, aspects, 35, 37
Bat-and-mole twilights, usage, 286
Batching, 249
Battle of Agincourt, 325
Bedridden workers, experiment, 73–74
Benchmarking, 259–260
Bennett, Henry, 98–100, 103, 169
    competition, 80
    yes-man, 95
Best practice deployment, 201–204, 321
Bethlehem Steel, 40, 332
Bhagavad Gita, 52, 96
Bill of materials (BOM), 212

Birmingham machines, design, 111
Black Belts, 274
Blackthorne, John, 94–95
Blue gas, 186
Bodek, Norman, 15
Bolts, usage, 253–254
BOM. *See* Bill of materials
Bombay Co., 119
Bonhomme Richard, 86–87
Bowers, Joseph, 129
Breakdowns, avoidance, 66
Britain, success. *See* Manufacturing
Buddhism, goal, 30
Buffer inventory, 246
Builder, aspects, 35, 37
Built-in waste. *See* Supply chain
Bukko (priest), 32
Business
  barometer, 139
  cost accounting system, impact, 131–132
  cycles, 137–139
  enterprise, viability, 60
  growth, manager/worker
    involvement, 70–71
  long-term health, 166
  principles, disregard, 51–52
  profits, 51
  running, Taylor opinion, 66
  stockholders, impact, 133–135
  success, 337
Byproducts, profit, 184–186

C
Cables, avoidance, 254–255
Cadillacs, disassembly, 269
Caesar, Julius, 81
Calibration program, usage, 272
Capacity-constraining operation, 218
Capacity-constraining resource (CCR), 236
Capital
  expenditures, 303
    ability, 166
    delay, 133
  inventory, impact, 234
  investments, 302
  usage, 70
Car bodies, shipping, 178
Car dealerships
  introduction, 120
  showrooms, value addition, 120–123
Carbon monoxide poisoning, 279
Carbon taxes, 144
Carelessness, impact, 278
Carrying costs. *See* Inventory
Cathaginians, 40–41

CCR. *See* Capacity-constraining resource
Cellular manufacturing, 196, 227–232
Champion, companion, 94–97
Change
  involvement, 329–331
  management, principles, 327–328
  progress, 53
  promotion, visible successes (usage),
    328–329
Chaplin, Charlie, 199, 239–240
Charlemagne, 94
China, success. *See* Manufacturing
Chipless machining, 173–177
Chronic problems/inefficiencies, 166
Citizens General Hospital, 160
Civil War, 145
Cleaning up Arranging Neatness
    Discipline Ongoing improvement
    (5S-CANDO), 8, 13, 196, 205–233
  aspects, 97
Clockwork, model, 18
Coal
  burning, innovation, 186–191
  coking, 184–186
Coating operation, fumes, 182–184
Coke, burning (innovation), 186–191
Colt Armory, 210
Columbus, Christopher, 41
Comfort. *See* Workplace
  sacrifice, 50
Commissaries. *See* Employees; Ford
    Commissaries
  cash-and-carry, 76
Commitment, 50. *See also* Management/
    labor; Mutual commitment
Committees/experts, impact. *See* Initiative;
    Progress
Commodities
  relationship. *See* Luxuries/commodities
  usage, 127
Communication. *See* Labor
Companies, running, 135
Companionship, 94–95
Competition, disregard, 23–24
Competitive economic environment, 72
Complacency
  avoidance, 34–37
  warning signs, 34–35
Compliance. *See* Malicious compliance
Compliant parts, usage, 254
Computers, usage, 249
Concrete heads, 90
Confucius, 49
Conservation principle, 152. *See also* Mass
    conservation

Constitution. *See* U.S. Constitution
Constraints. *See* Theory of Constraints
Construction material, selection, 255–256
Constructive imagination, 86
Consumer, goods delivery, 51
Consumption, importance, 65
Containment action, 6
Continuous flow
  effectiveness, 244–246
  model, 268
  operations, 245
  processes, 268
Continuous improvement, 8, 32–43, 199–204, 312
  gains, 202
  impact. *See* Price
  standardization support, 201–203
  usage. *See* Mass production; Sales per customer increase
Continuous price reduction, benefits, 125–127
Control, 295
  internal locus, 85, 86
Conveyors, 18
Corners, cutting (contrast). *See* Scientific management
Corporate culture. *See* Ford Motor Company
Corrective action, 287–288
Cost accounting system
  impact. *See* Business
  role, 132
Cost reduction, profitability, 333
Couzens, James, 35, 270, 310
Covey, Stephen, 9, 25
  description. *See* Scarcity mentality
  ideas, 79
  writings, 50, 55
C.R. Wilson Body Company, 306
Cranes, locking, 281–282
Credit unions. *See* Employees
Cross-functional communication, 91
Cross-training, 91
Crowther, Samuel, 98
Custom Foot (shoe manufacturer), 120
Customer
  needs
    identification, 295–296
    meeting, 87
  relationships, 293. *See also* Supplier/customer
  reliance. *See* Ford
  requirements, 258
  serving, 52

Cutbacks, implementation. *See* Development; Employees; Research
Cycle time
  accumulation, 240
  addition, 250, 301
  queue, 242
  reduction, techniques, 232, 240
Cyclic stress, 267
Cyclical demand, 297

D
Damage, opportunity, 230–231
Darwinism. *See* Economic Darwinism
Deaf employees, 74
Dealerships. *See* Car dealer
Defects, 276
Defoe Shipbuilding, 275
Delivery. *See* Packaging
Dell Computer, 109–110
Demand. *See* Cyclical demand; Universal demand
  creation, 293–297
Deming, W. Edwards, 9, 13, 17
  advice, 90
  principles, 208
Depreciation, inclusion, 132
Design. *See* Maintainability; Reliability
  cycles, 253
  disaster, 331–333
  handling/orientation/adjustment, 254
  parts, number, 252–253
Design for assembly (DFA), 15, 196, 252–260
Design for manufacture (DFM), 8, 15, 196, 252–260
Design of experiments (DOE), 14
Destiny. *See* Ford
Detroit Edison Company, 64
Detroit Electric Company, 64
Detroit Toledo & Ironton (D.T. & I.) Railroad
  departmental consolidation, 91–92
  Ford Motor Company purchase, 248
  visual controls, 208
Detroit Toledo & Ironton (D.T. & I.) Railway, 2
Developed power, 143
Development, cutbacks (implementation), 133–134
DFA. *See* Design for assembly
DFM. *See* Design for manufacture
Dharma, personification, 27, 31
Diehl, Fred, 103
Discrete-unit operation, 268
Disorderly element, demand, 48, 69

Dividends, payment, 70
Document control system, 203
Dodge Brothers
  lawsuit, 134
  Sorensen accusation, 94
DOE. *See* Design of experiments
Dollar-an-hour labor, 198
Dot-com companies, 4, 108
Dot-com stocks
  price-earnings ratios, 139
  purchase, 131
Doughnut hole, 171–173
Drinks, bottling, 177
Drum-Buffer-Rope (DBR) production
    control, 239, 246–247, 250. *See also*
    Ford Motor Company; Toyota
D.T. & I. *See* Detroit Toledo & Ironton
Duke of Gloucester, 79
Duke of Wellington. *See* Wellesley
Durable goods, 123
Dysfunctional behavior, 50
Dysfunctional economic driving
    forces, 146
Dysfunctional labor relations, Taylor
    opinion, 322–323
  Dysfunctional performance
    measurements, 324

E
Eastern philosophy, connection. *See* Ford
Economic Darwinism, 118, 324
Economic environment. *See* Competitive
    economic environment
Economic law, escape, 26
Economic prosperity, 144
Economic science, 28
Economics
  Ford, opinion, 137
Economies, awareness. *See* False
    economies
Economy, contrast. *See* Parsimony
Efficiency
  impact. *See* Unemployment
  improvement, process changes
    (impact), 262–263
Employees. *See* Deaf employees; Front-
    line employees; Mute employees
  benefit, 77
  commissaries, 76–77
  credit unions, 77–78
  housing/stores, 75–78
  injury, reporting, 278
  laying off, 133
  movement. *See* Work
  restrictions, 71–72

training, cutbacks (implementation),
    133–134
Employer/employee
  interdependence, 60–61
  involvement, 65
Employers
  job, 67
  paternalism, 77
  resources, 61
Employment
  disqualification, 71
  process, 65
  value, 65
En bloc cylinder, 287–288
End-of-model-year sales/incentives, 121
Energy
  costs, increase (consequences), 145–149
  role, 143–149
  shortages, 145–146
Environmental Protection Agency (EPA),
    9, 182
EPA. *See* Environmental Protection Agency
Equal Rights Amendment (ERA), 9
Equipment
  depreciation, 270
  purchase, 251
  running, 74
  usage. *See* Ford Motor Company
    Highland Park plant; Ford Motor
    Company River Rouge plant
  utilization, 301
Ergonomics, 282–283
Error-proofing. *See* Poka-yoke
Europe, regression, 47–49
Exchange of die, 213
Experts, impact, 38. *See also* Initiative;
    Progress
Explorer, aspects, 35, 37
External setup, 213

F
Factories. *See* Ford Motor Company
  job creation, 115–117
  layout strategies, 13
  operations, 245
  ordering. *See* Just-in-time
  workers, relationship, 198–199
Failure mode effect analysis (FMEA), 259
Failure, relationship. *See* Success
Fairchild Semiconductor, 251
False economies, awareness, 330
Family-owned business, tax effect, 153
Farm employment, reduction, 48
Fasteners, replacement, 253–254
Fear, absence, 23

Federal Reserve, 139
  Bank, 141
Feedback, 268
Fiber-optic communication channels,
  usage, 249
Finance, perspective, 129–131
Financiers, Ford (dislike), 64
Fisher, Fred, 306
Fixed labor costs, 132
Flanders, Walter, 14, 228
Flat organizational structure, 9, 17
Flat Rock, headlight factory, 92
Flexible components, usage, 254–255
Flexible system, contrast. *See*
  Rigid system
Floors, usage, 259
Flow stations, 18
Fluorescent lighting, usage, 285
FMEA. *See* Failure mode effect analysis
FMSs. *See* Freight management systems
Food shipments, 6
Ford Clothes Shop, 76
Ford Commissaries, 76
Ford, Edsel, 36, 96, 104
  competition, 80
  leadership, 103
Ford, Henry
  answers. *See* Zen riddle
  dislike. *See* Financiers
  eastern philosophy, connection, 29–32
  greatness, 37
  impact. *See* American society; Scarcity
    mentality
  Japanese connection, 29–32
  karma/destiny, 30–31
  opinion. *See* Economics; Government;
    Health care; Inheritance tax; Labor
    relations
  personal leadership, 99–100
  philosophy, 23
  price reduction, customer reliance, 63
  principles, 19–21, 23. *See also* Personal
  success; Individual success
    scientific management (correlation),
      311–312
  success, Sorensen role, 64
  Taylor, influence, 310–312
  weaknesses, 36–37
Ford, Jr., Henry, 103
Ford Motor Company
  blast furnaces, 168–169
  breakthrough (1908), 4–6
  corporate culture, 93–100
  culture, loss, 100–105
  DBR production control, 246–248

definition. *See* Automatic machines;
  Quasi-automatic machines
  factories, 195
  heritage, discovery, 101–102
  Internet site, 181
  inventory control, 235–236
  Iron Mountain (sawing operation), 168
  logistics system,
    coordination/effectiveness, 304
  machinery, 269
  operations, JIT nature, 305
  organization
    collapse (1943), 102–104
    operation, 97
  Piquette Avenue plant, 5, 229
  product creation, single production line
    (usage), 18
  production
    classifications, 71
    control, 235–236
  production system, success, 242
  purchase. *See* Detroit Toledo & Ironton
    Railroad
  results, 3–4
  safety policy, 276
  success, 8
  tool standards, 253
  TPS, comparison, 18–19
  unionization, 105
  waste reduction, principles, 181–182,
    192
Ford Motor Company Highland Park
  plant, 39, 77, 100, 203–204
  assembly lines, 248
  equipment usage, 231, 262–263, 278
  examples, 215, 219, 232, 235–236
  inspectors, usage, 288
  metallic fire curtains, 279
  productivity, reduction, 283
  transportation distance, reduction,
    228–229
Ford Motor Company River Rouge plant,
  180, 226, 233, 243–244
  assembly lines, 248
  bacteria, recognition, 284–285
  equipment usage, 279
  payroll system, 266
  PPE, usage, 280–281
  safety, 280
Foresight, 296
Forging, benefits, 176
Fortuna (fortune), 81, 85
France
  unemployment, level, 49
  work, amount, 47–48

Franklin, Benjamin
  influence, 337
  opinion, 200. *See also* Government;
    Initiative; Inventory; Money;
    Persistence; Self-reliance; Speculators;
    Waste
Free lunch. *See* There Ain't No Such Thing
    As A Free Lunch
  concept, 69–71, 128–136
  illusion, 70, 149–150
Freight management systems (FMSs), 196,
    303–305
Friction, 166, 260. *See also* Lean enterprise
  history, 70
  suppression, 97
Frictionless marketplace, 118
Front-line employees, 312
Frontline worker, 201
Fuel cell, usage, 186–191

G
Gage blocks, 16
Gage calibration, 14, 271–272
Gage capability, 271–272
Gage control, 16
Gage precision, requirement, 271
Gantt, H.L., 14, 202
GDP. *See* Gross Domestic Product
Gemba, 92, 227
  kaizen, 13–14
  managers, 97
General Motors, 190–191
Generalists, Inc., 112
Germany, work (amount), 48
Gilbreth, Frank B., 13–15, 151, 313
  studies, 221, 318
Gilgamesh (epic), 96
Go-and-no-go gage, 265–266
Gold Rush, dynamics, 75
Golden egg, division, 65
Goldratt, Eliyahu, 13–14
Goods
  delivery. *See* Consumer
  making, increase, 51
Gordian Knot, 40
Government
  efficiency/responsibility, level, 151–153
  Ford, opinion, 137
  foundation, natural law (usage), 29
  problem, 154–155
  role, 149–157
  waste, Franklin (opinion), 341
Grant, Ellsworth, 114
Great Society, 157
Greed, 52

Green manufacturing, 9
Greenhouse gases, reduction. *See*
    Livestock
Greenspan, Alan, 139
Grit, 86
Gross Domestic Product (GDP)
  consideration, 4
  manufacturing share, 108
Groupthink, 94

H
Half-alive, description, 32
HAMs. *See* High agility machines
Handicapped workers, role, 72–74
Hand-to-mouth component production, 236
Harvard School of Public Health, 159
Health care, 157–164
  error-proofing, 159–162
  Ford, opinion, 137
Health management organizations
    (HMOs), 53, 159, 163
  administrators, 162
Heat treatment, 210
Henry and Clara Ford Hospital, 9, 158–159
Henry Ford & Son, 134
Henry V
  actions, description, 325–326
  leadership role, 82–83
Henry VI, 81–82
Hephestion, 95
Hercules, role model, 37–38
High agility machines (HAMs), 173–174
Highland Park plant. *See* Ford Motor
    Company
High-priced crew, 66
High-priced men, 66
Hill, Napoleon, 93
HMOs. *See* Health management
    organizations
Holes, drilling/cutting, 170
Hoshino, Yukinori, 15
House of quality, 196, 257
Housing. *See* Employees
  spending, percentage, 75
Human behavior
  principles, 20
  universal code, 28–29
Human error, 260
Human resources, practices, 71–74
Hunger, end, 6
Huxley, Aldous, 2, 5, 54
Hygiene. *See* Workplace

I
Ieyasu, Tokugawa, 94

IG Metall (union), 48
Ignorance, impact, 278
Imai, Masaaki, 9, 13, 92, 97
  definitions, 167
Imperial Mine, 75
Importance ratings, computation, 258
Inaction/indolence. *See* Ozio
Incompetence, Sorensen (opinion), 35
Independent work groups, 224
Individual success, Ford principles, 79
Industrial espionage, 111
Industrial justice, 63–65
  principles, 64
Industrial safety principles/practices,
    276–280
Industries, power. *See* Value-adding
    industries
Inefficiencies, elimination, 340
Inflation
  reduction, 139
  relationship. *See* Unemployment
Inheritance tax, Ford opinion, 153–154
Initiative, 87–90
  committees/experts, impact, 89–90
  exercising, 89
  Franklin, opinion, 341–343
Innovation, 296
Input, output (relationship), 69–70
Inspections, 264
  aiding, 253
Inspectors, usage. *See* Ford Motor
    Company Highland Park plant
Institute of Medicine, 159
Interaction matrix roof, 258
Interchangeable parts, introduction, 47
Interest rates, increase, 139
Internet
  increase, 294
  usage, 118
Interplant supply system, 303
Interstate commerce, regulation, 155
Inventory
  accumulation, avoidance, 19
  carrying costs, 121, 122
  concept, 13
  control. *See* Ford Motor Company
  Franklin, opinion, 340–341
  impact. *See* Capital
  liquidation, 129–130
  purchase, 333
  reduction, 227, 234–252
    impact, 234
  selling, 121
  symptom, 249–251
Irrational exuberance, 139

Irwin, Bill, 40
ISO 9000, 8, 161, 282
  auditing, 13
  conscious workplace, 162
  considerations, 273
  consistency, 320
  quality systems, 158
  requirement, 169. *See also* Product
  standard, 197
  support, 275
  synergism, 201, 284
ISO 9001
  support, 71
  synergism, 218, 252, 264, 271, 287
ISO 14000, 8, 276
  cost, 182–193
  current usage, 192–193
  environmental standard, 181–182
  standard, satisfaction, 3
  usage, 192
Iwata, Yoshiki, 90

J
Japanese manufacturing techniques, 232
Japanese production lines, 243
Japanese productivity improvement
    techniques, 101
JIT. *See* Just-in-time
Job
  creation. *See* Factories; Model T
  designs, 73
  division, steps, 315–318
  elimination, 113
  redesign, 315
  restrictive descriptions, elimination, 13
  security, 46
Jobs, Steven, 131–132
Johansson, Carl E., 16, 271
  blocks, 16, 271–272
  gages, 16, 269
John Deere, 298
Johnson, Lyndon B., 150, 157
Jones, John Paul, 87
Judgment, exercising, 89
Juran, Joseph, 92
Just-in-time (JIT)
  delivery, 304
  factory ordering, 120
  manufacturing, 210, 234–252, 303
  origin, 238–239
  production, 6, 196
    system, 301
  quantities, 303
  support, 264
  transportation reliability, need, 248–249

K

Kaizen, 8, 13, 32–43, 199–204. *See also*
    Gemba
  blitz, 46, 312–313
      advantage, 328
    events, 313
    principles, 201
    teaching, 101
Kanban, 19
Karma, 23–26. *See also* Ford
  operation, 26
Keim presses, 269–270
Keynes, John Maynard, 83
Khan, Kublai, 37
Kingsford Products Company, 168
Kipling, Rudyard, 61–62, 206, 224, 322
Knacks, 318
Koan (riddle), 30, 32
Krishna, 31, 96
Kyoto Global Warming Treaty (Kyoto
    Protocol), 142, 146–149

L

Labor. *See* Dollar-an-hour labor; Offshore
    labor
  communication. *See* Management/labor
  costs. *See* Fixed labor costs
      reduction, 314
  goals, 60
  leader, 61
  medium, 59
  mutual trust/commitment. *See*
    Management/labor
  partnership. *See* Management/labor
  problems, communication, 66–67
  relationship. *See* Management/labor
  response. *See* Taylor
  responsibility, 71
  usage, 70
Labor relations
  Ford, opinion, 59
  natural law, relationship, 49–50
  science, 59
  Taylor
      opinion. *See* Dysfunctional labor
        relations
      relationship, 321–322
Large-scale production, 41
Law of the situation. *See* Situation
Layout change, principles, 317
Leadership. *See* Ford; Principle-centered
    leadership; Servant leadership
  qualifications, Taylor citation, 85–86
  role. *See* Henry V
Lean enterprise

concept, 300
  defining, 6–21
  friction, 7–8
Lean manufacturing, 139, 204–205,
    312–313
  American invention, 8–17
  details, 13–14
  development, 102
  general principles, 9–13
  implications, 45–47
  maxim, discussion, 105
  support, 240, 264
  systematization, 9
  transition, 63
Leape, Lucian, 159
Learning curve concept, 252
Lehr, usage, 39
Leland, Henry M., 269
Lighting, 277. *See also* Workplace
Livestock, greenhouse gases
    reduction, 191
Lock-and-key security, 281
Lockout-tagout, 9, 281–282
Long-term competitiveness, 133
Long-term results, seeking, 130
Lot sizes, 18
Louis XIV, reign, 141
Lubricating oil, usage, 183–184
Luddites, 45–46, 145
Ludditism, prevention, 72
Luxuries/commodities, relationship,
    64–65

M

Machiavelli, 80, 85
  defiance, 81
Machines
  availability, assuring, 243–244
  production, 41
  role, 144–145
Machining. *See* Chipless machining
Mahan, Alfred Thayer (captain), 110
Maintainability, design, 255, 257
Maintenance work, completion, 281
Make to order, 122, 127
Making-to-order, argument, 300
Malicious compliance, 46
Management. *See* Supply chain
    management
  blame, 61
  goals, 60
  principles. *See* Change
  rationing/cutting corners, contrast. *See*
    Scientific management
  responsibility, 68, 71

systems. *See* Freight management systems; Mechanistic management systems; Organic management systems
team, value, 102–103
time, value. *See* Project management
Management by Wandering Around (MBWA), 13, 98, 324–327
Management/labor
communication, 66–67
mutual trust/commitment, 61–63
partnership, 51, 60–61, 324
relationship, 20
Managers, involvement. *See* Business
Manufacturing. *See* Green manufacturing
backbone. *See* Prosperity; Security
Britain, success, 110–111
China, success, 112–113
engineer, role, 113
prestige, 113
process, 24
replacement, 114–115
share. *See* Gross Domestic Product
techniques. *See* Japanese manufacturing techniques
Markdowns, 299
Market-constrained situation, 236
Marketing
plan, 293
vision statement, 296–297
Markets, identification, 293–297
Mass conservation, principle, 69–70
Mass producers, 42
Mass production, continuous improvement (usage), 41–42
Master Mind, 93
Materials
traceability, 169–170
transportation. *See* Raw materials
usage, 70
MBWA. *See* Management by Wandering Around
Mechanical energy, recovery, 188–189
Mechanistic management systems, 92–93
Medical savings accounts (MSAs), 162
Medicine
argument. *See* Socialized medicine
man, 94
Mehrlander, Carmie, 119
Membership borrower, 77
Mental condition. *See* Workers
Mergers, 135–136
Middlemen. *See* Non-value-adding middlemen
value addition, 117–124

Military power, backbone, 112
Miller, Lawrence, 33, 35–36
Model A, introduction, 35
Model K, introduction, 255
Model T, 255
all-terrain capability, 296
contribution. *See* Prosperity; Wealth
impact, 1
introduction, 97
job creation, 115
success, 35, 255, 343
successor, 55
Modular designs, usage, 253
Monetary systems, impact. *See* Wealth
Money
Franklin, opinion, 343–344
makers, 53
making, 52
medium, 141
supply, 141
use, 344
Moral law, 26
Motion efficiency, 205, 220–227. *See also* Taylor
experiments, 329
principle, Ohno adoption. *See* Toyota Production System
Motion, elimination, 19
MSAs. *See* Medical savings accounts
Muda (waste), 7, 20, 167, 213, 260
Multifunctional parts, 253
Muri (strain), 20
Mute employees, 74
Mutual commitment, 63

N
Name references, 14–17
Napster, contoversy, 124
Nasser, Jacques, 123, 234
National Cash Register, 90
National prosperity, stock market relevance, 139–142
National Semiconductor, 244
National vitality, 149
Natural law, 24–29
absolute sovereignty, 49
extension, 43
influence, 68
principles, application, 49
relationship. *See* Labor relations
self-evidence/self-reinforcement, 25–27
usage. *See* Government
violations, 25
Navigation Acts, 110
Nazi coercion, failure, 152

New Deal, blame, 156
Nihon Chukuko, 260
Non-lean suppliers/subcontractors,
    reliance, 305
Non-union workmen, oppression, 323
Non-value-added time, 144
Non-value-added work, 263
Non-value-adding activity, 215
Non-value-adding entities, 75
Non-value-adding handling, 230
Non-value-adding middlemen, 76
Non-value-adding motion, 219
Non-value-adding overhead, 108
Non-value-adding setup times, 213
Non-value-adding steps, 242
Nuts, usage, 253–254

O
Obedience, perpetuation, 31
Obsolescence. *See* Planned obsolescence
Occupational safety, 276–287
Offshore labor, 112, 261–262
Offshore supplier, 302
Ohno, Taiichi, 4–5, 13–15, 18
    approach, 228
    citation, 165
    definitions, 167
    motion efficiency principle adoption.
        See Toyota Production System
    opinion, 46
Older workers, role, 74
Omission, errors, 81
OPEC oil embargo (1973), 302–303
Opportunity, 81
    cost, concept identification, 84–85
Organic management systems, 92–93, 97
Organization
    collapse. *See* Ford Motor Company
    flattening, 91–92
    wealth, 33
Organizational barriers, destruction, 9, 13,
    90–93
    recommendation, 17
Organizational behavior
    principles, 20
    universal code, 28–29
Organizational psychology, 59
Organizational structure. *See* Flat
    organizational structure; Porous
    organizational structure
Organizational success, 94
    principles, 79
Organizational transformation, 8
OSHA, 9, 182, 276, 287
Output, relationship. *See* Input

Overhead, inclusion, 132
Ozio
    contrast, 82
    inaction/indolence, 81
Ozone generator, 272

P
Packaging
    delivery, 273–274
    reuse, 170
Packing material, usage, 177
Padilla, James, 101
Painting, procedure, 191–192
Parallel processing/assembly, 196, 217–218
Paranoia, 103
Parsimony, economy (contrast), 65–66
Part casting operation, 261
Partnership. *See* Management/labor
    spirit, 67
Paterno, Joe, 30
Patient control database, 160
Patterson, John, 90
Patton, George (general), 61, 84
PDCA. *See* Plan-do-check-act
Peanut packing, 177
Pedestrianism, 102
PENNSAFE initiative, 283
Percent tolerance (P/T) ratio, 271
Performance
    measurements. *See* Dysfunctional
        performance measurements
    problem, 191
    safety, tradeoff, 144
Persistence, 85–87
    Franklin, opinion, 341–343
    importance, 342
Personal duty/destiny, idea, 31
Personal leadership. *See* Ford
Personal protective equipment (PPE). *See*
    Ford Motor Company River Rouge
    plant
    usage, 280–821
Personal success, Ford principles, 79
Personal vitality, 149
Per-unit production costs, dilution, 132
Peter Principle, 36–37
Peters, Tom, 9, 13–14, 17, 98
    emphasis, 320
    principle, 135
    recommendation, 90, 167
Phantom orders, creation, 134
Physical power, 33
Pillowcase manufacturing, 316–317
Piquette Avenue plant. *See* Ford Motor
    Company

Plan-do-check-act (PDCA) improvement
    cycle, 202, 320
Planned obsolescence, 54–55
Play, relationship. *See* Work
Point-of-use assembly, 274–275
Poka-yoka (error-proofing), 8, 159–162,
    266–267. *See also* Health care
    concept, 101
    description, 260
    idea, 255
    incorporation, 220
    premise, 162
    principle, 274
    usage, 196
Poor Richard's Almanac, 337–339
Porous organization, 13
    creation, 9
    dichotomy, Sorensen identification, 92
Porous organizational structure, 17
Porsche, 270
Portugal, ruin, 110
Poverty
    abolishment, 3
    taxes, impact, 155–157
Power, roles, 144–145
PPE. *See* Personal protective equipment
PPG Industries, 39
PPOs, 159
Practice, deployment. *See* Best practice
    deployment
Pratt & Whitney, 115
Pre-constraint operations, 246–247
Preventive action, 287–288
Preventive maintenance, 163, 208–210
    usage, 268
Price reduction, 128
    benefit. *See* Continuous price reduction
    continuous improvement, impact, 42–43
    customer reliance. *See* Ford
    principle, 127
Price, selling, 298–300
Pricing strategy, 297–300
Principle-centered leadership, 9, 55
Private enterprise, accountability, 341
Private membership association, 77
Proactive leader, 83
Process
    capability, 269–271. *See also* Six Sigma
    changes, impact. *See* Efficiency
    simplification/improvement, 196,
        260–273
Processing, variation suppression, 239–243
Process-oriented layout, 229
Product. *See* Value-adding product
    improvement, 269–270

quality, 270–271
    traceability, ISO 9000 requirement, 160
Production
    classifications. *See* Ford Motor Company
    control. *See* Drum-Buffer-Rope
        production control; Ford Motor
        Company
    costs, 311–312
        dilution. *See* Per-unit production costs
    equipment, 264
    flow, smoothing, 19
    managers, 171
    periods, 48
    worker, 113
Productivity, 316
    gains, 45
    improvements, 46–48, 321
        activities, 238
        methods, 8
        techniques. *See* Japanese
            productivity improvement
            techniques
    increase, 48
    reduction. *See* Ford Motor Company
        Highland Park plant
Profitability, 166. *See also* Cost reduction
    improvement. *See* Short-term
        profitability
Profits. *See* Business
    relationship. *See* Service
Progress. *See* Change
    committees/experts, impact, 89–90
Project management, time (value),
    251–252
Prophet, aspects, 35, 37
Proportional-integral-derivative control,
    268
Prosperity, 342. *See also* Economic
    prosperity
    manufacturing backbone, 54
    Model T, contribution, 115
    stock market relevance. *See* National
        prosperity
Protective apparel, 280–281
P/T. *See* Percent tolerance
Public Act 271 of 1941 (Michigan), 77
Pull system, 13

Q
QFD. *See* Quality Function Deployment
QS-9000, 271
Quality, 295. *See also* House of quality;
        Product; Service
    assurance methods, 287
    auditing, 288–289

Quality, *continued*
  concept, purchase, 298
  control, 287–289
  cost, 339–340
  goal, 51
  improvement methods, 8
  managers, 171
  selling, 124, 298–300
  systems. *See* ISO 9000
Quality Function Deployment (QFD), 196,
  257–259
Quasi-automatic machines, Ford
  definition, 231–232

R
Rate-limiting operation, 236
Rationing, contrast. *See* Scientific
  management
Raw materials, transportation, 178
Real estate prices, 75
Recording industry, model, 124
Recycling, 179–181
Reliability, 295. *See also* Service
  design, 256–257
Repetitive motion injuries, 282–283
Research, cutbacks (implementation),
  133–134
Resources, utilization, 167–182
Revere, Paul, 63–64
Revolutionary War, 86–87, 111
Richard II, 81–82
Richard III, 81–82
Ridge, Thomas (governor), 283
Rigid system, flexible method
  (contrast), 92
River Rouge plant. *See* Ford Motor
  Company
Rivets, 253–254
Road locomotives patent, 86
Robots, 309
Rolling blackouts, 145–146
Royal Automobile Club, 269
Royal College of Surgeons, 159
Royal Navy, ship interception, 111

S
Safeguards, absence, 276–277
Safety. *See* Occupational safety
  committees, 283–284
  principles/practices. *See* Industrial safety
    principles/practices
  tradeoffs. *See* Performance
Sales per customer increase, continuous
  improvement (usage), 128
Salvaging, 179–182

Sam's Club, 77
Sash enclosures, 18
Saxe, John Godfrey, 7
Scarcity mentality
  Covey description, 43
  Ford/Taylor impact, 44–45
Schwab, Charles, 40
Scientific management, 45, 205, 309–313
  correlation. *See* Ford
  element, 53
  outgrowth, 112
  principles, 14–15
  rationing/cutting corners, contrast,
    162–163
Scrap, 238
  cars, 181
  paper, conversion, 171
Screws, usage, 253–254
Securities and Exchange Commission
  (SEC) regulations, 131
Security. *See* Lock-and-key security
  manufacturing backbone, 54
Selden patent, 24
  lawsuit (1909), 86
Self-check gages, 250
Self-check systems, 196, 264–266, 268
  description, 260
  usage, 270
Self-limiting paradigm, 43
Self-reliance, 79, 85
  Franklin, opinion, 341–343
Selling. *See* Price; Quality
Semiconductor market, cycle, 137
Seppuku, 102
Serapis, 86–87
Servant leadership, 50
Service, 50–55. *See also* Trouble-free
  service
  profits, relationship, 24, 52–54
  quality, 54–55
  reliability, 54–55
SFM. *See* Synchronous flow manufacturing
Shewhart, Walter, 17, 197
Shingo, Shigeo, 13–15, 89–90, 204
  comparisons, 244–245
  definitions, 213
  education, 263
  ideas, 166–167, 212
Sho dan (black belt), 34
Shopping mall, usage. *See* Used shopping
  mall
Shortage chasers, 235
Short-term costs, reduction, 133
Short-term profitability, improvement, 130
Silver salts, recovery, 170–171

Sinclair, Upton, 105
Single-minute exchange of die (SMED),
    6–7, 196, 205, 212–217
    examples, 215–217, 219–220
    paradigm, 214
    usage, 13–14, 18
Single-piece flow, value, 211
Single-unit flow, merits, 211
Single-unit processing, 196, 205, 210–212
Situation, law, 93
Six Sigma, 13
    process capability, 16
    project, 273
Slater, Samuel, 111
Slavery, concept, 145
Sloan, Alfred, 37
Small lot processing, 196, 205, 210–212
SMED. *See* Single-minute exchange of die
Smoke soot smudge (3S), 205–206
Smokestacks, examination, 184–186
Smorgen Steel Group Ltd., 168
Snap fits, usage, 253–254
Social morality, 28
Social Security system, pyramid scheme,
    154–155
Social status, 53
Socialized medicine, argument, 163–164
Society, serving, 52
Soldiering, prevention, 72
SOPs. *See* Standard operating procedures
Sorensen, Charles E., 5, 97–99, 169
    accusation. *See* Dodge Brothers
    competition, 80
    Henry Ford man, description, 95
    identification. *See* Porous organization
    opinion. *See* Incompetence
    perspective, 96–97
    remarks, 40, 154, 310
    retirement, 103–104
    role, 94. *See also* Ford
    writings, 52
Spaghetti diagram, 228
Spain, ruin, 110
Spanish Armada, 110
SPC. *See* Statistical process control
Speculators, Franklin (opinion), 344
Speed, increase, 329
Stakeholders, business (serving), 50–51
Standard operating procedures (SOPs),
    319
Standardization, 102, 203–204
    description, 202
    support. *See* Continuous improvement
Statistical process control (SPC), 14, 17,
    116, 197, 210

reactivity, 269
    usage, 268
Stevens, Anne, 1
Stick-to-it-iveness, 342
Stock, changing/customizing, 176
Stock market
    increase/decrease, 139
    performance, 131
    reaction, 142
    relevance. *See* National prosperity
Stockholders, 128, 140
    demand, 70
    impact. *See* Business
Stop-and-start actions, 218
Stores. *See* Employees
    usage, principles, 76–77
Strain. *See* Muri
Strike. *See* UPS
    losers, 67–69
Success, 32. *See also* Ford Motor
    Company; Model T
    components, 113
    danger, 35
    failure, relationship, 342–343
    impact, 33–34
    usage. *See* Change
Suction systems, 18
Superman, 38
Supplier. *See* Offshore supplier
    development, 293, 305–307
    relationships, 293
Supplier/customer, relationship, 20
Supply chain
    built-in waste, 117
    management, 135, 250, 293, 300–307
Suvorov, Aleksandr V. (field marshal), 84,
    96, 252
Synchronization, model, 18
Synchronous flow manufacturing (SFM),
    91, 205, 210, 250
    production control, 246
Synergistic deal, 52
System Company, 208, 310

T
Tag and flag system, 282
Tagout. *See* Lockout-tagout
Takt time, concept, 18–19
TANSTAAFL. *See* There Ain't No Such
    Thing As A Free Lunch
Tao (the Way), 23
Tarot cards, role models, 81
Task completion times, 242
Task study ad redesign, 317
Task subdivision, 205, 220–227

Tax
  Ford, opinion. *See* Inheritance tax
  impact. *See* Poverty
Taylor, Frederick Winslow, 14–15, 201, 309
  citation. *See* Leadership
  impact. *See* Scarcity mentality
  influence. *See* Ford
  methods, labor response, 323
  motion efficiency, 313–318
  opinion, 195. *See also* Business;
    Dysfunctional labor relations
  principle, 116
  relationship. *See* Labor relations
Taylorism, 203
  truth, 318–331
Team-oriented problem solving, eight
    disciplines (TOPS-8D), 251
Tear-down
  room, 260
  usage, 255
Textile/Clothing Technology Corp., 119
Theory of Constraints (TOC), 13, 236–238
There Ain't No Such Thing As A Free
    Lunch (TANSTAAFL), 47, 49, 69, 128
  recognition, 70
Thermodynamics, laws, 187–188
Third-party logistics systems (3PLs), 303
Tiananman Square, 112
Tickler system, 209
Time
  losses, irrecoverability, 237–238, 333
  value. *See* Project management;
    Transportation
  waste, 237
Time-per-unit, 19
Tokimune, Hojo (general), 32
Tolerances, 267
Tool efficiency, improvement, 196, 218–220
Tooling changeovers, 18
TOPS-8D. *See* Team-oriented problem
    solving, eight disciplines
Toranaga, Yoshi, 94–95
Total Productive Maintenance (TPM), 2
Total quality management (TQM), 197
Towne, Henry, 116
Toyota, DBR production control, 246–248
Toyota Production System (TPS), 4, 13, 46
  comparison. *See* Ford Motor Company
  Ford/Taylor motion efficiency principle,
    Ohno adoption, 223
TPM. *See* Total Productive Maintenance
TQM. *See* Total quality management
Transportation, 240. *See also* Raw
    materials
  activities, time (value), 302–303

distances, reduction, 13. *See also* Ford
    Motor Company Highland Park plant
  reliability, need. *See* Just-in-time
  times, 251
  types, 305
  waste, 19, 177–179
Trine, Ralph Waldo, 85, 344
Trouble machine, 244
Trouble-free service, 54
Truck sharing, 303
Twain, Mark, 2, 114
Twelve-variable experiment, support,
    331–333
Tzu, Sun, 49, 100–101

U
Unclean conditions, 277
Unemployment
  efficiency, impact, 44
  inflation, relationship, 141–142
  level. *See* France
UniCo (warehouses), 341
Unions, 323
  blame, 61
  leaders, 76, 322
  shop work rules, 71
Unitary machines, 196, 227–232
  concept, support, 243
United States Steel, 40
United States, warning, 108–117
Universal code. *See* Human behavior;
    Organizational behavior
Universal demand, 294
Unplanned machine downtime, 243
Unterkunft, 84
UPS, strike (1997), 69
U.S. Constitution, 29
U.S. Postal Service, 151
Used shopping mall, usage, 118–120

V
Value
  addition, 117. *See also* Car dealerships;
    Middlemen
  government creation, 150
  perception, 107
  selling, 124
  time/energy, usage, 171–173
Value-adding industries, power, 3
Value-adding operation, 262
Value-adding product, 188
Value-adding workplace, 97
Variation/accuracy, 196, 267–269
Vertical integration, 135
Vertically integrated enterprise, 37

Vibration, problem, 267–268
Vietnam War, 150
Virtù (vitality), 79–81, 85, 86
  leader, 83
Vishnu, 31
Vision statement. *See* Marketing
Visual controls, 13, 232–233. *See also* D.T.
  & I. Railroad
Visual workplace, 232–233
Vitality. *See* Virtù
von Bismarck, Otto, 167
von Clausewitz, Carl (General), 7, 83, 166
von Moltke, Helmuth, 86
von Steuben, Baron, 213–214

W
Wages
  advantages, 64–65
  delivery, 46
  earners/spenders, 65
  earning, 224
  erosion. *See* World War I
  increase, 4, 51. *See also* Worker
Wal-Mart, 109
Wars of the Roses, 69, 83
Waste. *See* Muda; Supply chain;
  Transportation
  avoidance, 339–340
  elimination, 20–21, 165
  forms, 68
  Franklin, opinion, 338–341. *See also*
    Government
  motion, elimination, 263–264
  prevention, 339
  progression, 175–176
  reduction. *See* Ford Motor Company
  treatment, 191
Wasting energy, 144
Water gas, 186
Wealth. *See* Organization
  creation, 3
    monetary systems, impact, 141
  Model T, contribution, 115
  resources, unit, 70
Welfare, 154
Welles, Orson, 37
Wellesley, Arthur (Duke of Wellington),
  326
Wells, H.G., 36
Wheatley, Frank, 88
White mutiny, 46
Whitman, walt, 86
Whitney, Eli, 47
Whiz Kids, 104
Wibel, A.M., 103, 104

Wills, C. Harold, 14
Win-lose situation, 43
Win-win
  deal, 52
  usage. *See* Workplace
WIP. *See* Work-in-process
Wiremold, 248
Wires, avoidance, 254–255
Wong, Tai Gong, 28
Woolley, Edward Mott, 315
Work
  amount. *See* France; Germany
  arrival times, suppression, 239–243
  cells, 13, 229
  elasticity, 332
  employee movement, 221
  groups. *See* Independent work
    groups
  motion, testing, 217–218
  play, relationship, 97–99
  rules, restrictions, 71–72
  subdivision, 220
  success, 37–41
Workdays, missing, 74
Worker-initiated improvements, 320
Workers. *See* Frontline worker;
    Production
  clothing, usage, 277
  communication, government
    committee, 67
  demand, 70
  empowerment, 204
  experiment. *See* Bedridden workers
  goggles, usage, 277
  involvement. *See* Business
  mental attitude, 328
  mental condition, 278
  products, selling, 77
  relationship. *See* Factories
  role, 59. *See also* Handicapped workers;
    Older workers
  tool delivery, 225
  wages, increase, 129
Work-in-process (WIP), 196
  levels, usage, 250
Workmanship, payment, 65–66
Workplace. *See* Value-adding workplace;
    Visual workplace
  comfort/hygiene, 284–285
  dehumanizing, 198
  departmental barriers, erasing, 90
  lighting, 285–287
  win-win, usage, 43–50
Workstations, distances, 19
World function, change, 1

World War I, 322
  depression, 138
  wage erosion, 76
World War II, 275
  Ford Motor Company, experience, 103
  success, 4–6

X

Xerox, copiers, 253

Y

Yamamoto, Isoruku (Admiral), 4–5
Yes men, 94–96

Z

ZBP. *See* Zero base pricing
Zen goal, 30
Zen riddle, Ford answer, 32
Zero base pricing (ZBP), 306
Zero Emission Coal Alliance (ZECA), 190
Zero-sum game, 60

About the Author

William A. Levinson, principal of Levinson Productivity Systems, P.C., has authored and co-authored several books with the American Society for Quality including Lean Enterprise: A Synergistic Approach to Minimizing Waste, ISO 9000 at the Front Line, SPC Essentials and Productivity Improvement, Leading the Way to Competitive Excellence, and The Way of Strategy.

Books from Productivity Press

Productivity Press publishes books that empower individuals and companies to achieve excellence in quality, productivity, and the creative involvement of all employees. Through steadfast efforts to support the vision and strategy of continuous improvement, Productivity Press delivers today's leading-edge tools and techniques gathered directly from industry leaders around the world.

To request a complete catalog of our publications
call us toll free at 800-394-6868 or visit us online at
www.productivityinc.com.

Value Stream Management — Eight Steps to Planning, Mapping, and Sustaining Lean Improvements
Don Tapping, Tom Luyster, and Tom Shuker

Value stream management is a complete system that provides a clear path to lean implementation, ensuring quick deployment and great benefits. Value Stream Management-Eight Steps to Planning, Mapping, and Sustaining Lean Improvements shows you how to use mapping as part of a complete system for lean implementation. The central feature of this illustrative and engaging book is the value stream management storyboard, a tool representing an eight-step process for lean implementation. The storyboard brings together people, tools, metrics, and reporting into one visual document.

ISBN 1-56327-245-8 | 2002 | Stock # VALUE-BK

Reorganizing the Factory:
Competing Through Cellular Manufacturing
Nancy Hyer and Urban Wemmerlöv

Cellular manufacturing principles, applied to either administrative work or production, are fundamental building blocks for lean and quick response organizations. Reorganizing the Factory is the definitive reference book in this important area. Reorganizing the Factory's detailed and comprehensive "life cycle" approach will take readers from basic concepts and advantages of cells through the process of justifying, designing, implementing, operating, and improving this new type of work organization in each unique environment.

ISBN 1-56327-228-8 | 2001 | Stock # REORG-BK

Today and Tomorrow
Henry Ford

This autobiography by the world's most famous automobile manufacturer reveals the thinking that changed the industry forever. First published in 1926 and long out of print, the book had been largely forgotten. Yet Ford's ideas have never stopped having an impact; even Taiichi Ohno acknowledged that a key stimulus to JIT was his close reading of this book. Today, these same ideas are re-emerging to revitalize American industry in new ways.

While our fascination with contemporary business leaders continues, Henry Ford deserves a fresh look. Here is the man who doubled wages, cut the price of a car in half, and produced over two million units a year. Time has not diminished the progressiveness of his business philosophy or his profound influence on worldwide industry.

You will be enlightened by what you read and intrigued by the words of this colorful and remarkable man.

ISBN 0-915-299-36-4 | 1988 | Stock # FORD-BK

Toyota Production System - Beyond Large-Scale Production
Taiichi Ohno

Taiichi Ohno is considered the inventor of the Toyota Production System (known as Just-In-Time manufacturing) and lean manufacturing. In Toyota Production System, the creator of just-in-time production for Toyota reveals the origins, daring innovations and ceaseless evolution of the Toyota system into a full management system.

Now Available in Text, Compact Disc, and Audio Cassette formats!
Text: ISBN 0-915299-14-3 | 1988 | Stock #: OTPS
3 Compact Discs: ISBN 1-56327-267-9 | 2002 | Running time 180 minutes | Stock #: OHNOCD-BK
2 Audio Cassettes: ISBN 1-56327-268-7 | 2002 | Running time 180 minutes | Stock #: OHNOTP-BK

Zero Quality Control — Source Inspection and the Poka-yoke System
Shigeo Shingo

A combination of source-inspection and mistake-proofing devices is the only method to get you to zero defects. Shigeo Shingo shows you how this proven system for reducing errors to zero, turns out the highest quality products in the shortest period of time. He provides 112 specific examples of poka-yoke devices on the shop floor, most of them costing less that $100 to implement.

ISBN 0-915299-07-0 | 1996 | Stock # ZQC-BK

Becoming Lean — Inside Stories of U.S. Manufacturers
Jeffrey Liker

This best-seller contains performance records and real numbers to back up the power of going lean, lessons learned in the process of change (both logistics and people issues), and a realistic account of the journey to lean. This is the first book to provide technical descriptions of successful solutions and performance improvements. It's also the first book to go beyond snapshots and includes powerful first-hand accounts of the complete process of change; its impact on the entire organization; and the rewards and benefits of becoming lean.

ISBN 1-56327-173-7 | Stock # LEAN-BK

Productivity Press   **www.productivitypress.com**   **1-800-34-6868**